Claude R. Conder

Tent Work in Palestine

A Record of Discovery and Adventure: Vol. II.

Claude R. Conder

Tent Work in Palestine
A Record of Discovery and Adventure: Vol. II.

ISBN/EAN: 9783337179694

Printed in Europe, USA, Canada, Australia, Japan

Cover: Foto ©Andreas Hilbeck / pixelio.de

More available books at **www.hansebooks.com**

TENT WORK IN PALESTINE.

JOSEPH BILLING AND SONS, PRINTERS.

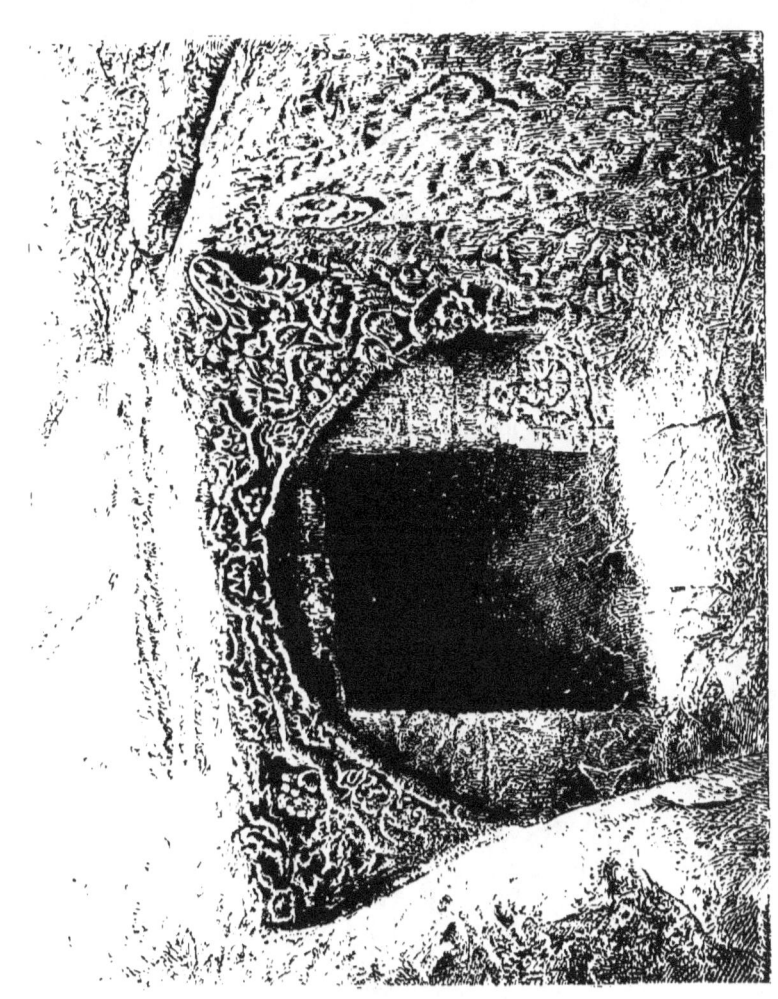

TENT WORK IN PALESTINE.

A Record of Discovery and Adventure.

BY
CLAUDE REIGNIER CONDER, R.E.,
OFFICER IN COMMAND OF THE SURVEY EXPEDITION.

Published for the Committee of the Palestine Exploration Fund.

IN TWO VOLUMES.—VOL. II.

WITH ILLUSTRATIONS BY J. W. WHYMPER.

New Edition.

LONDON:
RICHARD BENTLEY & SON, NEW BURLINGTON STREET,
Publishers in Ordinary to Her Majesty the Queen.
1879.
(All rights reserved.)

CONTENTS OF VOL. II.

CHAPTER	PAGE
I. JERICHO	1
II. THE JORDAN VALLEY	35
III. HEBRON AND BEERSHEBA	75
IV. THE LAND OF BENJAMIN	104
V. THE DESERT OF JUDAH	121
VI. THE SHEPHELAH AND PHILISTIA	148
VII. GALILEE	176
VIII. THE ORIGIN OF THE FELLAHÍN	204
IX. LIFE AND HABITS OF THE FELLAHÍN	236
X. THE BEDAWÍN	270
XI. JEWS, RUSSIANS, AND GERMANS	293
XII. THE FERTILITY OF PALESTINE	316

LIST OF ILLUSTRATIONS.

                                                                  PAGE

AN EARLY CHRISTIAN TOMB—*Frontispiece*.
    From a photograph by Lieut. Kitchener, R.E.; looking south.

GILGAL - - - - - - - - - 1
    From a sketch made by the Author on the spot; the view is north-west, over the Plain of Jericho.

THE KURN SURTUBEH - - - - - *to face* 53
    From a sketch by the Author; looking south.

DEBIR - - - - - - - - - 75
    From a sketch by the Author; looking south-west.

THE VALLEY OF MICHMASH - - - - *to face* 113
    From a photograph by Lieut. Kitchener, R.E.; looking east.

ENGEDI - - - - - - - - - 121
    From a sketch by the Author; looking south.

GATH - - - - - - - - - 148
    From a sketch by the Author; looking south-east.

COLUMBARIA, NEAR BEIT JIBRÎN - - - - 152
    From a photograph by Lieut. Kitchener, R.E.

THE SEA OF GALILEE - - - - - - 176
    From a water-colour sketch by the Author; looking north from Kaukab el Hawa.

	PAGE
A DERWÎSH - - - - - - - -	- 204

    From a sketch by the Author.

COSTUMES OF MOSLEM PEASANTRY NEAR SHECHEM   - 236

    From a sketch by the Author.

MALE DANCERS - - - - - - - - 253

    From a sketch by the Author.

A BEDAWI WOMAN - - - - - - - 270

    From a coloured sketch by the Author.

HAIFA - - - - - - - - - - 316

    From a water-colour drawing by the Author. View from the shore west of the German Colony; looking east.

SKETCH MAP OF PALESTINE - - - - - - 332

GILGAL.

CHAPTER I.

JERICHO.

The 15th of November, 1873, dawned, and the tents of the Survey Camp were once more struck, on a rainy morning, and packed wet on the small Bedawin camels, the loading of which gave us much more trouble than that of the huge pack animals of the peasantry. We were starting on an anxious and difficult undertaking, and were to attempt what no European had ever done before, in settling down for several months to life in the wild and unhealthy district of the Ghor, in order to survey it with an amount of accuracy of detail equal to that which we had obtained in the more civilised country of the settled population.

Through the white desert of the Bukei'a we marched north to a deep gorge, and descended into the broad flat plain of Jericho—a dusty expanse, with a black oasis of trees near the hills, and a black line of jungle round Jordan.

In this descent we came for the first time upon beds of the curious "stink-stone," or bituminous shale, probably part of the bed of a former Salt Sea at a higher level. It is a rock outwardly white like limestone, inwardly black, with a strong odour, and burning freely; here also the knolls and peaks of marl are striped with pink and yellow, and inter-stratified with great layers of flint.

Reaching Jericho we were again disappointed. The long groves which appear so charming at a distance are entirely composed of thorny shrubs. The Dôm or Zizyphus grows into a tree, with small green leaves and formidable prickles; the Nebk, another species, forms long hedges of briar, of which it is said the cruel Crown of Thorns was woven, for which reason it is called Spina Christi. The Zakkûm or balsam-tree (Balanites) is equally thorny, and beneath these grow poisonous night-shades, and other noxious plants. The distant beauty of the groves is only a mockery, and the environs of Jericho, when reached, are as stony and unlovely as any other part of the country.

Yet, in some respects, the place is still charming. Here, late in autumn, the sound of running water, and the song of birds greeted our ears. Among the huge mounds, or Tellûl, bare and dusty, a fresh beautiful stream was flowing from 'Ain es Sultân, the site of the first Jericho. The great spring wells up in a stony pool, under a high hillock, and opposite to this Tell is a jungle crowned by a very large castor-oil tree and other thick foliage. In this grateful shade the birds have found a retreat. The great grey shrikes (Abu Zereik) sit on the top branches, and the queer "hopping thrushes," with their tails stuck up like rapiers, bound about beneath. The bulbul also sings in the groves—a grey bird with a black head and a curious yellow patch at the root of the tail. Still more beautiful are the great Smyrna kingfishers (Abu Nukr), in their blue coats and chocolate-coloured waistcoats, white-throated, with bills like red sealing-wax; and the grey African species (Abu Kubeia), which also flutters above the stream. Last, but not least, come the lovely sun-birds (Suweid), peculiar to the Jordan Valley, darting about like little black wrens, but resplendent, when seen close, with all the colours of the prism.

The days were short, for night comes on in the valley almost an hour earlier than on the hills.

We arrived at our camping-place, and at dusk the camels came in, but mules, tents and dinner were still missing. We had our wine-boxes and made a fire of thorns, fed our horses and arranged our saddles for pillows. Unluckily I mistook a bottle of pickled olives for claret, which, however amusing to others, was a crowning trial after a long day's ride, and in the absence of dinner. At eight p.m. the baggage animals appeared, but the scoundrel who had led them wandering over huge precipices and steep hills, through his entire ignorance of the road, prudently kept away. By ten p.m. the tents were up, and dinner ready, and thus commenced the attack on the valley, destined, however, to a most serious repulse.

The view from the tents on every side was very fine. To the south we looked out over the long thorn-groves, towards the open plain stretching for eight miles to the Dead Sea, which appeared as a gleaming thread, shut in by long dim ridges of mountain, while the square tower of the modern Eriha or Jericho appeared in mid distance. In the early morning I looked out, and saw the long steel-blue ranges capped with rolling wreaths of cloud, behind which the ruddy streak of dawn ran out, the very light which, morning after morning, used to be watched by the priests in the Temple, gradually spreading towards the Hebron mountains.

West of us rose the steep precipice of Kŭrŭntŭl,

or Quarantania, the traditional mountain of Our Lord's forty days of fasting, a cliff a thousand feet high, burrowed with caves, chapels and cells, and crowned with a fortress of the Templars. Northwards the low shelf of gleaming marl hills ran out into a curious cone, called "Raven's Nest," of which more hereafter; to the east was Jordan, hidden between his banks; and behind rose the fine rounded summit of Mount Nebo, and the Moabitic chain.

The district around us was full of places of interest—Jericho, Gilgal, the Cities of the Plain, Jordan and the Salt Sea. The ruins were also important—Roman and later aqueducts, Crusading monasteries, and rock chapels. The results summed up in the following pages, represent the continuous labour of more than a month, during which I was in the saddle till late every day, and engaged till midnight in writing and drawing, rising before the sun began to appear behind the Moab wall. Twice again in the following years I returned to the valley, and revisited the sites round Jericho.

There is only one natural position for a large town in the plains of Jericho, namely, the neighbourhood of the beautiful fountain called "the Sultan's Spring," near the foot of the Quarantania precipice. Nothing can well explain the choice of a new position, but the fact that Jericho was cursed by Joshua, and that the curse was fulfilled.

1—2

Thus it is by the spring that we naturally place the Jericho of Joshua's time, and this view receives confirmation from the account of the flight of the spies "to the mountain;" for if situated in the immediate vicinity of the great crag of Kŭrŭntŭl, the city was so near that the fugitives might easily have crept through the cane jungle and thorn-groves to the shelter of one of the innumerable caverns on the face of its precipices.

Of ancient Jericho nothing now remains but the bright spring, and the shapeless mound above it. We can hardly wonder at this when we find that even the Jericho of Herod has disappeared, and that only a vague conjecture can be made as to the position of Thrax and Taurus, the great towers which once defended it. It seems probable that this second town stood south of ancient Jericho, and even closer to the hills, for the great aqueduct which brought water a distance of four miles from the fine spring at the head of the wild Kelt chasm leads just to the opening of the plain, and seems to be the only one of the numerous aqueducts which dates back to Roman times. At the mouth of the pass, also, is the rock-fort called Jubr or Chubr, in which title we may recognise, as my companion, Mr. Drake, pointed out, a relic of the name Cupros, which was given to a tower above Herod's Jericho.

Jerome tells us that there were in his day two Jerichos, and in 333 A.D. the anonymous pilgrim of Bordeaux found a town at the foot of the pass. Here also we have remains of a bridge which has the *opus reticulatum* of Roman masonry, and this, with a few strewn fragments and with two great mounds of sun-dried brick, seems all that is left of the second Jericho. The Byzantine, or fourth-century town, mentioned by Jerome as the second Jericho, is no doubt represented by the foundations and fragments of cornice and capital, over which the rider stumbles among the thorn groves east of the 'Ain es Sultân.

By 700 A.D. Jericho had again disappeared, and thus, in the twelfth century, we find the site once more moved. The modern Eriha then springs into existence near a square tower, such as the Crusaders erected along their pilgrim-roads, and a tradition of the "Garden of Abraham" comes into existence as early as the time of Sæwulf (1102 A.D.). In the fourteenth century Sir John Maundeville finds Jericho a little village, and Abraham's Garden is then stated to be at the foot of the Quarantania. Fetellus makes the distance between Jericho and the latter mountain two miles, and thus it is pretty clear that the modern Eriha represents the site which was created in the Crusading period.

A question of even greater interest is that of the long-sought site of Gilgal, and our inquiries were rewarded with success. Robinson had heard the name Jiljûlieh, but had not been able to fix the site. A German traveller (Herr Schokke), in 1865, had been more fortunate, and was shown the place at a mound about a mile east of Eriha. It was important to ascertain the reliability of this discovery, and I succeeded in fixing the spot visited by this traveller, by means of the compass-bearing which he had been wise enough to take. I found three persons who knew the site by the name Jiljûlieh, and one of them conducted me to ruins to which a curious tradition applies.

There was, however, still a difficulty to be met; for Captain Warren had been shown another place, as the true site of Gilgal, north of this Jiljûlieh, where are ruins of a large mediæval monastery. The explanation is, however, the usual one. Our Jiljûlieh is the Gilgal known to the early Christians, which St. Willibald (724 A.D.) places two miles from the Jericho of his time, and five miles from Jordan; Captain Warren's site is just in the position in which Gilgal is shown on the mediæval map of Marino Sanuto. The Crusaders have again in this instance changed the site, and both traditions are extant among the natives. The questions naturally rise, which is the true one, or whether either is worthy of notice? The ruins of Jiljûlieh, east of Jericho, appear to me to bear away the palm, for two reasons; first, the position is that described in the Bible, "in the east border of Jericho" (Josh. iv. 19); secondly, the fourth-century site is noticed by Jerome, not as fixed by a monkish tradition, but as held in reverence by the inhabitants of the country, and thus apparently connected with a genuine or indigenous tradition. It is true that the existing ruins, with hewn stones and tesseræ of glass, indicate traces of the early Byzantine monastery, which is noticed as containing the Church of Galgalis, but this does not militate against the genuine character of the site, for the tradition, in this case, appears to be derived from a more authentic source than that which fixes most of the early Christian sacred sites.

The recovery of Gilgal ranks as one of the most important successes of the Survey work. The name is not commonly known among the natives, for the site is generally called Shejeret el Ithleh, "the tamarisk-tree," from the very large tamarisk just west of the ruins. The tradition connected with the place is, however, apparently common among the Arabs of the neighbourhood.

South-east of the tamarisk is an oblong tank lined with rubble, and measuring about one hundred feet by eighty. It resembles other reservoirs found in early Byzantine buildings, especially in monasteries. Near it are about a dozen mounds, some ten feet in diameter and three or four feet high, which, when excavated, proved to consist of sandy marl, with pottery, glass, and tesseræ imbedded. North-east of the tree is a modern Arab graveyard, showing, perhaps, that the place is held sacred by the Bedawîn, as they generally prefer to bury in the neighbourhood of consecrated ground. The grave-stones are blocks apparently belonging to some ancient building, and many other stones are strewn round. These remains—stones, tesseræ, and the tank—indicate the former existence of a monastery similar to the numerous other religious establishments which once covered the plain. The mounds are called Telleilât Jiljûlieh, "the little hillocks of Gilgal;" the tank is named Birket Jiljûlieh, "the Pool of Gilgal."

The site is conspicuous from a distance, because of the magnificent old tamarisk, and the view from it is very fine, extending up the Jordan Valley as far as the grand peak of Surtubeh, which stands out, like a bastion, in front of the line of hills, and culminates in a sharp cone, not unlike the outline of Monte Viso, seen near Turin. The 'Osh el Ghŭrâb, or "Raven's Nest," in front, equally white, and almost as pointed, repeats the Surtubeh in miniature, and above the Quarantania crag stands the lofty summit of Jebel Nejmeh 3000 feet above the valley. The white marl banks—shores of a former Dead Sea—skirt the Jericho plain thinly dotted with Dôm-trees, balsam-trees, and tamarisks, and reach the foot of Quarantania. In front are the shapeless mounds round the Sultan's Spring, and the thorn-groves reaching to the tower of Erîha, which is brown and square, with a solitary palm beside it. The rest of the view is almost the same as that seen from 'Ain es Sultân.

The Bedawîn of the district have a well-known tradition regarding the site of Jiljûlieh. Over the coffee and pipes in the evening, after the day's work was done, they related it to us. By the old tamarisk once stood the City of Brass, which was inhabited by Pagans. When Mohammed's creed began to spread, Aly, his son-in-law, "the lion of God," arrived at the city, and rode seven times round it on his horse, Maimûn. The brazen walls fell down, destroyed by his breath, and the Pagans fled, pursued by the Faithful towards Kŭrŭntŭl; but the day drew to a close, and darkness threatened to shield the infidels. Then Aly, standing on the hill which lies due east of the Kŭrŭntŭl crag, called out to the sun, "Come back, O blessed one!" And the sun returned in heaven, so that the hill has ever since been called the "Ridge of the return." Here stands the Mukâm, or sacred station of Aly, and here also is the place where Belâl ibn Rubâh, the Muedhen of the Prophet, called the Faithful to prayer after the victory.

Such is the legend. In it we see mixed up and assigned to the Imâm 'Aly ibn Abu Tâleb, and to Belâl ibn Rubâh, two episodes of the life of Joshua—the fall of Jericho and the battle of Ajalon.

At first one is tempted to believe this to be a genuine tradition, for Jerome tells us that Gilgal was shown, in his time, as a deserted place, "two miles from Jericho, and held in wondrous reverence (*miro cultu*) by the people of that region." When, however, we examine the question more fully, the original source of the story seems doubtful. It attaches to the site of a monastery, it is related by the descendants of a race which only entered Palestine with Omar in the seventh century; and, above all, it is connected most probably with another Crusading tradition, for the Chapel of the Apparition of St. Michael to Joshua stood, in 1185 A.D., (as Phocas tells us), below Quarantania, apparently just where the present Mukâm of 'Aly is to be found.

It may appear strange, and perhaps improbable, that the Bedawîn should retain and hand down Christian traditions derived from monks. Yet, within this very district, there is a second undoubted instance which may here be given as illustrating the above.

The Quarantania, or Kŭrŭntŭl mountain, has, from the twelfth century down, been shown as the place to which Our Lord retired for the forty days of fasting in the desert. Near to it the Crusaders also looked for the "exceeding high mountain" whence the Tempter showed Our Lord "all the kingdoms of the world and the glory of them" (Matt. iv. 8). Sœwulf tells us that the site of this mountain was three miles from Jericho. Fetellus places it north of that town, and two miles from Quarantania. The measurements bring us to the remarkable cone before noticed, called 'Osh el Ghŭrâb, or "Raven's Nest."

The story is wonderfully illustrative of the simplicity of men's minds in the twelfth century, for the summit of the "exceeding high mountain," whence all the kingdoms of the world were to have been seen, is actually lower than the surface of the Mediterranean, and it is surrounded on every side by mountains more than double its height. This tradition is nevertheless still extant among the Bedawîn. The valley which comes down from the side of the mountain is called Mesâ'adet 'Aisa, " the ascension of Jesus," and the name has, no doubt, its origin in the tradition that Our Lord was carried by Satan to this conspicuous summit. It can hardly then be doubted that mediæval monkish traditions still linger among the Arabs of the Jordan Valley.

Another great antiquarian question claimed our careful attention from the Jericho camp. It was that of the "Cities of the Plain" or "Ciccar." The Crusaders placed them south of the Dead Sea, and their supposed sites of Sodom (Usdum) and Zoar (Zûeirah) are easily recovered. The Moslems believe that the wicked cities lie beneath the Sea of Lot, as they call the Lake Asphaltites, but the geological evidence all goes to prove that the Dead Sea must have existed pretty much in its present condition in the time of Abraham, and that such a convulsion as they suppose cannot have occurred within historical times. Modern scholars, therefore, have sought anew for the sites of Sodom and Gomorrah, Zoar, Zeboim, and Admah. It seems almost certain that these cities should be placed towards the north end of the lake, because the term Ciccar applies properly to the Jordan valley and to the Jericho plain; our utmost efforts were therefore directed to the discovery of the sites of the Cities of the Plain (or Ciccar) in this direction. Over almost every acre of ground between Jericho and the Dead Sea, I rode day by day. The whole is a white desert, except near the hills, where rich herbage grows after the rains. The time of year was most favourable for such exploration, because no long grass existed to hide any ruins. In all that plain I found no ruin, except the old monastery of St. John and a little hermit's cave, and it seems to me probable that no other ruins will ever there be found.

With regard to this subject several points require to be kept in memory. The ancient record, which commences so curiously "in the days of Amraphel king of Shinar" (Gen. xiv. 1), refers to events which occurred more than three thousand years ago. The cities were overwhelmed by fire, and their names were blotted out of the later topography of the time of Joshua. To expect to find their ruins is manifestly to disregard the Bible history, and even had they not been overthrown, what hope could there be of their preservation at the present time, when the buildings of Herod, nineteen centuries later, are not now in existence?

In the second place, there is no very accurate indication in the Bible of the position of the cities: they were in the Vale of Siddim, "which is the Salt Sea," but they may have been very far apart. One thing alone seems pretty certain. If they were near the Salt Sea they would also probably have been situated near fresh-water springs, as Engedi is situated. Such springs are few and far between in the neighbourhood of the Dead Sea, and none occur along the north shore, or in the plain immediately near it. On the north-west, however, there is one fine outflow of water at 'Ain Feshkhah, and higher up the Jordan Valley springs are abundant.

Although no ruins were found by the Survey party, and, as I have urged above, were not to be expected, yet there are names in the district, applying to portions of the ground, which seem to me to have a possible connection with those of Gomorrah, Admah, and Zeboim.

The great spring of 'Ain Feshkhah is a probable site for one of the Cities of the Plain, and the great bluff not far south of it is called Tubk 'Amrîyeh, and the neighbouring valley Wâdy 'Amrîyeh. This word is radically identical with the Hebrew Gomorrah, or Amorah as it is spelt in one passage (Gen. x. 19), meaning, according to some authorities, "depression," according to others "cultivation." It is possible then that the name of Gomorrah is preserved in this modern district title.

Admah means "red earth," a description which would hardly apply to the ground near the Dead Sea. A "city Adam" is noticed in the Book of Joshua, and the name Ed Dâmieh applies to the neighbourhood of the Jordan ford east of the Sŭrtubeh, about twenty-three miles up the valley. It has always seemed to me possible that Adam and Admah were one and the same.

Zeboim means "hyenas," and is identical with the Arabic *Dub'a*. Now the cliff just above the plain, near the site of Roman Jericho, is called Shakh ed Dub'a, "lair of the Hyena;" but the title is Hebrew, not Arabic—Shakh being a word not found in the Arabic dictionaries. Might not Zeboim, I would ask, have stood here?

Sodom alone remains without a suggestion, and of this word we find no trace west of Jordan. I may note, however, that the word Siddim is apparently the same with the Arabic *Sidd*, which is used in a peculiar sense by the Arabs of the Jordan Valley as meaning "cliffs" or banks of marl, such as exist along the southern edge of the plains of Jericho, the ordinary meaning being a "dam" or obstruction. Thus the Vale of Siddim might well, so far as its name is concerned, have been situated in the vicinity of the northern shores of the Dead Sea.

Such are the only suggestions I am able to offer on this interesting question. To discover the sites of these cities, on the north shores of the Dead Sea, will, I feel convinced, be impossible, unless springs of fresh water be also there discovered, which are not to be found on the Survey sheets.

A morning ride brings the traveller from the Sultan's Spring to the banks of Jordan, at the spot where the Kelt valley debouches, and where the Crusading monastery of St. John-on-Jordan, replacing the original building erected by the Emperor Anastasius, stands on the marl hillocks, by the fine reservoir built by Justinian for the former structure. On the 28th of November I surveyed this part, and in 1875 I spent the morning of New Year's day on the banks of the stream in company with Lieutenant Kitchener.

From the fourth century downwards, the great ford at this place has been pointed out as the scene of Our Lord's Baptism—the Bethabara of the fourth Gospel. This view is sanctioned by the Greek and Latin churches alike, and pilgrims yearly repair hither at Easter-time to bathe in Jordan.

Writers who have endeavoured to cast discredit on the Gospels, have, from an early period, caught at this identification as showing a physical impossibility. Bethabara was a spot where certain events took place on consecutive days, while on the "third day," Christ was at Cana of Galilee (John i. 29, 35, 43; ii. 1). Now Cana was at least seventy miles from the neighbourhood of Jericho, and the distance is manifestly too great for one day's journey. But the error lies, not with the Evangelist, but with his opponents, who assume that the fourth-century tradition is necessarily correct. The name Bethabara is not to be found in the neighbourhood of Jericho, and the site discovered, by the Survey party, in 1874 (to be described in the next chapter) is much higher up the valley. The existence of the name in another direction, where the requisites of the New Testament narrative are fully borne out, is therefore, I think, fatal to the traditional site. But though the spot in question cannot apparently claim to be the real Bethabara, there is every reason to suppose that it is the place where Joshua and his host crossed over in front of Jericho, and it has thus an historical interest of a scarcely inferior degree.

Leaving behind us the mud hovels and black tents among low vineyards, which now make up modern Jericho, since the fire which lately destroyed the village, we rode through cornfields, and over open plains where the alkali plant (Hubeibeh) grows; descending a sort of step we came upon an extent of white crusted mud, too salt for any plant to grow on, and so to the Zor, or broad trench in which the river flows. The Zor is full of Dôm trees and tamarisks in which the sun-birds swarm, while the ground is riddled with the burrows of the jerboa. The river itself flows in a brown swirling rapid stream, amid a thick jungle of tamarisk, cane, and willow. Here the Nimr or hunting leopard, much feared by the Arabs, finds a retreat, and, beside the river, I came suddenly on a wolf prowling alone.

The lower valley teemed with wild life along the stony bed of the Kelt; the desert partridges marched in a file of eight or ten, and the blunt noses of the jerboas peeped out of their holes. A large black water-bird was slowly flying up stream, and a flock of wild pigeons hovered over the opposite cliff.

Just where the Kelt falls into the Jordan there is a great bend westward, and an open shingly shore to the river. The opposite bank, some twenty yards off, is a flat expanse of mud, with a perpendicular marl-cliff above, some fifty feet high. North of this ford is a group of magnificent tamarisks, apparently of great antiquity; on the south the thick jungle again hides the stream.

From the Pilgrim's Bathing-place we rode down by the beautiful blue pool of 'Ain Hajlah, and over the desolate expanse of grey, salt mud, to the mouth of Jordan, where a delta of soft marsh and vegetable debris is formed, and so along the open pebbly beach of the Dead Sea.

The scenery round the sea is very fine. It is compared, by those who have seen both, to that of the Lake of Geneva. The appearance of the shore is desolate in the extreme, in consequence of the long line of white driftwood—dry trunks of tamarisks and willows, brought down by the winter floods, and now bleaching fifteen feet above the summer level of the water, crusted over with white and bitter salt.

The present chapter is too short to allow of an account of the sea itself, of its nauseous taste, its high specific gravity, or of the peculiar sensations of bathing in its waters. On my first visit I had to swim out to the curious island, called Rijm el Bahr (the Cairn of the Sea), covered with stones, and connected by a stony causeway with the land—a place which seems to me to be the ruin of an artificial pier or jetty. When I got back, very sore and with smarting eyes, I soon became coated with white salt. On this day also I noticed flocks of wild-fowl swimming about half a mile from shore—a practical contradiction of the old fable that birds flying over the Dead Sea fall into it dead. I have never, however, found any living animal in the water, though many fish, brought down by the Jordan current, lie salted and pickled along the shores.

On the east side of the Jordan stretches a plain,

corresponding to the Jericho plain, in which possibly Sodom once stood. Above this, on the south-east, rise the steep cliffs of the Ammonite ranges, where Zoar is now fixed. On the west there are precipitous hills, 800 feet high, with a narrow beach, and a marl-cliff, or Sidd, below. Here lies the curious ruin of Kumrân, and beneath it is a cane-brake extending to the Feshkhah springs, where the beach is terminated by the promontory of the same name rising sheer from the water, its base surrounded with the huge fallen "fragments" from which the title Feshkhah seems derived. This spot, with the running stream, the broad shallow pool, the cane-brake, and the steep precipice behind, is perhaps the most picturesque on the shore.

There is one other remarkable natural feature in this interesting plain of Jericho which demands attention—the Kelt Valley, running from the spring of that name, and south of Eriha, past Jiljûlich to Jordan. There seems no doubt that this is the Valley of Achor, in which Achan was stoned; and the bed of the valley is full of boulders and pebbles of every size, which would account for its being chosen as the scene of the execution, as there is hardly a stone in the greater part of the plain round it.

Wâdy Kelt has been also thought to be the Brook Cherith, and the scene seems well fitted for the retreat of the prophet who was fed by the "'Oreb,' whom some suppose to have been Arabs. The whole gorge is wonderfully wild and romantic, it is a huge fissure rent in the mountains, scarcely twenty yards across at the bottom, and full of canes and rank rushes between vertical walls of rock. In its cliffs the caves of early anchorites are hollowed, and the little monastery of St. John of Choseboth is perched above the north bank, under a high, brown precipice. A fine aqueduct from the great spring divides at this latter place into three channels, crossing a magnificent bridge seventy feet high, and running a total distance of three miles and three-quarters, to the place where the gorge debouches into the Jericho plain. On each side the white chalk mountains tower up in fantastic peaks, with long knife-edged ridges, and hundreds of little conical points, with deep torrent-seams between. All is bare and treeless, as at Mar Saba. The wild pigeon makes its nest in the "secret places of the stairs" of rock; the black grackle suns its golden wings above them; the eagle soars higher still, and over the caves by the deep pools the African kingfisher flutters; the ibex also still haunts the rocks. Even in autumn the murmuring of water is heard beneath, and the stream was one day swelled by a thunderstorm in a quarter of an hour, until it became a raging torrent, in some places eight or ten feet deep.

The mouth of the pass is also remarkable; for

on either side is a conical peak of white chalk—one on the south called the "peak of the ascent" (Tuweil el 'Akabeh), while that to the north is named Bint Jebeil, "daughter of the little mountain," or Nusb 'Aweishireh, "monument of the tribes."

These peaks are again, to all appearance, connected with a Christian tradition. Jerome speaks of Gebal and Gerizim as two mountains close together, shown in his day just west of Jericho. In the name Jebeil we may perhaps recognise the Gebal of this tradition; and in that case the "monument of the tribes" would be the traditional altar of Joshua in Ebal. If this be so, the southern peak must be the early Christian Gerizim; but the name is apparently lost.

The neighbourhood of Jericho has been a favourite retreat for hermits since the fourth century. In the twelfth it was full of monasteries, and the ruins of no less than seven of these buildings remain, without counting the chapels on Kŭrŭntŭl, or the Templars' church in the fortress on the summit of the same mountain. The interior walls of these ruins were covered with frescoes, in some cases well preserved, and all the designs have painted inscriptions. The character used fixes the frescoes as not earlier than the twelfth century, and the masonry and pointed arches lead to the same conclusion regarding the date of these buildings.

The monastery in Wâdy Kelt was dedicated to the anchorite St. John of Choseboth; the names of Athanasius, Gerasmius of Calamon, and St. Joachim—traditionally held to have here lived in seclusion—are written above the figures of three saints on its walls. A barbarous inscription in Greek and Arabic states the monastery to have been restored, by a certain Abraham and his brothers, of the Christian village of Jufna.

The Kŭrŭntŭl chapels, which we visited in 1873, are perched half way up the crag, and full of frescoes with the names of Gregory, Basil, Chrysostom, Athanasius, and other fathers of the Church. In the great monastery of St. John of Beth Hogla, half way between Jericho and the Dead Sea, we found the names, Andrew of Crete, John Eleemon (Patriarch of Jerusalem, in 630 A.D.), Sophronius of Jerusalem, and Sylvester, Pope of Rome (probably the famous Sylvester II., 998 A.D.). The remaining monastic sites include St. John on Jordan, now called "Jews' Castle," and Tell Mogheifir, or Tell el Kursi, in which name we perhaps find a trace of that of the old monastery of St. Chrysostom, rebuilt in the twelfth century.

Such was the work which occupied us in the end of November, 1873. The Arabs round us were willing and intelligent; they made good guides, and shot for us, not only birds, but also a fine "bedn," or ibex. The Sheikh Jemîl, an old friend of Dr. Tristram's, accompanied me day after day, and often inquired after the Doctor, whom he called "the father of the beard." He rode an elegant little dromedary, which was extremely tame. The great speed which could be got out of the animal was surprising, but the rider seemed regularly shaken to pieces by the pace, when keeping up with my horse at a canter. He was a good shot, and one of the best fellows I ever met among the Bedawin, though avaricious, as are all Arabs who come much in contact with Europeans.

The autumn rains commenced in 1873 with a great thunderstorm on the 24th of November. I came back to camp wet through, and found four ladies sitting on their horses under the dripping thorn-trees. Should they read these lines, they will remember the adventure; how they lost their guide; how I offered my services; how they passed the night in the mud hovel, which called itself an hotel, at Jericho; how the rain came down the walls through the roof of reeds while the party sat at dinner; how my people were alarmed, and came down with lanterns and firearms to see me home; and I shall myself not forget how we got entangled, in the dark, among the hedges of thorn, as we endeavoured to find the way back to my camp.

And now the face of the country suddenly changed, and the cool, clear, delightful autumn weather set in—most treacherous of all the seasons in Palestine, as the sun then draws out the reeking miasma from the softened ground. The plains became green with tender grass, the great cloud-banks rose behind the hills, and I awoke one morning to hear, to my dismay, the croaking of frogs close to the camp. With the experience of one more year, we should at once have moved to higher ground. We stayed however where we were, and suffered in consequence.

The climate of Jericho must have altered greatly since Josephus described the place as " a region fit for gods." Thrice we visited the Jordan Valley; three times the terrible remittent fever of Jericho threatened valuable lives in our party, and once it proved fatal. The change of climate is due, I imagine, to the decay of cultivation. Herod planted palm-groves, and watered them by aqueducts still remaining. The groves existed in the seventh, and even in the twelfth century; but now only two trees can be found. The Crusaders also undertook cultivation, and made sugar at the ruined mills under Quarantania, still called the "sugar-mills." At the present day the land is quite as productive as ever; but the Arabs disdain agriculture, and the inhabitants of Eriha are so enervated, by the climate, that they bring men down from the hills to reap their scanty crops. Every kind of vegetable will grow here—tomatoes, vegetable marrows, grapes and indigo; yet the beautiful streams of Kelt and of Elisha's Fountain ('Ain es Sultân) are allowed to run to waste, or to form malarious pools, and thus the untilled lands in the plain reek with miasma.

On the 4th of December the fever found us out. On the 2nd, Drake had over-fatigued himself in paying a visit to the Kelt monastery; on the 3rd I had ridden up to Jerusalem, to make preparations for our proposed winter in the valley; on the 4th I started again for camp late in the afternoon. The way lay along the well-known road to Jericho, round the chalky hill to the little stone village of Bethany, where the ruined Crusading tower, so quaintly named by mediæval writers "the Castle of St. Lazarus," dominates the more modern buildings. Thence the road leads by certain rock-cut tombs, one of which perchance is the very sepulchre whence Lazarus was called back to life, and soon after it dives down into a valley between barren hills, and passes the traditional Apostles' Fountain. There is nothing remarkable after this until one arrives at a small plain, and ascends to where the strong fort, once called the Castle of the Good Samaritan, commands the pass above a ruined Khan; this place is still called by the old Bible name, "The going up of blood," due to the red colour of the marl all round the hill. A very steep descent leads down on the east from the castle, and soon after a long view opens out of countless knolls and peaks of marl, each throwing a little conical shadow into the intervening valleys; beyond the peaks is the white Jericho plain, and the black patches of grove and jungle, and yet farther the Moab mountain-wall.

The mellow evening light gradually became more rosy, until a clear flame-colour spread over the mountains with shadows sharply defined. A steel-coloured shade crept over the plain and climbed slowly the eastern slopes, and the cold blue at length reached the summits. Hardly had the sunset faded away, when, in almost theatrical contrast, a second brilliant effect succeeded. A great orange-coloured moon rose up behind the mountain wall, and flooded hill and plain with brilliant light. I was now skirting the precipices of the great Kelt gorge, which lay beneath me in glossy gloom; but the almost electric light of the full moon on the white chalk contrasted forcibly, and long shadows were cast from the pale peaks of the mountains. The very pebbles in the road shone like silver; and my shadow and that of my horse were thrown, in gigantic proportions, against the cliffs on the opposite side of the gorge. Presently the horse scented a piece of carrion which he could not see in the path, and became almost unmanageable. My servant's animal was still more frightened, for nothing seems to terrify a horse more than this odious smell. Debouching on to the plain I galloped rapidly towards the camp lights, and was surprised that no groom met me. I had ridden down in the short space of three and a half hours, and was tired and hungry; I found that both grooms were ill with fever; that Sergeant Armstrong had also had an attack, and that poor Drake was suffering very much.

The morning arrived on which I had meant to move up country. It was fortunate indeed that we had not already gone farther, or we should have been beyond the reach of assistance. The march had to be postponed, and I rode out to visit Gilgal once more, hoping to move next day.

Saturday came, and I found that Drake had hardly slept at all, and that medicine seemed to do him no good. Four servants were now ill, and two of the Bedawîn had ague. I sent a mounted soldier up to fetch Dr. Chaplin, since it seemed impossible to move the patients far.

Sunday was indeed an anxious day; nearly all the servants were ill, and some were dangerously affected. I could do nothing beyond administering quinine and endeavouring to make Drake comfortable. When he dozed he became delirious, and one of the most appalling features of this dreadful fever is, that while the patient will answer any question quite rationally, he will wander in his talk the moment you leave him quiet. I read to Drake the great part of the day, but he was now suffering from want of sleep even more than from fever; and at last expressed a wish to have the doctor sent for. I was able to tell him that I expected the doctor every moment, having sent for him twenty-four hours before.

No doctor came, and another night of general sickness settled down on camp. I sat up till midnight, and had just dosed off in my clothes when my faithful servant, Habib, came in. I may well call him faithful, for had he not stuck to his duty it is quite possible that every native member of the party who could walk would have deserted. On that morning the cook, the most important person of all, had announced that he was going, and would no doubt have gone, indeed, but for the following message.

"The road to Jerusalem lies by my tent," I told him, "and if I see you pass by the door I shall shoot you at once."

He was soon busily employed in making broth for the invalids.

Habib came in, as above said, at one p.m., and announced Dr. Ilievitz, who deserves our best thanks for his kindness and humanity, in undertaking by night the long and difficult journey from Jerusalem to our camp. Dr. Ilievitz lost his way, and had a severe fall. No sooner therefore had he seen Drake and those of the servants who were suffering most, than I put him to bed, with brown paper and vinegar on his bruises.

On Monday I moved most of the tents to a higher position, and sent all the men out surveying, as being a more healthy occupation than lingering in a fever-stricken encampment. The doctor and I spent the day in making up and administering medicine, and we sent to Jerusalem for a litter in order to move Drake; it arrived on the next morning, and leaving Sergeant Black in charge of the camp I rode up slowly beside it to the hills.

We now experienced the kindness of the English colony in Jerusalem. Mr. Neil, the English chaplain, had already sent us down wine and jelly, roast fowls, cakes, and everything he could think of. I met Dr. Chaplin near the Apostles' Fountain; though himself ill at the time he had risen from bed to ride down to us at Jericho. Mr. Neil accompanied him, and though I was glad that they were saved the fatigue of their proposed journey, I was not the less grateful for a kindness which I shall not easily forget.

We had reason also to be grateful to many other Europeans, and not least to Mr. Hornstein the hotel-keeper, who, at the risk of losing all his guests, took Drake in, though suffering from an infectious fever. I could not but feel thankful that I had sent my messenger for the doctor in time; both doctors told me that Drake would have died if the dreadful symptoms had remained much longer without attention. All that night Dr. Chaplin sat up with me, in spite of his own sufferings, watching over poor Drake, who was in high delirium. On Wednesday I sent orders to Sergeant Black to march the rest of the party to Jerusalem, giving up all hope of a winter campaign.

Several days of nursing followed, and many of our people who had escaped the fever in the valley, were seized by it when they came up to the hills. On Sunday, however, Drake was much better, and I was able to go to church. The past fortnight had been the most trying time I had experienced; every member of the party except myself, Sergeant Black, Corporal Brophy, and Habib, had been down with the fever. Our immunity was, I believe, due to doses of quinine taken as soon as the danger became evident. But my turn was to come; I went incautiously to the Haram in the hot sun, after a night of nursing and of very little sleep, and the same day I received letters complaining of the expense of the Survey. Little did those who composed them foresee how, arriving at such a time, they were to be the last drop in the cup of my troubles, for the consequent worry laid me on my back with the fever in a very few hours.

I had now to look after myself, and in addition a storm threatened to blow down the camp. I had occasion again to be grateful to Dr. Chaplin, who lent me his summer residence for the party, and to others who came to see me and offered their assistance, for poor Drake was still scarcely able to get out of bed.

I shall always regret that I did not urge Drake more persistently, to leave the country after this very serious attack of the Jericho fever, but I fear it would have been useless to do so, for his recovery was so rapid and his health seemed so good, that there appeared no immediate cause for further anxiety.

During the whole of that winter I suffered from fever. It was an exceptionally severe season; the Plain of Sharon was a swamp, the winds in the hills were cold and cutting, Jordan overflowed its banks, and was half a mile wide, while the whole valley was merely a quagmire; we had seven falls of snow in Jerusalem, and one of these lasted for some time, the hills remaining white for several days. All the intervals of fine weather were employed in field-work, and I even camped out near Bethel for three days; but it cost me another attack of fever, and a third was brought on by a visit to Neby Samwil. Once or twice the fit came on while I was riding, and I can imagine nothing more disagreeable than to be ten miles from home, on a rough road, with a fever headache.

The ulcers, which seem always to accompany fever in malarious climates, attacked us all, and altogether the expedition was much shaken; but as spring returned we got gradually better, and thus as soon as the Jordan Valley was reported by the Arabs fit for riding, I once more marched out with a strong expedition on the 24th of February, 1874.

Those who read the above pages will, I hope, be convinced that the Survey of Palestine was no holiday task. The results were worth the difficulties we encountered, and Gilgal and Bethabara are, I think, enough to put into the scales against six months' ill health, but if any one feels inclined to criticise our work, I would beg him to consider the difficulties, of every kind, which had to be overcome in carrying it out.

CHAPTER II.

THE JORDAN VALLEY.

THE Jordan Valley is not only the most remarkable feature of Palestine, but one of the most curious places in the world. It has no exact counterpart elsewhere, and the extraordinary phenomenon of clouds sweeping as a thick mist 500 feet below the level of the sea, is one which few European eyes have seen, but which we witnessed in the early storms of the spring of 1874.

The Jordan rises as a full-grown river, issuing from the cave at Baniâs, about 1000 feet above the level of the Mediterranean. In the short distance of twelve miles it falls not less than 1000 feet, passing through the papyrus-marshes, and reaching the Hulch Lake. This lake is four miles long, and from its southern extremity to the north end of the Sea of Galilee is ten and a half miles. The second lake has just been determined, by our line of levels, as 682 feet below the Mediterranean; thus in twenty-six and a half miles there is a fall of 1682 feet, or more than sixty feet to the mile.

The Sea of Galilee is twelve miles and a half, or about as long as Windermere, and thence the Jordan flows sixty-five miles measuring in a straight line (the bends make it a good deal more) to the Dead Sea, 1292 feet below the Mediterranean. The fall in this distance is, however, not regular. Above the Jisr Mujâmi'a it is over forty feet to the mile. From the south end of the Sea of Galilee to the Dâmieh ford is a distance of forty-two miles, and a fall of only 460 feet. From the Dâmieh to the mouth of Wâdy el 'Aujeh is thirteen miles, with sixty feet fall, and thence to the Dead Sea is ten miles, with ninety feet of fall.

It will be seen from the above that the total direct length of Jordan is about 104 miles, or only half the length of the Thames; that the fall to the Sea of Galilee is over sixty feet to the mile; thence to the Dâmieh, at first forty feet, afterwards not quite eleven feet per mile; from the Dâmieh to the 'Aujeh not much over four and a half feet to the mile; and for the last ten miles, about nine feet per mile. The break down of the immense chasm may thus be said to commence immediately north of the Sea of Galilee.

The valley may be divided into eight sections. First the portion between Baniâs and the Huleh, where it is some five miles broad, with steep cliffs some 2000 feet high on either side and a broad marsh between. Secondly, from the Huleh to the Sea of Galilee, where the stream runs close to the eastern hills, and about four miles from the base of those on the west, which rise towards the high Safed mountains, more than 3500 feet above the lake. Thirdly, for thirteen miles from the south end of the Sea of Galilee to the neighbourhood of Beisân, the valley is only one and a half mile broad west of the river, and about three on the east; the steep cliffs of the plateau of Kaukab el Hawa on the west, reach an altitude of 1800 feet above the stream.

South of Beisân is the fourth district, with a plain west of Jordan, twelve miles long and six miles broad, the line of hills on the east being straight, and the feet of the mountains on this side about two miles from the river. In the neighbourhood of Beisân the cross section of the plain shows three levels: that of the shelf on which Beisân stands, about 300 feet below sea-level; that of the Ghor itself, some 400 feet lower, reached by an almost precipitous descent; and that of the Zor, or narrow trench, from half to a quarter of a mile wide, and about 150 feet lower still. The higher shelf extends westward to the foot of Gilboa; it dies away on the south, but on the north it gradually rises into the plateau of Kaukab and to the western table-land above the Sea of Galilee, 1800 feet above Jordan.

After leaving the Beisân plain, the river passes through a narrow valley twelve miles long and two to three miles wide, with a raised table-land to the west, having a level averaging about 500 feet above the sea. The Beisân plain is full of springs of fresh water, some of which are thermal, but a large current of warm salt water flows down Wâdy Mâlch, at the north extremity of this fifth district.

In the sixth district—the Damieh region, the valley again opens to a width of about three miles on the west, and five on the east of Jordan. The great block of the Kurn Sŭrtŭbeh here stands out like a bastion, on the west, 2400 feet above the river. Passing this mountain the seventh district is entered—a broad valley extending from near Fusâil to 'Osh el Ghŭrâb, north of Jericho. In this region the Ghor itself is five miles broad, west of the river, and rather more on the east; the lower trench or Zor is also wider here and more distinctly separated from the Ghor. A curious geographical feature of this region was also discovered by the Survey party. The great affluents of the Fâr'ah and 'Aujeh do not flow straight to Jordan, but turn south about a mile west of it, and each runs, for about six miles, nearly parallel with the river; thus the mouth of the Fâr'ah is actually to be found just where that of the next valley is shown on most maps. This curious feature was not discovered even by Captain Warren, and nothing more surprised me, in surveying the district, than the unsuspected parallel course of the streams. The whole of the valley in the seventh region is full of salt springs and salt marshes, but the Fâr'ah, flowing from the Ænon springs, is a perennial stream of fresh water.

The eighth and last district is that of the plain of Jericho, which with the corresponding basin (Ghôr-es-Seisebân) east of Jordan, measures over eight miles north and south, and more than fourteen across, with Jordan about in the middle. The Zor is here about a mile wide, and some 200 feet below the broad plain of the Ghôr.

To sum up shortly the regions thus enumerated. First we have the Huleh marshes ; secondly, the basin of the Sea of Galilee ; thirdly, the narrow gorge of Kaukab ; fourthly, the plain of Beisan ; fifthly, the narrow valley below the Bukei'a of Tûbâs ; sixthly, the broader region of the Fâr'ah ; seventhly, the wide Fusail valley ; eighthly, the great basin of the Jericho plain ; in short, four broad regions connected by two narrow ones, with a marshy lake and a valley highest of all, suggestive, as a glance at the map will show, of a former chain of great lakes connected by a river, which have gradually dwindled in area till three small sheets of water alone remain, with the broad dry beds of two others, represented by the Beisan and Jericho basins.

The question thus suggested of the original formation of this great chasm, is not only interesting in itself, but it has a direct bearing on that of the position of the Cities of the Plain.

Various causes of the great depression of the

valley have been suggested, among which the action of glaciers has been one of the latest. M. Lartet, the French geologist, was, I believe, the first to point out the clear indications of a great fault or crack, extending all along the valley, which has, in fact, slid down towards the centre of the earth. Special observations were, however, much wanted, and we were able to supply these all along the western side, where apparently they were the most necessary.

To enter into the details of these observations would be impossible in the present work. I propose to sum up the results which seem to me most important, and which I have submitted to geologists for criticism.

The main reason for conjecturing the existence of a fault, is that the formations on the east and west are not the same. On the west we have strata of the age of the English chalk, which dip down very suddenly towards the centre of the valley. On the east we have the Nubian sandstone, with hard limestone above it geologically coeval with our greensand. The section of the present bed of the Dead Sea tells the same story; the deepest part is towards the east, where there is more than ten times the depth of water found near the western shore, and here the mountains rise almost sheer from the lake, while on the west. a succession of steps occurs between the sea and the watershed.

The precise manner in which the slopes of the
Palestine watershed fall towards the Ghôr differs
in the different regions, but in principle it is the
same throughout; there is everywhere a violent
contortion of the strata, sometimes forming a
fault or fissure running north and south, and
sometimes a sharp dip down eastwards. We
first studied the section above the Bukei'a, near
Mar Saba, and here, as I have before noticed,
there appears to be a well-defined fault. In the
neighbourhood of Fusâil I found the rocks tilted up
at an angle of 30°, and the same violent contortion
has formed the great fissure of Wâdy el Hamâm,
west of the Sea of Galilee. The Fâr'ah Valley is
a great rent seemingly due to the same causes, and
thus the whole of the geological evidence goes
apparently to prove the occurrence of a violent
and probably sudden collapse of the whole Jordan
Valley commencing north of the Sea of Galilee.

This depression must have taken place at a comparatively late geological period; all the cretaceous
rocks had been deposited before it occurred, for
their strata all dip down east, on the west side of
the valley. There are even the means of fixing
the period pretty exactly, for there are marine
formations deposited on the cretaceous rocks which
seem to have no dip, namely, the coloured marls
and bituminous limestones which occur at Neby
Musa, and again at the edge of the plain of
Beisan, in the first case 200 feet higher than the

Mediterranean, in the latter, 200 feet below that level; these strata are, I believe, attributed to the Eocene period. It appears that even at an earlier epoch the region was bituminous: the latest of the cretaceous formations disturbed by the depression, contain bitumen which seems to have been once liquid, and, near Masada, there are even black bituminous stalactites on the rock. The Eocene coloured marls contain innumerable fossils, and the formation appears to have been deposited under water. It is probable that in Eocene times the Dead Sea reached up nearly to Hermon, and to the Red Sea, with which the Mediterranean must have been then in full connection, as the Isthmus of Suez had not then been formed.

A further change was wrought still later, for the convulsions which were accompanied by the great outflow of lava which has covered so large a district west and north of the Sea of Galilee, and in the Lejja country, are, I believe, dated by geologists as of the Tertiary period, and in one place the lava appeared to me to overlie the coloured marls. The chain of Gilboa, Little Hermon, and Tabor, with the Galilean hills, have all been more or less affected by this volcanic disturbance, and perhaps the depression of the valley may then have increased still more.

The valley having sunk to its present depression, the melting snows of Hermon probably began to pour into it, and as the chasm had now no outlet (the watershed of the 'Arabah on the south having been raised about 200 feet above sea-level), a huge salt lake must have formed at its southern end; the history of the sheets of water then occupying the distance of 150 miles, appears to be recorded in the formations now found in the valley.

The present north shore of the Dead Sea is a shingly beach, with a ridge of pebbles at the top of a somewhat steep slope. Some thirty feet above the high-water mark a second similar beach may be seen inland; and about a hundred feet above the water is a third. There can be little doubt that we see in these raised beaches former limits of the lake. Above the beaches, some 300 feet higher than the water, there are flat shelves of marl with steep slopes much worn by water action. These marls are deposited against the high Dolomitic cliffs, the tops of which are about the level of the Mediterranean. The shelves (the "Sidd" of the Arabs) have also been recognised as former shores of the sea, and this level may be called the Siddim level.

When the marl beds are closely investigated they are found to consist of very thin strata of various materials, mud, small pebbles, and shingle, in layer above layer, strongly impregnated with salt and bitumen. They have the appearance of being deposited in still, deep water, and the present bottom of the Dead Sea must be of much the same character. The whole area over which they occur, reaching up the Jordan Valley for about four miles, is so salt that no vegetation will grow upon it; thus there is every reason to regard these formations as once forming the bottom of a lake resembling the present Dead Sea.

But our observations were carried still farther. North of Jericho is a curious terrace, in form not unlike a croquet-ground on a large scale, called Meidân el 'Abd, "the open place of the slave." The study of the Dead Sea beaches shows, by comparison, that this is another old shore-line of a former sea, and, a little south of it, there is a cliff of conglomerate, which has also the appearance of a shore formation. The line of this former beach runs south, to the marl deposits which have been formed at the foot of Kŭrŭntŭl; thus we find yet another level some 600 or 700 feet below the Mediterranean, forming the shore at a time when the plains of Jericho were under water, and when the Dead Sea must have reached to the foot of the Sŭrtŭbeh, or eighteen miles farther north than at present. The shelf on which Beisân stands looks like another similar shore-line, and thus, perhaps, the Beisân plain was also, at this period, under water.

From these observations we infer the gradual desiccation of the Jordan Valley; the Beisân Lake and the Jericho end of the Dead Sea having disappeared. Thus the present lake may be compared to one of the little pools on its own banks, left by the waves in the hollow of a rock, and gradually evaporating, surrounded by a crust of dry white salt. Into its thick oily waters—more than one-fourth part solid salt—the winter rains, and the streams from the salt springs, bring down all the chlorides which were once spread over the larger basin of the former great lake, and which are now accumulating in the smaller area, so that the sea seems to be almost in process of evaporating into a salt-marsh.

There is, however, a curious indication still to be noticed. Hitherto evaporation has been on the increase. Is this still the case? The fords near the Lisân, which used to be passable by donkeys, are said now to be much deeper than formerly, and Sheikh Jemîl, the most intelligent of the Arabs near Jericho, told me that in his father's days the sea did not generally reach further inland than the Rujm el Bahr, whereas now the connecting causeway is always under water. This represents a rise of some ten feet in the water-level. In fact, according to this statement, the sea has now more water in it than it used to have half a century ago.

If the theory of desiccation be correct, the idea that the Dead Sea was first formed at the time when the Cities of the Plain were overthrown is a fallacy. Geologists hold that the lake had reached its present condition before man was created, and thus the vale of Siddim is, no doubt, still represented by the district of the Sidds round the northern shores of the sea; for the four successive Dead Seas, which we have traced above, had all dried up before the days of Abraham.

Turning from the question of the probable formation of the valley, we may next notice the most remarkable of its antiquities, namely the Tellûl or Tells there found.

The word Tell (meaning a "heap") is used for many different things; for a conical mountain, for a little sand-hillock, for an artificial mound, or for a heap of ruins. The Jordan Valley has Tells of all these kinds in it, but the class of artificial mounds is the one more peculiarly interesting. Of these there are seven at Jericho, twenty-four at Beisân, several others between, and others again east of Jordan. They have been described as ruined sites of cities or fortresses, commanding the passes; the following peculiarities seem to be invariably recognisable.

The Tell is a mound with steep slopes, from two or three to twenty or thirty feet high; a large Tell is often surrounded by smaller ones irregularly scattered; they are of no particular shape, and they show no signs of stone masonry, being outwardly earthen mounds, whilst inwardly, Captain Warren's excavations proved them in some cases to consist of sun-dried bricks.

The Tells all occur in alluvial soil, and I believe there is scarcely an instance in which water—a spring or a stream—is not found close by. It is true that Tells exist near the passes of the hills and by the Jordan fords, but this is, I think, no proof that they were fortresses, for half the number are placed in positions of no strategical value, and those which are so placed will be found also to stand by water either springing from the hills or flowing into Jordan.

Brick mounds in clay land by water are suggestive of brick-making. Travellers from India and from Egypt have recognised a similarity between the Jordan Valley Tells and the great mounds of refuse bricks, found in both those countries, on which other bricks are laid out to dry in the sun. This seems to me the most probable origin of the Tells, but we find possibly a reference to them in Scripture, when Solomon cast the Temple vessels "in the clay ground" of the Jordan Valley, near Succoth (2 Chr. v. 17).

The preceding observations are intended to give a general idea of the physical features of the Jordan Valley, and of their relation to its probable origin, as well as of the most striking archæological features. We may now return to the history of the second Jordan Valley campaign, and to the principal Biblical discoveries which rewarded us for months of most severe exertion.

On the 24th of February we marched down

into the valley; by the 20th of April we had completed the work to within three miles of the Sea of Galilee; the rate obtained was nearly 300 square miles per month, being treble that which had been possible with the smaller, and inexperienced party, which I had conducted through the Samaritan mountains.

Descending by the familiar pass of Wâdy Kelt, we found the valley completely changed in appearance. It was no longer all white and glaring chalk, but a broad expanse of deep pasture; the Kelt was a rapid stream running with a loud murmur in its rocky chasm.

As a precaution, we now encamped on the very top of the fatal Tell by Elisha's Fountain, where we had suffered so much three months before. It was no longer a mound of dust, but a huge hillock, hidden deep in luxuriant mallows with immense round leaves.

We visited the Dead Sea once more, to fix up poles for observing the water-levels; these poles had been carefully made in Jerusalem and were marked with figures. The first we drove, without difficulty, at the water's edge, but the second it was almost impossible to fix. Floating on my back, I held it upright in the water, with my feet, while Drake swam and drove it with a huge mallet. There was a strong current, which made the operation most difficult, but at length it was so far fixed that I was able to climb on to it, and to drive it down farther with the mallet from above. We were nearly an hour in the water, and Drake suffered from the over-exertion. Within a week the Arabs pulled up the poles, for the sake of the iron, in spite of the reiterated assurances of the Sheikhs that they should be respected.

We next visited the spring encampment of Sheikh Jemíl, and, after the coffee, we were treated to a repast consisting of a sort of omelette and a dish of sweet rice, both very good, as was also the thin wafer-like bread just baked. From the tent-door we looked out on the flowery slopes and the gleaming lake, on the children, camels and donkeys, goats and kids, and lambs with speckled fleeces, such as Jacob chose from Laban's flocks. Here and there a female figure stole out, robed in the dark green and indigo-coloured sweeping garments peculiar to the Bedawîn women; and inside the black camel's-hair tent, on bright cushions and carpets, our friends sat round—Jemíl, the educated chief, who could read and write; Jedû'a, his brother, the great hunter of the ibex; the young flaxen-haired Sheikh who had been one of our principal guides; and many others with faces then quite familiar to me.

On Tuesday the 26th of February we struck camp, and marched north to Fusâil, the ancient Phasaelis founded by Herod. Our procession was spread over a quarter of a mile as I reviewed it from a hillock beside the road. Five Englishmen on horseback came first, eight mules, and eight camels followed, we had four Bedawin guides, seven muleteers, six servants, and a Bashi-Bazouk, three donkeys, and Sheikh Jemil's dromedary—in all, twenty-seven individuals and thirty-four animals, including six dogs.

The new camp was not in the territory of Sheikh Jemil, and I had procured letters to the Emir of the Mes'aid Arabs. Our old friends left us, and Jemil seemed disappointed by the present I gave him, though it was worth five pounds, but was radiant on the receipt of another five shillings.

About two p.m., on the 28th, the Emir was announced; he was seen coming across the plain, with ten horsemen armed with long lances, and swords, and with guns which they kept firing off. They dismounted with much ceremony, and coffee was served; the Emir was rather a handsome man, with delicate features and very small hands and feet. He left his son and nephew with us, but was very anxious we should come on to the Fâr'ah Valley where his camp was pitched. We had intended to give him a dinner, but the provisions did not arrive, and he intimated, through the servants, that money would be more acceptable, so I had two half-sovereigns wrapped up in paper, and slipped one into his hand and one into that of his cousin; I also sent out to him a black abba, and the great prince rode off happily. I suppose that had I offered such a present during this troublous year, when Fendi-el-Fais has just taken £300 from Tiberias, the Emîr would not have been so contented with the amount.

We found it very difficult to keep any Arabs at Fusail; some said it was not their country, others that the fever was always bad there, others again that they were afraid of a ghoul in the ruins. In reality the country here belongs to the Fellahîn, and I imagine no Arabs had a right to camp there. We were much hindered by weather; rain and snow fell, and though the latter never came into the valley it lay thick on the hills; and on the summit of the Kurn Sŭrtŭbeh we were caught in a fall of sleet. Corporal Brophy had to ride up 3000 feet every morning before he got to his work, and the transitions of temperature were far from improving our health.

We were now almost at the foot of the Sŭrtŭbeh block, one of the finest features of the valley; and I surveyed the detail on the mountain myself; for ever since 1873 I had been in the habit of taking part in the survey of detail. In addition to this I had my duties as commander, and the writing of notes and reports, studies of archæological and antiquarian questions, plan-making, hill-shading, accounts, and general provisioning, all of which duties fell upon me personally.

The Sŭrtŭbeh is a block of chalk which has slid down the face of the tilted dolomitic limestone of the watershed hills. Its summit, two thousand four hundred feet above the valley, is capped by a cone two hundred and seventy feet high, with steep smooth sides like those of the so-called Frank Mountain (Herodium) near Bethlehem. The building on the top appears to be the foundation of a Crusading fort with large drafted stones; beneath are caves all round the hill, and lower still a sort of terrace like a garden. An aqueduct follows the contour of the mountain, collecting surface-drainage and leading to some large reservoirs cut in rock. A wall, enclosing a space some thirty yards by ninety, surrounds the foundations of the tower, which are about eighteen feet in height.

This mountain, under which we lived for just a month, had always a wonderful attraction for me. It has so remarkable an appearance, and yet so slight a history, that one could not help imagining a mystery about it. We asked the Arabs, but they said that Sŭrtŭbeh was a king who built a castle on the top. It has by some been supposed to be the Tower of Alexandrium near Corea, noticed more than once by Josephus, but Corea was on the boundary of the lands of Judea and Samaria, and near the watershed, as Josephus expressly tells us.

The name Surtuba occurs in the Talmud, as that of a beacon-station on the way from Jerusalem to the Hauran, which was lighted when the new moon appeared. This fact is, no doubt, con-

THE KURN SCHUBEH

nected with the title Dalûk, applied, not to the
conical summit, but to one close to it on the chain,
and meaning "burning" in Hebrew; and also
perhaps with the name "Mother of the New
Moon" applied to a prominent point on the
mountain. Sŭrtŭbeh means, as Dr. Chaplin
pointed out to me, neither more nor less than
"Bellevue," and is certainly a title very appropriate to this fine point. I have only been able
to find one later reference to the place, Marino
Sanuto speaking of it as the fortress of Docus
where Simon the Asmonean was murdered; but
this is a mistake, and other mediæval writers
point out the true site near 'Ain Dûk.

On my first visit to England, I proposed to
identify the Kurn with the place where the great
monumental altar of Ed was erected by the
children of Gad, Reuben and Manasseh. The
site seems wonderfully appropriate for a monument intended to show that the trans-Jordanic
tribes were not cast out from their participation
in the religious rites of the western tribes. The
place stands above the great ford, by which they
perhaps crossed in going from Shiloh to the land
of Gilead, and the name Ed is perhaps recognisable in the Tal'at Abu 'Aid on the side of the
mountain. There are, however, objections to the
theory; first that the tribes crossed by the
"passage of the children of Israel" (Josh. xxii.
11) after leaving Shiloh, and this seems to point,

not to the Dâmieh, but to the Jericho ford; secondly, Josephus says that the altar was east of Jordan; thirdly, Abu 'Aid, "father of the feast," may be (as it sometimes is) a proper name of a person born on a feast day. The idea is therefore merely a conjecture, and far from being an identification.

The Jordan Valley was now one blaze of beautiful flowers, growing in a profusion not often to be found, even in more fertile lands. The ground was literally covered with blossoms: the great red anemone, like a poppy, grew in long tracts on the stony soil: on the soft marls patches of delicate lavender colour were made by the wild stocks; the Retem or white broom (the juniper of Scripture) was in full blossom, and the rich purple nettles contrasted with fields of the Kutufy or yellow St. John's wort. There were also quantities of orange-coloured marigolds, and long fields of white and purple clover, tall spires of asphodel and clubs of snapdragon, purple salvias and white garlic, pink geraniums and cistus, tall white umbelliferous plants, and large camomile daisies, all set in a border of deep green herbage which reached the shoulders of the horses. Even the Zor was green, and Jordan's banks covered with flowers, while the brown Turfah or tamarisks and the canebrake hid the rushing stream, and the white marl banks stood out in striking contrast.

Rain, and Bedawîn unpunctuality, delayed our

move for several days, but on Tuesday the 10th of March we got to Wâdy Fâr'ah,—the open plain north of the Sŭrtŭbeh, which Vandevelde marks as "beautiful" on his map. Drake and the men went on before, and I sat on a box waiting for the camels. Six Arabs appeared, at last, on horseback, escorting a drove of about fifteen camels, ranging from a patriarch with a pendent lower lip to a little woolly thing not as high as a pony, who came along making constant attempts to get refreshment from his mother. Very picturesque no doubt! but they had no proper saddles. The owners proposed to put our boxes in sacks, as they put their own camp-furniture. We bound the things on somehow, and various little negro boys mounted the humps of the camels. They had no bridles, and took seven hours to go as many miles, stopping to crop the grass at intervals; but we were thankful to get any beasts at all in this wild region.

We commenced the triangulation from the new camp at once, and rode out on the 11th to a hill north of it, whence a fine view of the Ghor could be obtained. On the south was the wide valley, flanked by steep ranges, with the Sŭrtŭbeh in the foreground, and the gleaming Dead Sea in the far distance. On the north the valley became narrower, and its surface was broken into mud-islands, and marl mounds scored with hundreds of intricate watercourses—a region well called by the Arabs "the Mother of Steps." In the middle of it the snaky Jordan wriggled along, with brown tamarisk swamps on either bank; far away were black volcanic ranges and the white dome of snowy Hermon, with the long white line of Anti-Libanus to the west. Eastward was the rugged Mount Gilead, crowned by a Crusading castle (Kŭl'at er Rubud) and on the west the shapeless hills north of Nablus,—the mediæval land of Tampne.

The ulcer on my hand had now been growing bigger for four months. The snow had got into it, and not only my hand but the whole arm also was quite useless from pain. I had, in addition, severe rheumatism in the shoulders, which prevented my sleeping, so I rode up forty miles in one day, to Jerusalem, to see the doctor, and get the ulcer cauterised. I shall not forget the kindness of Mr. Henry Maudslay on this occasion, for, by constant rubbing of my shoulders, he routed the rheumatism for the time. On Monday, the 16th of March, I went back to camp, and had to ride the forty miles in a continual succession of showers. Next day the equinoctial gales came down on us, and, to my great disgust, we had to sit idle in our tents until the 25th of the month, for while the evenings and nights were fine, every morning was so wet as to make the tents too heavy to move. We had at this time a visit from some Egyptian dancing-girls, and the Arabs were much surprised at my dismissing them from camp.

On Wednesday the 25th, we at length got a fine morning, and spite of the very boggy nature of the ground, we set out for Wâdy Mâleh, the only place at a suitable distance where water was reported. It was not a change for the better by any means. The Fâr'ah Valley is a most delightful place in early spring, when it does not rain, but Wâdy Mâleh was quite the worst camp we ever went into. Down the Fâr'ah a perennial stream flows from near Tullûza, in which stream I have proposed to recognise the "much water" between Salem and Ænon. Part of the course is through a narrow gorge, between low precipitous cliffs of dark limestone, with iron-coloured bands of flint and many natural caverns. Lower down it broadens into an open vale a mile across, the whole of which was now knee-deep in beautiful flowers. The canes in the stream had been swept down, and piled in heaps, covered with mud, in consequence of the late floods. The oleander bushes grow all along the bed of the river in great luxuriance, and they were now in full flower.

Leaving this charming valley hidden among its rolling hills, we ascended northwards into the Bukei'a, or plateau, on which the ruin 'Ainûn (Ænon) stands. Here the flowers were also abundant; the pheasant's-eye was as large almost as an anemone; two beautiful species of bugloss formed patches of sky-blue, and the pink cistus (comparatively rare in Palestine) grew between the rocks; the veronicas, blue and red, with here and there a bunch of the dark iris (the "lily of the field"), were interspersed with large maroon-coloured velvety arums. The plain is good corn-land, but seems to have a bad natural drainage; and our mules floundered in deep bogs, sometimes up to the girths.

Still farther north, we began to descend a long valley, and came on a different kind of country. A basaltic outbreak appeared, and cliffs tilted in every direction. The valley-bed was strewn with fragments of hard basalt. Passing over a bare ridge, where the beautiful white Retem broom (Elijah's juniper) abounded, we descended into a most desolate valley, where, between green rolling hills like those of the Judean desert, a muddy stream was flowing. We had ridden fifteen miles, and it now began to rain again. We found, to our dismay, that this was where we had to camp, as no other supply of water existed in a position central to the new work.

The valley comes down from a narrow gorge, dominated by a Crusading castle, and beneath this is a great outbreak of basalt. We rode up the gorge, hoping to find a better place; but the pass was too rugged to expect to get camels up it in the then state of the road, so we resigned ourselves to a camp in the lower ground by the stream.

We soon made a still more unpleasant discovery. The valley was full of clear springs, but they were all tepid and salt. The head spring has a temperature of 100° F., and the stream from it is about 80° F. If the Survey was to be done at all, it appeared that we should have to drink brackish water for ten days or more. Here, then, we sat down on the wet grass, in a driving drizzle of rain, by the brackish stream; not a soul was to be seen, either Bedawî or peasant, and it was evident that food would have to be brought from a distance.

The mules soon arrived with our tents and beds, which, though soaked with rain, we set up on the bare ground. Of course all the party were cross, and thought themselves injured. I had a very bad cold and rheumatism, and Habib had tic-douloureux. The Arabs looked wretched; but I was glad they should have their share of the hardships, for, unlike our Abu Nuseir friends at Jericho, they were the most lazy and good-for-nothing tribe we had come across.

News of the camels reached us after dark; they had been unable to struggle any farther, and one had sprained its leg slipping on the rocks; they had, therefore, halted a few miles farther south. We got some dinner, and tea made with salt water, which was very nasty, and went to bed; but the rheumatism in my legs kept me awake. It rained all night, and the horses fought one another.

Next morning things looked a little better, and we went out to choose points for the theodolite; we also discovered a spring of cold fresh water about a mile away, and found a peasant, from whom we bought an aged goat.

The Emîr and his party left us, having been thoroughly disgusted with the journey and with the rain.

The morning of the 27th promised well, and Sergeant Armstrong and I set out to ascend a hill called Râs Jâdir, six miles from camp, and 2500 feet above it. We again floundered through deep bogs, and had the greatest difficulty in making any progress. As we got to the summit, we experienced a wind so cutting and strong that we had to dismount, being nearly blown off our horses; and the theodolite was scarcely adjusted before a pelting hail-storm followed. Wrapped in our waterproofs, we waited under a tree, when suddenly the sun burst out, and a very clear view was obtained. Half the observations were taken, when a second hailstorm came on; and a third broke over us before we had finished. It was piercing cold, and the wind at times almost a hurricane; but it was clear between the squalls, and we obtained very good observations, though my hands were so cold that I could scarcely write them down.

Such were the difficulties which attended our third Jordan Valley camp in 1874. Against them we may count the exploration of Ænon, Abel Meholah, and Tirzah, the plotting of a region scarcely known before, and the discovery of an important volcanic centre and of hot springs. Perhaps no European will again be obliged to linger so long in this inhospitable region.

East of camp, Wády Málch ran out into the south part of the Beisân plain, which looks like the Jericho plain turned round, with Hermon at the farther end. The view in this direction was a fine one—a broad open valley, gay with flowers, dotted with Tells all hidden by dark mallows, and frequented by the solemn white storks, called "fathers of good luck," or "little pilgrims," by the Arabs. On the north-west the heights of Gilboa closed the view, with Tabor and Neby Duhy, our old friends of 1872, peeping over them. A black mound represented the ruins of Beisân, and the high plateau rose behind, crowned by the Crusading castle of Belvoir overlooking Jordan. A silver thread seen through the gap below was the Sea of Galilee; the hills of Safed were pale and blue beyond; and farther yet was Hermon, in the full glory of his fresh winter robe of snow, his rounded bulk dwarfing the lower ranges and closing the scene.

From the banks of the Ghor we looked down also on Jordan, a turbid coffee-coloured stream, breaking in one place over stones down a small rapid, and varying from some forty to seventy yards in width, being now very full. Little islands covered with tamarisks occurred at intervals, and the river wound like a snake, looking wild and desolate, and flowing, as Josephus says, "through a desert." The Zor is here not continuous, and in places there are cliffs a hundred feet high immediately over the stream. The low ground was covered with barley, already very high.

The only places of interest in this part of the Beisân plain were 'Ain Helweh, a spring with ruins, at the distance from Beisân at which Jerome places Abel Meholah ; and Sâkût, which has been thought by some to be Succoth. The name is, however, radically different, and Succoth seems clearly to have been somewhere opposite the Dâmieh ford; but Sâkût is probably a Crusading site, for Marino Sanuto seems to mark it on his map as Succoth, though Jerome places this Biblical site east of Jordan.

On the 4th of April, after having endured our camp for ten days, we were able once more to march north to Beisân (the Biblical Bethshean), one of the best-watered places in Palestine, and at that time literally streaming with rivulets from some fifty springs. Here, then, we rested, for Easter Sunday, surrounded by interesting ruins, and near a fine pool in the Jalûd river in which we could swim. We had a boar's head, pigeons, quail, and fish from Jordan for dinner, and enjoyed the change from the succession of patriarchal goats which we had devoured in Wâdy Mâleh.

There was still a fortnight's work to do, and the weather was dry, though getting very hot; but the party were hardly equal to the task. Drake was much tried by the exposure, and required great care. I was almost entirely exhausted, suffering not only from rheumatism, but also from a very aggravated kind of hay-fever, brought on by the rank herbage. The ground all round us was very swampy, and frogs and tortoises abounded round the tents.

I shall not easily forget the labour of one day's Survey along the banks of Jordan, while endeavouring to fix the position of the fords, of which I found twenty-one in seven miles, none of which had been previously marked on any map. It was no easy task to follow out the windings of the stream, to clamber up and down the marl hills, and across the muddy rivulets flowing into Jordan. I had to force my poor horse through acres of enormous thistles, ten feet high, and returned with his shoulders and my knees bleeding, and covered with the poisonous yellow pollen of the marigolds. Accompanied by one Bedawî, I rode down to a camp of the Sukr Arabs, to inquire about the fords. A wild, naked boy stopped my path, and presented a pistol at my head; but finding I was not afraid, he came and kissed my hand. It seems to be always the boys who make these tentative assaults, the men being able to attribute their proceedings to youthful indiscretion, if they see the traveller is not intimidated. This cautious method of action, in attempted robbery with violence, is very characteristic of the Bedawîn.

The fords were collected and marked in the natural course of the Survey, the names carefully obtained, and every precaution taken to ensure their being applied to the right places. It was not, however, until the next winter that I became aware how valuable a result had been obtained. Looking over the nomenclature for the purpose of making an index, I was struck with the name 'Abârah applying to a ford. The word means "passage," or "ferry," and is radically the same word found in the name Bethabara. I looked 'Abârah out at once on the map, and found that it is one of the main fords, just above the place where the Jalûd river, flowing down the valley of Jezreel and by Beisân, debouches into Jordan.

One cannot but look on this as one of the most valuable discoveries resulting from the Survey; and I have not, as yet, seen any argument directed against the identification which seems to shake it. It may be said that the name 'Abârah is merely descriptive, and perhaps applies to several fords.

That it is descriptive may be granted; so is the name Bethabara, or Bethel, or Gibeah, or Ramah. That it is a common name may be safely denied. We have collected the names of over forty fords, and no other is called 'Abârah; nor does the word occur again in all the 9000 names collected by the Survey party.

Nor do we depend on the name alone. An identification may be defined as the recovery of a site unknown to Europeans, but known to the natives of the country. Evidently places can only be known by their names, unless we have measured distances by which to fix them. If in England we endeavoured to recover an ancient site, and knew the district in which it should occur, we should be satisfied if we found the ancient name applying to one place, and one only, in that district. Without the name, we should still be in doubt. Does not this apply to Palestine? It is true that name alone will not be sufficient; position must be suitable also. No one would try to identify Yarmouth in Norfolk with Yarmouth in the Isle of Wight. But, on the other hand, without the name it is merely conjecture, not identification, that is possible.

Here at 'Abârah we have the name, and nowhere else, as yet, has the name been found; the question then arises, is the position suitable?

We speak commonly of Bethabara as the place of Our Lord's baptism. Possibly it was so, but the

Gospel does not say as much. It is only once mentioned as a place where John was baptising, and where certain events happened on consecutive days. These events are placed in the Gospel harmonies immediately after the Temptation, when Christ would appear to have been returning from the desert (perhaps east of Jordan) to Galilee. Bethabara, "the house of the ferry," was "beyond Jordan;" but the place of baptism was no doubt at the ford or ferry itself; hence the ford 'Abârah is the place of interest. It cannot be Christian tradition which originates this site, for Christian tradition has pointed, from the fourth century down to the present day, to the fords of Jericho as the place of baptism by St. John.

"And the third day there was a marriage in Cana of Galilee" (John ii. 1). Here is the controlling passage. The hostile critics of the fourth Gospel have taken hold of it; they have supposed the traditional site to be undoubtedly the true one, and have thence argued the impossibility that in one day Christ could have travelled eighty miles to Cana. To the fourth-century inquirer the difficulty would never have occurred; he would have answered at once that Our Lord was miraculously carried from one place to the other; but the Gospel does not say so, and we should therefore look naturally for Bethabara within a day's journey of Cana. The ford 'Abârah is about twenty-two miles in a line from Kefr Kenna, and no place can be found, on Jordan, much nearer or more easily accessible to the neighbourhood of Cana.

I leave these facts to the reader, asking him to choose, between the difficulties attendant on the traditional site, and the suitability of the new site, where alone as yet the name of Bethabara has been recovered.

There is, however, another point with regard to Bethabara which must not be overlooked. The oldest MSS. read, not Bethabara, but Bethany, beyond Jordan. Origen observed this, yet chose the present reading, and we can hardly suppose that the early fathers of the Church made such an alteration without some good reason; perhaps the original text contained both names, "Bethabara in Bethany" beyond Jordan being a possible reading.

The author of "Supernatural Religion" has made a point of this reading in arguing against the authenticity of the fourth Gospel. He supposes that Bethany beyond Jordan has been confused in the Evangelist's mind with Bethany near Jerusalem, forgetting that this very Gospel speaks of the latter place as "nigh unto Jerusalem, about fifteen furlongs off" (John xi. 18). The assumption of the confusion is quite gratuitous. Bathania, meaning "soft soil," was the well-known form used in the time of Christ, of the old name Bashan, which district was in Peræa, or the country beyond Jordan.

If Bethabara be a true reading, the place should thus most probably be sought in Bathania, and the ford should therefore lead over to Bashan. This again strengthens the case for the 'Abârah ford, which is near the hills of Bashan, whereas the Jericho fords are far away, leading over towards Gilead and Moab.

A second site of primary interest may here be noticed in its proper place, namely that of Megiddo.

In a former chapter we have seen, that the identification proposed by Robinson rests on a wholly insufficient basis. Here again it is a question of recovering the name. The position of Megiddo is not fixed very definitely in the Biblical narrative, though the town is noticed in connection with Taanach, west of the Great Plain, and with Jezreel, Bethshan, and other places near the Jordan Valley. A broad valley was named from the city, and the "waters of Megiddo" are also noticed in Scripture. All these requisites are met by the large ruined site of Mujedd'a at the foot of Gilboa, —a mound from which fine springs burst out, with the broad valley of the Jalûd river to the north. It is the only place, as yet discovered, at which any name like the Hebrew Megiddon exists, and the position seems to suit also with the march of Thothmes III. towards the Sea of Galilee, through Aaruna (perhaps 'Arrâneh), and Kaina (possibly Kâ'aûn), to the plains of Megiddo.

A third place of importance is the Spring of Harod, where Gideon divided his troops. This appears, according to Josephus, to have been near Jordan, while from the Bible we gather it to have been in the neighbourhood of Gilboa, being towards the south of the Valley of Jezreel, and opposite the Midianite host (Judg. vi. 33; vii. 1). The Mount Gilead of the passage is very possibly the name of part of the chain, above the river now called Jalûd (see Judg. vii. 3). It is very striking to find in this position a large spring with the name 'Ain el Jem'ain, or "fountain of the two troops," and there seems no valid objection to the view that this is the Spring of Harod.

Beisân itself, where we were now encamped, is a miserable hamlet of mud hovels, amid the ruins of the important town of Scythopolis, which was a bishopric, from the fifth century, until the change of the see to Nazareth, in the twelfth century. In the Bible it is famous as the place where the body of Saul was fastened to the wall (1 Sam. xxxi. 10), but the remains of a theatre, hippodrome, and temple, of fine structural tombs and baths, with a Crusading fortress and bridge, are among the best preserved antiquities of western Palestine. Christian martyrs, in the fourth century, here fought wild beasts in the theatre, and the cages with the sockets of the iron bars, and the narrow passages from the outside, are still intact in the ruined theatre of black basalt.

On the 14th of April Sergeant Black accompanied me on a flying expedition, to carry the work farther north. We left Drake and the two Corporals to finish the special survey of Beisân, and took up our abode with one tent, for three days, in the old Crusading castle of Belvoir, six miles nearer the Sea of Galilee. Poor Drake had ulcers on his feet, which prevented his riding, and nearly all our horses had sore-backs from the wet and the grass diet, while most of them required new shoes.

We got off early, and did not find it very hot, but were much troubled with the flies. With almost every breath we sucked in half a dozen of them; others were just small enough to get up one's nose; some yet smaller got into our eyes, and huge bluebottles bit through our clothes. One could not wonder that the lowlanders of Palestine used to propitiate Baal-Zebub, "the God of flies."

Riding up the Ghor, we saw, on the east, the white cliffs of the Yermûk pass, with a stream almost as broad as Jordan running northwards to join it. After visiting a point on the plateau south-west of the Sea of Galilee, we turned south towards Kaukab el Hawa (as Belvoir is now called), and had to cross the great Birch Valley, which is a gorge a thousand feet deep. The thermometer was nearly 100° F. in the shade, and not a breath of air was stirring. As we went down into the chasm I began to feel burning hot, then sore from head to foot, and then cold thrills shot over me. I set spurs to my poor horse, and galloped up hill, swinging my arms and legs and endeavouring to restore the stagnating circulation. A few buckets of water over my head put me right, but it was a narrow escape of sunstroke, and a warning that Europeans should not attempt to stay in the Jordan Valley any longer when even the Arabs were moving up to the hills. We now felt a great reluctance to face the noonday sun, so we rose before dawn for the next two days, returning to the tent by noon, when the great heat of the day begins.

The black basalt fortress, beside the ditch of which our tent stood, had cost the lives of numbers of Saracens when attacked by Saladin in 1182, more of the assailants perishing from heat and sunstroke than by the sword. Jordan wound along, 1800 feet beneath us, spanned by two bridges, and joined by the tortuous Yermûk. The heat had already withered the flowers, but green patches of corn on the plateau contrasted with the dry grass. The round Lake of Galilee lay among its hills, and mirrored in its glassy surface the dome of Hermon; the Horns of Hattin, the rugged range of Safed, and the low Nazareth hills, were all visible, Nazareth itself gleaming white among the latter, while Tabor, like a gigantic molehill, dotted with oaks, was backed by the blue Carmel range, visible from the peak of sacrifice, right away to the monastery at the sea end. The whole breadth of the land was thus seen—some thirty miles across, from Jordan to the promontory above Haifa. South of Tabor rose the Neby Duhy cone, with the black tents of the Sukr, coming up, like the Philistines and Midianites of old, by the highway of the Jezreel Valley, to levy black-mail from the villagers of the Great Plain, and unopposed by any modern Saul or Gideon. Farther south the tower of Jezreel was visible above the valley, and the peak of Sheikh Iskander behind it. Gilboa hid the Great Plain; but, behind the Beisân valley and the hills of Wâdy Mâleh, the cone of the Surtŭbeh stood up like a great inverted funnel; and the Moab mountains could be seen almost as far as the Dead Sea. The length of the land, as well as the breadth, was included in this magnificent panorama from the castle of Belvoir.

We moved up, on the 17th, to Shunem, where Drake was to join me, and here we lived on eggs and bread, our meat being finished, and on the next night we experienced an adventure. Our party was so small—consisting of only three persons—that the Sukr Arabs were tempted to try and steal our horses. A short, sharp bark from our big dog warned my servant, and the thieves, creeping through the long grass, were seen and fired on just as they reached the tethering-rope. Half an hour later, just as we were dropping asleep, we heard a distant Bedawîn war-song coming nearer and nearer, and several shots were fired. Our guards from the village shouted lustily for help, and I got up, put on my boots and loaded my gun, while the Sergeant prepared his pistol. The noise grew louder as the enemy approached, when suddenly the village woke up. It was pitch dark, but we could hear the shouts of the peasants as they ran out to meet the Arabs. The dark outline of the mountain could just be distinguished, with the twinkling stars above, and soon there were flashes on every side; but the guns seemed only to go off about once in four times. The war-song grew fainter, and the Arabs appeared to be easily driven back. They never came to our tents, but they got hold of a cow from the village, and so retreated.

Next day neither Drake nor any provisions turned up, but I had a visit from three English ladies travelling under escort of a negro dragoman. Finally, on the 19th, the rest of our party appeared, Drake scarcely able to put his feet to the ground. On the 20th we marched to the pleasant gardens of Jenin, and felt as if returning to civilisation. The horses were shod, and the party became wonderfully high-spirited, relieved from the abnormal pressure of the air below sea-level, and looking forward to rest and better food.

Such is the history of the Survey of the

Jordan Valley. The results were more important than could have been hoped. The cost was the complete exhaustion of Drake and myself. Scarcely able to sit on my horse, tortured with rheumatism and by a constant cough, I was so knocked up that, in Dr. Chaplin's opinion, nothing but perfect rest, and a visit to England, could prevent my breaking down. I left Drake with many apprehensions about his health, and even wrote to his friends at Damascus to look after him. We clasped hands and parted, never to meet again, for almost the first news I got, on reaching England, was that he had been again attacked with the horrible typhoid fever of Jericho. After reaching Jerusalem the exposure and malaria proved too much for his constitution, and we paid a heavy price for our success, for he died at his post in the summer. It is a sad consolation to remember that we had been cordial, and entirely of one mind, during the two years we had spent together, and that not a single unkind or hasty word had passed between us. In the gallant gentleman who had been my only companion for so long, I lost a friend whose fine qualities I had learned to appreciate, and whose tact and courtesy had lightened the burden of the command which I held.

DEBIR.

CHAPTER III.

HEBRON AND BEERSHEBA.

On the 20th of September, 1874, I once more landed in Palestine, having been absent for nearly five months, four of which were spent in England, where I was detained on account of my health. During this period the party had been engaged, under charge of Sergeant Black, in office work and survey, in the vicinity of Jerusalem.

My first painful duty was to assist the Consul in winding up Mr. Drake's affairs; my next was thoroughly to prepare the expedition for a new campaign. On the 5th of October we marched out, and encamped by the beautiful spring of

Dhirweh just by Hûlhûl. This village stands on the watershed of the Hebron hills, 3300 feet above the sea, and only three miles north of Hebron itself. My object was to avoid camping at the latter town, and thus to escape the suspicion of wishing to attempt an entrance into the Hebron Haram.

The fountain of Dhirweh is traditionally that at which St. Philip baptised the Eunuch, and traces of an old chapel are visible above it; but it seems improbable that chariots could ever have travelled along these stony mountain paths, and the road to Gaza by which the Apostle was travelling on that occasion should rather be sought in the plain.

Opposite to our camp was Bethsur, famous in Maccabean times — a stony hill with a ruined tower on the top. To the north we discovered a ruin called Kueiziba, perhaps Chozeba, the home of Bar Cochebas; and near it we found the head of Pilate's great aqueduct to Jerusalem, never before traced to its real commencement, which is thirteen miles from Jerusalem as the crow flies, and forty-one and a half by the aqueduct, the fall being 365 feet in that distance.

My party now consisted of three non-commissioned officers; and Lieutenant Kitchener was expected to join me in about a month. We had with us eleven natives, including Habib the headman, a scribe, a second valet, two grooms, the cook (a villain who only sat and watched his boy cooking), two muleteers, and two Bashi-Bazouks; the party was thus, at its full strength, composed of only sixteen persons, with nine horses and seven mules. Our dogs had accumulated in Jerusalem till we had fifteen, but I soon reduced this rabble to three fox-terriers, Tom, Jack, and Looloo, with our old colley-dog Tarbush.

Our tents were arranged in a straight line, including three large Egyptian double tents, a little English one, a cook's tent, and a smaller one for the grooms, six in all. Our horses were tethered to a long rope to leeward of the camp, and the mules were near them; by night a guard was provided by the Sheikh of the village, and four guides were hired who received a shilling a day, a mule to ride, and breakfast; the information which they gave the Surveyors was written down from their mouths by the scribe, an intelligent young Damascene recommended by Mr. Wright. Thus correctness both of pronunciation, and of locality was ensured, and the names were checked by every means in our power.

Such was the daily routine. The parties left by eight a.m. and returned by five p.m.; dinner was at sunset, and from about eight to eleven, or even until midnight, I studied, after the day's work, the topography of the district. This labour was not unrewarded, for one might easily have passed over many places of interest had one not known the points to which Mr. Grove, and other scholars required special attention to be directed. At the same time it will be evident to the reader that there was no possibility of "cooking" our discoveries, as the guides and surveyors were not informed of the special interest attaching to certain sites, but, after their discovery in the natural course of the work, I visited the spots, in order to obtain a good description, and to verify the names collected.

Riding on the 10th of October to the hill above Dûra, we obtained a glimpse of the extreme southern boundary of the Survey. The view was fine; to the east was the great ridge on which stands the traditional tomb of Lot; on the west the Philistine plain lying in a hot haze which towards Gaza hid it entirely; on the south were rolling hills, isolated mounds, and a broad plain, with a dark patch near the Beersheba wells; and yet farther were grey misty ridges, the land appearing to descend in steps towards the Desert of the Wanderings.

In returning to camp we passed through the luxuriant vineyards of the supposed Vale of Eshcol, carefully enclosed between dry-stone walls. The grapes, mellowed by the autumn mists, were in full beauty; the rich amber-green foliage covered the whole of the open valley; beyond was a stone town, and a fortress gleaming with a recent coating of whitewash, having a tall minaret above. A barren hill and a few grey olives rose behind. Such was our first view of Hebron, the ancient city which, as the Bible tells us, "was built seven years before Zoan (or Memphis) in Egypt" (Num. xiii. 22).

The results of the fuller acquaintance which we gained with the town, in three subsequent visits of several days' duration, may here be gathered up. Hebron is a long stone town on the western slope of a bare terraced hill; it extends along the valley, and the main part reaches about 700 yards north and south, including the Mosque Quarter, and the Quarter of the Gate of the Corner. On the north is a separate suburb, named from the mosque of 'Aly Bukka, who died in 670 A.H.; on the south also, and west of the road, is another small suburb. The Haram stands above the middle of the main Quarter. The Sultan's Pool—a large well-built reservoir, occupies part of the valley. West of the city is an open green below the Quarantine, surrounded by hills which are covered with olives.

The contrast between Hebron and Bethlehem has been already noticed; the town has a dead-alive appearance, and the sullen looks of the Moslem fanatics contrast with the officious eagerness of the Bethlehem Christians. There are some 17,000 Moslems in Hebron, according to the Governor's account; and about 600 Jews are tolerated in the Quarter of the Corner Gate. The town is the centre of commerce for the southern Arabs, who bring their wool and camel's-hair to its market. It has also a sort of trade in glass ornaments and in leather water-buckets, but the bustle and stir of Bethlehem are not found in its streets; the inhabitants seem wrapped in contemplation of the tombs of their forefathers, and boast that no pagan Frank has yet desecrated the holy shrines with his presence, or built his house in the town.

The place of chief interest in Hebron is the Cave of Machpelah containing the tombs of the Patriarchs. There seems no reason to doubt the genuine character of the site now surrounded by the Haram, and here again we have that valuable consent of traditions — Jewish, Christian, and Moslem, which seems to distinguish the true sites, from those less genuine concerning which two or more discordant traditions have arisen.

Only two trustworthy witnesses—Dean Stanley and Mr. Fergusson, have had the opportunity of describing the interior of this sanctuary; and it seems very doubtful if any living being has ever descended into the mysterious cavern beneath the floor since the Moslem conquest of Palestine; nor will it be possible to explore this cave so long as the Moslems have possession of the place, unless unexpected changes occur in their religious feelings. One curious story was, however, told me. It is said that when Ibrahim Pacha threatened the town, the inhabitants carried their property to the cave for safety. If this be true the area must be considerable, and an entrance must be known to the natives to which no European has as yet obtained a clue, though such a doorway is mentioned in the twelfth century.

The surrounding wall is one of the mysteries of Palestine, and a monument inferior only to the Temple Enclosure, which it resembles in style. It measures about 112 feet east and west, by 198 feet north and south, and has eight pilasters on the short sides, and sixteen on the long, resembling those which I found, as before noticed, at the north-west corner of the Jerusalem Haram. The stones also are scarcely inferior in dimensions, for one is said to be thirty-eight feet long, and three and a half feet high; they are all drafted with the real Jewish draft, broad, shallow, and beautifully cut, as at Jerusalem. Judging from the similarity of style, one is led to ascribe the building to the Herodian period—a view supported by Mr. Fergusson in his able paper on the subject, his opinion being based on historical grounds.

Josephus speaks of monuments of the Patriarchs as existing in his day (B. J. iv. 9, 7), but is silent as to the enclosure. Had it, however, existed in the Old Testament times, we should surely find some record of its origin in the Bible; nor does it seem likely that it was built later than Herod's time, for the earliest Christian pilgrim in 333 A.D. found it already standing.

The great walls are surmounted by two high white minarets on the south-east and north-west. The southern portion of the area is occupied by a Gothic twelfth-century building, presumably a church; the nave has a pointed roof and clerestory windows, the aisles are lower and their roofs rest against the fortress wall. Within are the cenotaphs of Isaac and Rebecca, supposed to stand above their true graves in the cavern. Outside the building, in separate chambers, are the tombs of Abraham and Sarah, flanking the entrance. On the north side of the open court Jacob and Leah have similar cenotaphs, covered, like the rest, with richly embroidered green cloths. A modern building is erected against the western fortress wall on the exterior. This is called the Tomb of Joseph, whose bones are said, by Josephus, to have been removed hither from Shechem—a story no doubt due to Jewish jealousy of the shrine at Shechem, which was in the hands of the Samaritans.

Cenotaphs like those in the present building are mentioned as early as 700 A.D. Rabbi Benjamin of Tudela states, however, that Jews were able in his days to descend, through an iron door, into the cavern, which was in three compartments, and where the real tombs were shown. The twelfth-century writers, in describing the fortress, which they quaintly name the "Castle of St. Abraham," also call the cavern Spelunca Duplex, "the double cave"—a title which suggests that the form of the interior was known at that period; and Sir John Maundeville, in 1322, states that one chamber was above the other.

An idea appears to have existed at an early period that Hebron was not originally built on its present site, but on the hill north-west of the modern town. Arculphus mentions this in 700 A.D., and Marino Sanuto in the fourteenth century says the same, both apparently referring to ancient ruins then visible in the direction of the present site of Abraham's Oak. There are traces of the same theory in the writings of many intermediate visitors, and the Bible narrative itself seems to require a position opposite the Haram, if the true Machpelah be beneath that enclosure, for the cave was not *in* Hebron, but in a field "before Mamre—the same is Hebron" (Gen. xxiii. 19). Thus, though a new city may have grown up around the sacred tombs, even in Jewish times, the original Hebron, Mamre, or Kirjath-Arba of Abraham, must have had a different site; and it may be noted, that the principal springs, and many of the rock-cut tombs dating from the Jewish period, are now found north-west of Hebron.

The Crusaders had other traditions connected with this neighbourhood. The grave of Abner was then shown within a church in Hebron, probably the same place now found in the house of a Moslem. The grave of Esau was fixed in a suburb of the town, as also those of Adam and Judah, which have now disappeared. The open green, west of the town, was known as the "Field of Damascus," apparently because owned by the Sultan of Damascus. The place where Cain killed Abel was a little farther south, and on the north was the cave in which Adam and Eve lived for a century, which appears to have been the modern rock-hewn spring called 'Ain-el-Judeideh, "the excavated fountain," which is covered by an arch and reached by steps. Here Adam mourned for Abel, and hence the spot is called by some chroniclers the Vale of Tears; here also Adam was made of the red earth of the place. Hebron was considered to have obtained its name Kirjath-Arba, "city of four," from the four patriarchs, including Adam—an explanation derived from the Rabbinical commentators, but not in accordance with the reason given in the Bible, "And the name of Hebron before was Kirjath-Arba, which Arba was a great man among the Anakims" (Josh. xiv. 15).

On our last visit to Hebron we were shown an ancient Jewish tomb with nine graves, or Kokim, close to 'Ain-el-Judeideh, and to this we obtained the curious name Kabr Hebrûn, "the grave of Hebron." We did not, however, learn the origin of the title, or the source of the tradition. A little higher up the hill is a ruined monastery, in a corner of which the tomb of Jesse is shown.

The Oak (or plain, as our version renders it) of

Mamre has been shown at various times in different directions. Jerome places it at the modern Râmeh, where is a fine unfinished stone enclosure with a large well. The walls measure 162 feet north and south by 214 east and west, and one stone is fifteen feet long. A little farther east the remains of Constantine's basilica are distinguishable, and the great enclosure may perhaps be the market where the Jews were sold by Hadrian, after the fall of Bether.

The present site of the Oak is farther south, and the magnificent tree stands among the vineyards north-west of Hebron. It is called Ballûtet Sebta, "the oak of rest," and has branches fifty feet long, one of which was broken by the snow in 1857. The Oak is thought to be more than two hundred years old, but cannot be the one seen by Sir John Maundeville, for it is covered with leaves, whereas that which was shown to Sir John he calls "the dry tree." "They say," he continues, "that it has been there since the beginning of the world, and that it was once green, and bore leaves till the time that Our Lord died on the Cross, and then it dried, and so did all the trees that were then in the world." Jerome, however, is more moderate in his assertions, and speaking of the northern site of Mamre at Râmeh, distant two miles from modern Hebron, and now called "Abraham's House" by the Jews, he says that the Oak was still visible and worshipped by the peasantry in the days of Hadrian, but disappeared during his own time. We have thus no certainty as to the position of Mamre or of the Oak, which Josephus places only six furlongs from Hebron (B. J. iv. 9, 7).

There are two other springs near Hebron which deserve notice; one is east of the "Oak of Rest," and is called 'Ain Kheir ed Dîn, "Spring of the chosen of the faith," perhaps in connection with Abraham's history. The second is more important, because almost undoubtedly a Biblical site.

After his interview with David, Abner set out on his way to Jerusalem, and had gone as far as the Spring of Sirah, when Joab's messengers overtook him and brought him back to Hebron, where he was murdered in the gate (2 Sam. iii. 26). Now on approaching the modern town by the old paved road to the north, the first spring beside the way is called Sârah. Like the Hebrew Sirah, the word means "withdrawn," and the title is, no doubt, due to the fact that the spring is under a stone arch, at the end of a little alley with drystone walls, and is thus withdrawn from the high-road. This place may therefore be considered as one of the few genuine sites in the neighbourhood of Hebron.

On the 22nd of October we marched south, to camp at Yuttah, the ancient Levitical town of Juttah, five miles south of Hebron.

We were now entering on a new district, differing in character from the rest of the Judean hills. In the neighbourhood of Yuttah, Dûra, and Yekîn, the country descends by a sudden step, and forms a kind of plateau, divided into two by the great valley which runs from north of Hebron to Beersheba, and thence west, to Gerar, and the sea. The plateau is about 2600 feet above sea-level, and 500 feet below the general level of the Hebron watershed. It consists of open wolds and arable land, the soil being a white soft chalk, geologically a later formation than the hard limestone of the hills. There are no springs in this region, but the water, where not contained in tanks and cisterns, sinks through the porous rocks, and runs in the valleys below the surface of the ground. On the south another step leads down to the white marl desert of Beersheba; on the west are the Philistine plains; on the east, 300 feet below, is the dreary Jeshimon, or "solitude." The plateau has only two inhabited villages on it, but is covered with ruins. It is dry and treeless, but rich in flocks and herds. It seems to have been the country of the Horites, for the place is riddled with caves intended for habitations, and the name of this troglodytic race is preserved in the titles of two of the ruined towns.

The plateau formed part of the district called Negeb, or "dry land," in the Bible; and here, in the southern part of the possessions of Caleb, we should seek for Debir, which he gave to his daughter; for the Choresh Ziph, where David and Jonathan met; and for the hill of Hachilah, where David hid from Saul.

One is at once struck with the fitness which the plateau presents for the adventures of the fugitive bandit chief who was destined to become the king of Israel. The inhabitants, like Nabal of Carmel, are rich in sheep and oxen. The villagers of Yuttah owned 1700 sheep, of which 250 belonged to the Sheikh. All along the borders of the Jeshimon and Beersheba deserts there is fine pasturage, to which the peasants descend in spring-time, having made some sort of agreement with the neighbouring Bedawin to protect them from other tribes. Thus we find perpetuated the old system under which David's band protected the cattle of Nabal.

The story of David's wanderings is one of the most interesting episodes of the Old Testament, and we have now so recovered its topography, that the various scenes seem as vivid as if they had occurred only yesterday. First we have the stronghold of Adullam, to be described later, guarding the rich corn valley of Elah; then Keilah, a few miles south, perched on its steep hill above the same valley. The forest of Hareth lay close by, on the edge of the mountain chain where Kharas now stands, surrounded by the "thickets" which properly represent the Hebrew "Yar,"—a word wrongly supposed to mean a woodland of timber trees.

Driven from all these lairs, David went yet farther south to the neighbourhood of Ziph (Tell Zif); and here also our English version speaks of a forest—the "Wood (Choresh) of Ziph," where David met with Jonathan. A moment's reflection will, however, convince any traveller that as the dry, porous formation of the plateau must be unchanged since David's time, no wood of trees can then have flourished over this unwatered and sun-scorched region. The true explanation seems to be that the word Choresh is a proper name with a different signification, and such is the view of the Greek version and of Josephus. We were able considerably to strengthen this theory by the discovery of the ruin of Khoreisa and the Valley of Hiresh (the same word under another form), close to Ziph, the first of which may well be thought to represent the Hebrew Choresh Ziph. Should this word appear as a proper name in the new English Version, a very marked improvement will be made in what might be called the orientalising of the Bible, substituting the actual language of the land, for that essentially English tone which has been imparted to the narrative by the expressions of translators to whom the East was less familiar than their own fair country.

The treachery of the inhabitants of Ziph, like that of the men of Keilah, appears to have driven David to a yet more desolate district, that of the Jeshimon, or "Solitude," by which is apparently intended the great desert above the western shores of the Dead Sea, on which the Ziph plateau looks down. As a shepherd-boy at Bethlehem, David may probably have been already familiar with this part of the country, and the caves, still used as sheep-cotes by the peasant herdsmen, extend all along the slopes at the edge of the desert.

East of Ziph is a prominent hill on which is the ruined town called Cain in the Bible; hence the eye ranges over the theatre of David's wanderings.

On the south are the wolds of the Negeb plateau, with the plains of Beersheba beyond. On the east is the "Solitude," with white peaks and cones of chalk, and deep, narrow watercourses, terminated by the great pointed cliff of Ziz, above Engedi, and by the precipices over the Dead Sea, two thousand feet high. Here, among the " rocks of the wild goats," the herds of ibex may be seen bounding, and the partridge is still chased on the mountains, as David was followed by the stealthy hunter Saul. The blue sea is visible in its deep chasm, and is backed by the dark precipice of Kerak, " scarred with a hundred wintry watercourses."

The great hump of rock on which Maon,—the home of Nabal,—stands, is seen to the south, and rather nearer is the Crusading castle at Carmel, where were Nabal's possessions; the ruined mound of Ziph is to the west, and Juttah among its olives. Thus the whole scenery of the flight of David, and of Saul's pursuit, can be viewed from this one hill.

The stronghold chosen by the fugitive was the hill Hachilah, in the wilderness of Ziph, south of Jeshimon. This I would propose to recognise in the long ridge called El Kôlah, running out of the Ziph plateau towards the Dead Sea desert, or Jeshimon—a district which, properly speaking, terminates about this line, melting into the Beersheba plains. On the north side of the hill are the "Caves of the Dreamers," perhaps the actual scene of David's descent on Saul's sleeping guards.

Pursued even to Hachilah, David descended farther south, to a rock or cliff in the wilderness of Maon, which was named Sela Ham-mahlekoth, "Cliff of Divisions" (1 Sam. xxiii. 2—8). Here he is represented as being on one side of the mountain, while Saul was on the other.

Now between the ridge of El Kôlah and the neighbourhood of Maon there is a great gorge called "the Valley of Rocks," a narrow but deep chasm, impassable except by a detour of many miles, so that Saul might have stood within sight of David, yet quite unable to overtake his enemy; and to this "Cliff of Division" the name Malâky now applies, a word closely approaching the Hebrew Mahlekoth. The neighbourhood is seamed with many torrent-beds, but there is no other place near Maon where cliffs, such as are to be inferred from the word Sela, can be found. It seems to me pretty safe, therefore, to look on this gorge as the scene of the wonderful escape of David, due to a sudden Philistine invasion, which terminated the history of his hair-breadth escapes in the South Country.

On the 28th of October a great storm arose, and for several hours we were in constant expectation of the whole camp being blown down. On the next day an adventure befell us. Corporal Brophy was attacked by four cowherds, who threatened to stone him, and abused him as a "pig." He came home and reported the assault, having had some difficulty in escaping. Just at the same moment, as good luck would have it, the Sheikh of Semû'a, to which village the cowherds belonged, rode into Yuttah on a visit. I sent my two Bashi-Bazouks out at once, and brought the unhappy old man into camp. The Sheikh of a village is responsible for his people, and so I sent him as a hostage to Hebron, in spite of many entreaties. He however bribed his guard by the way, and escaped. I deducted the amount which I supposed him to have given from the soldiers' pay, and the next day the four offenders were in gaol, where the accommodating governor offered to keep them as long as I liked. They, of course, remained there till they paid some one to get them out, and peace was thus secured through the district, the inhabitants finding that even Christian "pigs" and "dogs" might occasionally get their own way.

On the 4th of November another hurricane struck the camp, and half buried us in dust and mould. A tenth-of-an-inch of rain fell in about a quarter of an hour, and but for the friendly olive-trees the camp would have been in ruins. On the 5th we moved once more south, and encamped at Dhâheriyeh, a village the inhabitants of which were remarkably courteous, having profited by the lesson taught to their friends of Semû'a.

There seems to me to be every reason for supposing Dhâheriyeh to be the ancient Debir, a place not identified before the Survey. The name has the same meaning, derived from its situation on the "back" of a long ridge; and the position between Shochoh (Shuweikeh), Dannah (Idhnah), Anab ('Anâb), and Eshtemoa (Es Semû'a), seems very suitable (Josh. xv. 48). The place, moreover, is evidently an ancient site of importance, to which several old roads lead from all sides. The springs near Debir given to Achsah (Judg. i. 15) might well be the beautiful springs of Dilbeh, about seven miles north of the town, and the identification seems to me to be amongst the most valuable of those due to the Survey.

The autumn weather now began once more to tell on the health of the party; Sergeant Black suffered with dysentery, and I left him in the main camp with Corporal Brophy, while I myself, with Sergeant Armstrong, descended to Beersheba to complete the south boundary of the map. We had with us only one servant, one groom, the scribe, a guide, and the Sheikh of Dhâherîyeh, for whom I had a great liking. We took two tents, five mules, and three horses, carrying also provisions for three days and one theodolite.

Following a long valley, we arrived at a broad undulating plain, grey and dry, like the muddy basin of a former sea. The hills end very suddenly, and the boundary is thus sharply defined between the lands of the settled population and the district of the Bedawîn, who, though nomadic, cultivate a little tobacco and barley round Beersheba.

The scenery was tame and featureless, with a single dark Tell in front, and white marl peaks capped with flint to the west. The heat and glare were oppressive, and I was glad at noon to rest under a white chalk cliff, and was able to realise the force of the poetic language of Isaiah, "The shadow of a great rock in a weary land" (Isaiah xxxii. 2).

After lunch we ascended the Tell or mound of Seb'a, which is two and a half miles east of the Wells of Beersheba, and thence we had a fine view of the great boundary valley which limited our work on the south, joining the long ravine which comes down from Hebron, and running west in a broad, flat, gravelly bed, between high walls of brown earth. The pebbles were white and dry, yet water-worn, for, as we found in the following spring, a river will occasionally flow for hours along the Wâdy bed. East of us there were remarkable white chalk hills called El Ghurrah, and on the west a low ridge shut out the maritime plain. To the north were the hills of Judah, dotted with lotus-trees, and to the south stretched the endless Desert of the Wanderings.

No mules appeared, and we therefore rode down towards the wells, passing by innumerable burrows of the jerboa, and by numerous herds of camels, with a distant view of black "houses of hair." At length we spied a tent, and our servants talking with mounted Arabs near the principal well. At the same moment I saw a pigeon by one of the wells, and fired, killing it on the spot. I noticed that the Arabs rode away immediately after, and I found that they had been insolent, and had ordered the servants to take down the tent; but, seeing a well-armed party approaching, and conceiving a great respect for a gun that could kill at such a distance, with characteristic Bedawin caution, they made off before we came up.

The desert of Beersheba is a beautiful pasture-land in spring, when the grass and flowers cover the grey mud, as in the Jordan Valley; but in November it is very desolate; not a tree exists near the wells, and only the foundations of a flourishing fourth century town remain.

Our tents were by the principal well, which is twelve feet three inches in diameter, and over forty-five feet deep, lined with a ring of masonry to a depth of twenty-eight feet. A second well, five feet in diameter, exists about 300 yards to the west, and on the east is a third, which is dry, twenty-three feet deep, and nine feet two inches in diameter. The sides of all the wells are furrowed by the ropes of the water-drawers; but we made one discovery which was rather disappointing, namely, that the masonry is not very ancient. Fifteen courses down, on the south side of the large well, there is a stone with an inscription in Arabic, on a tablet dated, as well as I could make out, 505 A.H., or in the twelfth century. This stone must be at least as old as those at the mouth, which are furrowed with more than a hundred channels by the ropes of seven centuries of water-drawers.

The wells have no parapets, and I nearly fell into the dry one, so little was it visible until quite near; round the two which contain water there are rude stone troughs, which may be of any age —nine at the larger, five at the lesser well.

The sun began to set, and we hurried back to observe the polestar from the Tell, but were foiled by a rising bank of clouds. Returning to camp, we secured our horses with fetters and tethers, so that they could not be stolen, and then retired to sleep in peace.

We now found how useful dogs may be in camp. In the spring our colley had saved the horses at Sulem, and I had intended to take him on our rather risky visit to Beersheba, but somehow he was left behind, and thus not one of our faithful guards was with us. During the night a thief came into the tents : he ripped up the saddle-bag containing our provisions, and took them all with him, and he even came to the head of my bed and stole Bulwer's " Disowned," but only took it about a hundred yards from camp. It is evident that he must have crept on his stomach, since he only took what was near the ground and left my watch lying on the table, and (which was for the moment more important) he also left me my boots, though he removed the tin washing-basin. Our plates, bread, chickens, and some barley in a nosebag, he (or they) stole from the servants' tent, all this being neatly accomplished in about ten minutes.

In the early morning heavy rain began, and my people, left without food, and with very long faces, evidently expected orders to return to Dhâheriyeh; but I was determined not to go back till I had completed the work proposed, and also not sorry to give the natives a lesson for not taking better care of our property; so I sent the guide back to bring fresh provisions and to meet us in the evening at Tell el Milh, fourteen miles east, where I proposed to camp next. The tents were packed up wet, the sun rose and the sky cleared, promising a cool pleasant day.

After taking some observations from near the well we started. Our faces were turned towards the road by which Rebecca had come to Beersheba: like Isaac we lifted up our eyes, and "behold the camels were coming." As far as the view extended the plain was covered with hundreds of them, each moving alone towards the wells, each casting before it a long shadow in the light of the rising sun. Dusky, half-naked boys sat on the humps, and, arriving at the well, they stripped off what clothes they had on, and let down to the water the goat-skin bags which served them as buckets, drawing them back with great rapidity in time with a rude chant, and evidently vying in the rate of watering their herds; both the wells were besieged, and a thick crowd of camels had collected before we left.

We once more passed the Tell and found another smaller well near it. Marching east we came on flocks of sheep, with a few goats among them, driven mostly by girls under twelve years of age— the age no doubt of Leah when Jacob first came to Haran. As is still the custom of the Bedawin, the girls over fourteen were no doubt in Jacob's time withdrawn to the privacy of the women's apartments in the tents, and this seems to agree with the account of Jacob's kissing his cousins, for if they were more than children such a salute would surely have been quite contrary to Eastern ideas of propriety. Small as the flocks appeared, from the great extent of the plain, the smallest contained at least twenty head, and the average was over one hundred, so that we came across at least eight hundred in all. This gives an idea of the immense number of the flocks which exist in this apparently sterile desert, where it seems impossible that they can find anything to eat in autumn.

Dinner was doubtful, and we had unfortunately only two or three cartridges left, so we were reduced to the very unsportsman-like proceeding of shooting birds on the ground; flocks of plover were running before us, and, creeping up a gully, the Sergeant and I both fired at the same time and killed three, which were excellent eating when rudely spitchcocked. We also saw large coveys of the sand-grouse or pintail, which is not found in the hills of Palestine, though in summer it comes up the Jordan Valley; the crops of those we shot were full of hard round seeds and of small pebbles.

The journey was tedious, and the scenery very monotonous. Ten miles from Beersheba we came upon another ruined town with two wells, also containing water. The place has lost its old name, and is now only known as El Meshâsh, "the water-pits." It must have been a very important town, yet hitherto it has escaped notice, other travellers having gone by routes east and west of the place, and never across country; thus the discovery was left for us, and the utility of systematic survey once more exemplified.

After travelling for miles without seeing a living thing, we came suddenly on this site, with brown ruins, and a crowd of dusky naked men drawing water in a frenzied manner, and a few women in sweeping garments, driving diminutive donkeys laden with black water-skins.

Tell el Milh is a third site of character similar to the last; it is the Malathah of the fourth century, and possibly the "City of Salt" (as the modern name signifies) noticed in the Bible (Josh. xv. 62). There is here a great hillock with Arab graves on the top, ruins of an extensive town, and on the north two wells, just like those at Beersheba. Crowds of horses, goats, sheep, and camels surrounded them, and the song of the water-drawers was loud and wild.

We sat down under the steep bank of the valley, north of the wells, and very soon a crowd of naked savages collected above us. They demanded "bucksheesh," and made rude remarks as to our being Christians. "Look at the big watch," said one, observing our aneroid; "Look at the guns and pistols," said another. Some of the chiefs (who wore clothes) came down to talk to our Sheikh, and, putting their foreheads against his, made a sound representing the kiss of peace. The Sheikh, though not a Bedawi, seemed not at all afraid of the crowd, and abused the wild Arabs roundly, telling them to be off. As for us, we turned our backs on them and smoked in peace.

I ordered all the provisions we had left to be served out to the party, for the natives had eaten no breakfast. Just as darkness came on we heard the song of the messenger from our main camp, and he came in dead tired, after trotting for eleven hours on a rough mule; with him came one of our soldiers on his mare, followed by its colt which was also much fatigued.

We made great preparations in the shape of traps for thieves, but none came. That evening, the 11th of November, 1874, nearly proved the close of my existence, for I was seen, in the dusk, at some little distance, and my servant fired, mistaking me for a Bedawî robber, the ball passing very near my head. During the night we slept but little, being in constant fear of losing the horses, or of a night attack from the Arabs.

By seven next morning we had set off for the hills, and passed by the ruined towns of Ghurrah, S'awi (perhaps the ancient Jeshua), and Haura, which are noticeable for the walls of flint-conglomerate, possibly very ancient, surrounding their sites; in the afternoon we reached Dhâheriyeh, and found all well except Sergeant Black, who was suffering much from dysentery. Sheikh Hamzeh, the well-known guide from Hebron, and Abu Dahûk, chief of the Jâhalin Arabs, were in camp. I had arranged with them to start for Beersheba on the 10th, and had gone without them as they did not come on that day. This lesson in punctuality was very useful when I again required their services.

On the 16th of November I rode to Jerusalem in order to meet Lieutenant Kitchener, who was just arriving at Jaffa, and to ask advice for Sergeant Black. On the 19th I started for camp, together with my new colleague, and we met the Sergeant on the way, coming up by my order to Jerusalem. I was shocked to see how entirely a strong man may, in three days, be prostrated by dysentery.

Soon after we had passed the party conveying him, a storm came on, and we lost our way in the trackless hills; we reached camp, however, in the evening, and, after thirty miles' ride, we were forced to sit up all night, in momentary expectation of having the tent blown about our ears, and with the rain dripping through all its seams. It was the grandest storm we had seen; the rain dashed down like water out of a bucket, and the lightning was incessant. Our animals were under shelter in the village, but the Sergeant was exposed, at Hŭlhûl, to all the fury of the storm. His companions took him into a rock-cut tomb, where he lay on the stone bench, but the floor was ankle-deep in water, and the tent he had just left was blown down and broken by the gale.

The weather continued bad, so, on the 23rd, I decided to march to Jerusalem, and refit, hoping still to be able to complete the Survey of the Dead Sea desert before Christmas; but this was not to be. We did indeed fit out a light expedition, and marched to Tekû'a on the 8th of December, but here we encountered a yet worse storm, and all hope of work in the field had to be given up for the season. Our beasts were stiff with rheumatism, and it would have been folly to attempt a campaign which would have left the expedition unfit for the spring work. So as soon as the storm was over, and the heavy tents packed, we marched back, cold, stiff, and wet, to our hired house in the Armenian Quarter of Jerusalem, and settled down in winter quarters.

In January I visited Jericho with Lieutenant Kitchener, who paid dearly for it. He was attacked with Jericho fever, and it seemed probable that he would have to return to England; Sergeant Black also remained in danger of his life for some time, and was invalided home early in January. Thus, of the original members of the party, only Sergeant Armstrong was left, and neither he nor I were destined to see the last miles of the Survey of Palestine completed—so baneful is the climate in which this arduous undertaking has been carried out.

CHAPTER IV.

THE LAND OF BENJAMIN.

NORTH of Jerusalem lies a narrow district, which contains more places of interest than can, perhaps, be found, in any other parts of Palestine, within an equal area. A portion of this district was the first part of the hill country surveyed; another portion was filled in during the winter of 1873—74; and the stormy camp of Deir Diwân, where Sergeant Black and I struggled against the rain and sleet for three days, cost us several attacks of fever. During our second winter in Jerusalem I was able to revisit most of the interesting places within this region, and may here endeavour to give some idea of their appearance.

The district is that which was allotted to the tribe of Benjamin, and includes about 200 square miles of hills, extending ten miles from Jerusalem to Bethel, and about twenty from the lower Beth Horon to the deserts above Jericho.

We are now able to draw, with a great amount of accuracy, the north boundary of Benjamin, from Bethel to Archi ('Ain 'Arik), and thence to "Ataroth Adar, near the hill that lieth on the south side of the nether Bethoron," exactly where we discovered the ruins of Ed Dârieh still existing. South of these limits are the famous towns Bethel, Ai, Michmash, Geba, Ramah, Nob, Mizpeh, Gibeon, with others of minor importance. To these places the present chapter is devoted.

It is clear from the Old Testament that the place where Jacob's vision occurred was Bethel or Luz, as it was originally called, on the boundary of Ephraim and Benjamin. Later traditions have been busy with the site, and (as we have seen before) the Samaritans claim that the true place is on Gerizim, while in the twelfth century the sacred rock on the Temple Hill was held to be the Beth-el, or House of God, of the narrative in Genesis.

Bethel at the present day is one of the most desolate-looking places in Palestine; not from lack of water, for it has four good springs, but from the absence of soft soil on its rocky hills. All the neighbourhood is of grey, bare stone, or white chalk. The miserable fields are fenced in with stone walls, the hovels are rudely built of stone, the hill to the east is of hard rock, with only a few scattered fig-gardens, the ancient sepulchres are cut in a low cliff, and a great reservoir south of the village is excavated in rock. The place seems as it were turned to stone, and we can well imagine that the lonely patriarch found nothing softer than a stone for the pillow under his head, when on the bare hill-side he slept, and dreamed of angels.

There is a second episode of Bible history, connected with Bethel, which seems to merit attention; for it is generally supposed that here, within sight of Solomon's Temple, Jeroboam erected one of the golden images of Apis, the fellow of which was in Dan.

The Crusaders did not hold this opinion. Dan and Bethel were not, according to their view, the north and south boundary towns of the kingdom of Israel, but were places close together, in the heart of the country, at the old religious centre at Shechem, where once stood "the Sanctuary of the Lord" by the oak (Josh. xxiv. 26).

Bethel is described in the twelfth and fourteenth centuries as immediately west of Gerizim, evidently where the Samaritans still show the ruins of Luz. Dan was on the mountain west of Ebal, which is still called "Hill-top of the Judge," the meaning of Dan in Hebrew being also "Judge."

There seem to be indications worthy of consideration which tend to show that in this view the Crusaders were right. In the first place, Jeroboam instituted these temples with the express intention of diverting the attention of the tribes from Jerusalem. Surely, therefore, it is most strange that he should have chosen for one of them a place which was actually within the allotted portion of Benjamin. The southern Bethel was moreover taken from Jeroboam by Abijah (2 Chron. xiii. 19), and there is no notice of its recovery, while at the same time there is no account of the destruction of the calf idol, which remained, on the contrary, in its place until the time of Jehu (2 Kings x. 29), and was only finally overthrown by Josiah (2 Kings xxiii. 15). Had the calf temple been at the southern Bethel, there would surely have been some account of the destruction which would certainly have overtaken it on the conquest of the town by the King of Judah. In the third place, we learn that Bethel of the calf was close to Jeroboam's palace (Amos vii. 13), and this palace was apparently in Shechem (1 Kings xii. 25). Lastly, Bethel is noticed as the place to which the Israelite priest returned when instructing the colonists of *Samaria* to "fear the Lord" (2 Kings xvii. 28).

These passages, coupled with the constant connection of the calf-worship with the name of Samaria in the denunciations of the prophets, seem to me to point to the conclusion that the Bethel intended is not the true Bethel, which was in the territory of the kings of Judah, and where was the school of the prophets, but the heretical Bethel on Gerizim; and that we have here the earliest account of the schism which afterwards caused a Samaritan temple to be built on Gerizim, just where the calf temple of Jeroboam had perhaps originally stood.

The prophecy of Hosea, and that of Amos as well, connect Bethel and Bethaven in such a way as to make it appear that they were the same place. Such is the opinion of the Jewish commentators, and we may thus perhaps trace the origin of the present corruption of Beitîn for Bethel back to the early time of Jeroboam. Bethaven, however, means "house of naught," and the title was, no doubt, originally given to the desert east of Bethel, because of its barren character, though in the prophecy there is a play on the word: "Gilgal (freedom) shall go into captivity, and Bethel shall come to naught" (Aven).

Another town of almost equal interest existed in the same neighbourhood, namely Ai, east of Bethel, a place which was quite unknown in the fourth century, but concerning the general position of which there is but little dispute. The various notices in the Bible (Gen. xii. 8; Josh. viii. 9—14) define its situation with much exactitude, as being east of Bethel, with a valley north of the town, and low ground to the west, where an ambush might be set unseen from the city, while on the opposite side was a plain (verse 14). This description applies, in a very complete manner, to the neighbourhood of the modern village of Deir Diwân, and there are here remains of a large ancient town, bearing the name Haiyân, which approaches closely to Aina, the form under which Ai appears in the writings of Josephus. Rock-cut tombs and ancient cisterns, with three great reservoirs cut in the hard limestone, are sufficient to show this to have been a position of importance. To the west is an open valley called "Valley of the City," which, gradually curving round eastward, runs close to the old road from Jericho by which Joshua's army would probably have advanced. To the north of the site there is also a great valley, and the plain or plateau on which the modern village stands close to the old site, expands from a narrow and rugged pass leading up towards Bethel, which is two miles distant on the watershed.

Beside this pass and north of the ruins, is a large terraced knoll, very stony, and crowned by a few olives—a conspicuous object in the landscape. It is called simply Et Tell, "the mound," and a connection has been supposed between this name and the fact that Joshua made Ai "a heap (Tell in the Hebrew) for ever." The place does not, however, show traces of having at any time been covered by buildings, and the rock-cut tombs and cisterns above noticed seem too far from it to indicate Et Tell as the exact site of Ai; being close to the pass, it has moreover no valley such as would seem fitted for the ambush immediately west of it.

From this Tell a fine view is obtained towards the plains of Jericho. The village of Deir Diwân is seen on its little plateau in the foreground, while the desolate hills of Benjamin rise beyond, with the chain of the Quarantania Mountain, hiding the western half of the Dead Sea and of the plain of Jericho, though the mouth of Jordan and the eastern ranges of Moab with Mount Nebo are visible, forming the extreme distance.

Advancing a few miles farther south, we come on the scene of one of the most romantic of Old Testament stories—the attack made by Jonathan and his armour-bearer, on the Philistine camp, near Michmash.

A great valley, as we have seen above, has its head west of Ai, and curving round eastwards it runs to Jericho: about two miles south-east of Ai it becomes a narrow gorge with vertical precipices some 800 feet high—a great crack or fissure in the country which is peculiar in this respect, that you only become aware of its existence when close to the brink, for on the north the narrow spur of hills hides it, and on the south a flat plateau extends to the top of the crags.

On the south side of this great chasm (the true head of the Kelt valley) stands Geba of Benjamin, on a rocky knoll, with caverns beneath the houses and arable land to the east. Looking across the valley the stony hills and white chalky slopes present a desolate appearance; and on the opposite side, considerably lower than Geba, is the little village of Michmash, on a sort of saddle, backed by an open and fertile corn-valley. The existence of this valley no doubt accounts for the place having been famous for its barley, so that the Talmudic proverb, "to bring barley to Michmash," represents exactly our "carrying coals to Newcastle."

The pass between these two towns appears to have been more than once the place of meeting between the Jews and their enemies, though to a military man it seems curious that the main road along the watershed should not always, as it did in Maccabean times, have formed the line of Jewish defence north of Jerusalem.

The town of Geba, south of the valley, is generally understood to be that notorious in the history of the extermination of the tribe of Benjamin, and to have been the place where Jonathan smote the garrison of the Philistines (1 Sam. xiii. 3). If this be so, then it must apparently be the "hill of God" (Geba-ha-Elohim) where was the garrison of the Philistines (1 Sam. x. 5), and where some of Saul's family seem to have lived (verse 14). Thus Geba of Benjamin seems to be connected with Gibeah of Saul, but the latter name appears to have applied to a district as well as to a town, for the neighbouring city of Ramah is said in one passage to have been "in Gibeah" (1 Sam. xxii. 6).

Josephus tells us of a village called Gabaoth Saule which was by the Valley of Thorns, and about thirty stadia from Jerusalem. This reminds us at once of the name Seneh, "thorn" or "acacia," which was applied to one of the crags at the place where Jonathan crossed to the Philistine camp at Michmash. The modern name of the great valley between Geba and Michmash is Suweinît, or the "valley of the little thorn-tree" (acacia), and if this identification of the Valley of Thorns with Wâdy Suweinît be correct, the town of Gibeah of Saul is apparently to be placed at the present Jeb'a, though the distance given by Josephus is not exact.

The site of the Philistine camp at Michmash, which Jonathan and his armour-bearer attacked, is very minutely described by Josephus. It was, he says, a precipice with three tops, ending in a long sharp tongue and protected by surrounding cliffs. Exactly such a natural fortress exists immediately east of the village of Michmash, and it is still called "the fort" by the peasantry. It is a ridge rising in three rounded knolls above a perpendicular crag, ending in a narrow tongue to the east with cliffs below, and having an open valley behind it, and a saddle towards the west on which Michmash itself is situate.

Opposite this fortress, on the south, there is a crag of equal height and seemingly impassable; thus the description of the Old Testament is fully

THE VALLEY OF MICHMASH.

To face page 113, **Vol. II.**

borne out—"a sharp rock on one side, and a sharp rock on the other" (1 Sam. xiv. 4).

The southern cliff, as we have noticed above, was called Seneh, or "the acacia," and the same name still applies to the modern valley, due to the acacia-trees which dot its course. The northern cliff was named Bozez, or "shining," and the true explanation of this name only presents itself on the spot.

The great valley runs nearly due east, and thus the southern cliff is almost entirely in shade during the day. The contrast is surprising and picturesque between the dark cool colour of the south side and the ruddy or tawny tints of the northern cliff, crowned with the gleaming white of the upper chalky strata. The picture is unchanged since the days when Jonathan looked over to the white camping-ground of the Philistines, and Bozez must then have shone as brightly as it does now, in the full light of an Eastern sun.

To any one looking over the valley it seems a most difficult feat to cross it, and in the words of Josephus, "it was considered impossible not only to ascend to the camp on that quarter, but even to come near it." Yet in the winter of 1874 we were able to march with horses and mules over this great chasm, perhaps treading almost in the steps of Jonathan. We arrived on the brink east of Geba and looked down in despair, expecting to have to make a long detour towards the watershed.

The guides said that not even a goat could get across, and indeed, peering over the edge down to the boulders of the torrent-bed beneath, it seemed impossible to descend the cliff; but time was precious, and our trigonometrical point was in full sight beyond; I noticed also that the dip of the strata down eastwards gave hopes that by one of the long ledges we might be able to slide, as it were, towards the bottom. It is not likely that horses had ever before been led along this ledge, or will perhaps ever again cross the pathless chasm, but it was just possible, and by jumping them down one or two steps some three feet high, we succeeded in making the passage. Such a descent we never made again; and looking up, it seemed incredible that iron-shod beasts could have come down those vertical walls; for the Survey party had marched across almost the worst part of the passage which checked the advance of the King of Assyria on Jerusalem.

Though we got down Seneh, we did not attempt to climb up Bozez. That rock was not on our line of march, which was directed east of the Philistine camp. Horses could scarcely find a footing anywhere on the sides of the northern precipice, but judging from the descent, it seems possible that Jonathan, with immense labour, could have "climbed up upon his hands and upon his feet, and his armour-bearer after him" (1 Sam. xiv. 13). That a man exhausted by such an effort could have fought successfully on arriving at the top, can only be accounted for on the supposition of a sudden panic among the Philistines, when they found the enemy actually within their apparently impregnable fortress.

The watchmen of Saul in Gibeah of Benjamin must have seen clearly, across the chasm, the extraordinary conflict of two men against a host, as the "multitude melted away and they went on beating down one another." The noise in the host was also, no doubt, clearly heard at the distance of only two miles, and the army would have crossed the passage with comparatively little difficulty by the narrow path which leads down direct from Geba to Michmash, west of the Philistine camp. Thence the pursuit was towards Bethel, across the watershed, and headlong down the steep descent of Aijalon — that same pass where the first great victory of Joshua had been gained, and where the valiant Judas was once more in later times to drive back the enemies of Israel to the plains.

The town of Ramah was, as above noticed, in the district of Gibeah, which surrounded Geba and reached to Migron (1 Sam. xiv. 2), or to "the precipices" of the Michmash Valley. Ramah was a well-known town of Benjamin, but it is not generally regarded as that Ramah, or Ramathaim Zophim, which was Samuel's home and burial-place.

As regards this famous subject of controversy, it is safest to say that we do not know where Ramathaim Zophim was; like all controversies, it arises from the fact that there is very little absolute information to be obtained on the subject. The main points to be observed seem to me to be: first, that the city was in Mount Ephraim; secondly, that a place called Sechu lay on the road from it to Gibeah; thirdly, that Samuel belonged to the family of the Kohathites who possessed Beth Horon (1 Chron. vi. 67), from which it might be argued that his native town was probably near Beth Horon; lastly, that the name Ramathaim Zophim means "the heights of the views," so that it is natural to expect a position commanding an extensive prospect. These considerations seem to point to Râm Allah, east of Beth Horon on the west slopes of Mount Ephraim, overlooking the maritime plain, and in confirmation of this proposition we find a ruined village called Sûeikeh, perhaps the Sechu of the Bible (1 Sam. xix. 22), on the high-road from Geba to Râm Allah.

There are yet two sites to be noticed which are equally indeterminate—the sacred cities of Nob and Mizpeh; but the Survey has done little to throw light on this question. There is however a remarkable connection between the two places which leads to the supposition that they were either close to one another or, perhaps, identical. The names Nob, "a high place," Mizpeh, "a watchtower," suggest a similarly commanding position. Nob was for many years the place where the Tabernacle stood, as we may infer from the Bible, and as we are expressly told in the Mishna; Mizpeh in like manner was the gathering-place of Israel, "where they prayed" (1 Macc. iii. 46). Nob was on the high-road to the capital, seemingly in sight of Jerusalem (Isaiah x. 32), and Mizpeh was "over against Jerusalem." Mizpeh is not mentioned in episodes where the name of Nob occurs, nor does Nob occur in passages where Mizpeh is noticed.

Most writers, including Mr. Grove and Dean Stanley, place Mizpeh in the neighbourhood of the modern Sh'afât, or between it and the hill Scopus. From either place Jerusalem is visible, and either would suit the order in which Nob occurs in the lists (Neh. xi. 32), between Anathoth ('Anâta) and Ananiah (B. Hannîna); but this is a good instance of the uncertainty which must always remain as to ancient sites, unless the old names can be recovered. There are plenty of Nobs and of Mizpehs in Palestine, but in positions quite inapplicable, whereas, in the right direction there is no name of the kind (so far as has yet been discovered) for Sh'afât is not apparently derived from Mizpeh, but is a name very like that of Jehosaphat, and the natives of the place say that it was called after a Jewish king. In Crusading times the town seems to be also mentioned under the title Jehosaphat.

The early Christians placed Mizpeh in quite another direction, and Nob at Beit Nûba, which is famous in the history of Richard Lion-Heart. Their site for Mizpeh was near Sôba, west of Jerusalem, and here we found a ruin with the title Shûfa, which in meaning is equivalent to the Hebrew Mizpeh, but this place cannot be described as "over against Jerusalem," and its recovery would thus be a matter of minor interest.

There is one other site which has been proposed for Mizpeh, though it is merely a conjecture and not a name which might lead to the identification; this site is the remarkable hill called Neby Samwîl, north of Jerusalem. The place is conspicuous from the tall minaret which crowns the old Crusading church on the summit, and within the church is the cenotaph now revered by the Moslems as the tomb of Samuel,—a modern monument covered with a green cloth.

The Crusaders, with their usual contempt for facts, fixed on this hill as the ancient Shiloh; they also called it Ramah, and added besides a title of their own. "Two miles from Jerusalem," says Sir John Maundeville, " is Mount Joy, a very fair and delicious place. There Samuel the prophet lies in a fair tomb, and it is called Mount Joy because it gives joy to pilgrims' hearts, for from that place men first see Jerusalem."

The tradition which places Samuel's tomb here seems, however, to be only recent. Rabbi Benjamin of Tudela, who is a tolerably safe guide as regards Jewish sacred sites, discredits the story and speaks of a change of site. "When the Christians took Ramleh, which is Ramah, from the Mohammedans," says the Rabbi, "they discovered the sepulchre of Samuel the Ramathi, near the Jewish Synagogue, and removed his remains to Shiloh, where they erected a large place of worship over them called St. Samuel of Shiloh to the present day."

This statement, though exhibiting an amount of ignorance quite equal to that of the Christian twelfth-century writers, still serves to show that the tomb at Neby Samwîl does not come into the category of sites recognised by the Jews; and the ancient name of the hill of St. Samuel remains unknown. There is nothing at the site necessarily older than Crusading times, though the fine water-supply to the east would point to the suitability of the neighbourhood for an ancient city. At the foot of the mountain, hidden among olives, we discovered Hazzûr, evidently the ancient Hazor of Benjamin (Neh. xi. 33). On the top of the mountain we planned the old church, the rock-cut scarps and stables, with other Crusading remains; but we found no Jewish tombs near the modern village. Perhaps this commanding situation was first chosen for a fortress by the Latin Kings of Jerusalem, and afterwards came to be regarded as an old site; the very difficult approach, the magnificent panoramic view, and the numerous springs, including "the King's spring," "the Emir's spring," etc., would have indicated the place as a fitting position for a fortress, flanking the two main north roads to Jerusalem.

Looking down from the roof of the church one sees the old site of Gibeon (El Jîb) on a rounded hillock to the north, with its famous fountain under a cliff south-east of the village. Dean Stanley has proposed to recognise in Neby Samwîl the high place of Gibeon, so famous for the dream of Solomon when visiting the Tabernacle then erected at that spot; but it must not be forgotten that the distance between the two places is a mile and a quarter, and that a broad valley separates them. We can now only conjecture the name by which Neby Samwil was known in Bible times, because the ancient name—if ever there was one—has been for ever lost, while the mediæval tradition of the tomb of Samuel has furnished an appellation familiar to the Moslem peasantry, who now reverence the place just as they do Christian traditional sites, in Jerusalem, in Samaria, and at St. Matthew, south of the capital.

ENGEDI.

CHAPTER V.

THE DESERT OF JUDAH.

THE history of the Survey has been brought down, in the preceding chapters, to the end of the third year, at which time three districts remained to be completed: the Desert of Judah; the Philistine Plain, with the low hills east of it; and Galilee as far north as Tyre and Cæsarea Philippi.

On the 25th of February I once more took the field, with a light and compact expedition, my intention being to push as rapidly as possible through the desert west of the Dead Sea, as far south as the line of Beersheba. Lieutenant

Kitchener was scarcely convalescent from his very severe attack of Jericho fever, and our head-man, Habib, was also unfit for hard work. So, as I expected to meet with very rough weather, and to have to undergo extraordinary fatigue, it seemed prudent to leave the two invalids in comfortable quarters, until the desert work was done, and the easier task of surveying the Philistine Plain could be undertaken.

I determined to follow in this case the same policy which had been successful in the Jordan Valley, and to go down among the Arabs without any previous formalities. Most travellers who have passed through this desert—the Jeshimon or "Solitude" of the Bible—have summoned the Arab chiefs to Mar Saba or Hebron, and there entered into stipulations with them, which have not, as a rule, been carried out; but we had a strong party, we knew the language and the ways of the Bedawin, and it was therefore safe for us to proceed in a manner which would be impossible for Europeans strange to the country.

We bought in Jerusalem three gaily-coloured head-shawls and one pair of red leather boots as presents. Thus prepared, we marched straight to the nearest Arab camp and pitched close by, without asking leave; and so we became, as it were, the guests of the Sheikh, and were received hospitably. The result of this policy—which was considered risky in Jerusalem—was, that we spent only five pounds in presents and payments to guides, whereas, in just the same length of time, a former party had given thirty pounds. The saving effected in the Jordan Valley was at the same rate; and including the visit to Beersheba, and the other occasions when we went into the Bedawin districts, we saved, I believe, about £100 for the Palestine Exploration Fund by this method of treating the Arabs. A peculiarity of the Survey of Palestine which should be fully recognised, is the very cheap way in which it was carried out. If it be remembered that the expense in the field was only one penny per acre, it will, I think, be allowed that a very severe economy of time and money was effected, in order to survey a country containing 6000 square miles so completely, in so short a period as five years, and in spite of the hindrances due to long winters, and to seasons of sickness. To keep a party of about sixteen men and sixteen animals (not including those required for moving camp) at the rate of one shilling and sixpence per diem for a man and one shilling for a horse, required constant attention and careful planning, in order to prevent a single day in the field from being wasted.

This economy was appreciated in Jerusalem, and our banker has frequently expressed to me his surprise at my being able to keep up the party on what I drew. The bills, however, appeared heavy, because the rapid rate at which the work was pushed on, necessitated a strong party; but I feel satisfied that—comparing the results with those which can be obtained by equal expenditure in excavation—the public will find that no work of the Palestine Exploration Fund has rendered a better return for the money spent upon it.

Another feature of this Desert Survey was the fact that no one but the leader could speak both English and Arabic enough to carry on the work. Habib, my regular interpreter, was invalided, and not one of the natives could speak any language but their own; so that for three weeks I was obliged to carry on the whole business of the expedition in Arabic, to make every inquiry myself, and to interpret in some instances for the men. The difficulty of understanding the corrupt dialect of the Bedawîn was not a small one, yet we succeeded in obtaining all the information we needed, and in working our way under unforeseen complications. There is no part of the work to which I look back with greater satisfaction, because the difficulties overcome at this time were greater than those which we encountered during any other period of the Survey.

On the 25th of February we camped at Bethlehem, and there took leave for a time of Lieutenant Kitchener, who, though eager to go with us, had the good sense not to repine at arrangements necessary for his health.

On the following day the tents were struck, and

we marched past Tekû'a, of stormy memory, where, in the previous December, we had spent two sleepless nights, sitting on wet beds, in momentary expectation of having the tent blown about our ears. From this place we had a first view of the inhospitable desert before us, with long ridges, sharp peaks and cones, deep narrow valleys, and iron crags. The train of pack animals—thirteen mules in all, with two small donkeys—wound slowly down the slopes of the watershed, followed by seven horsemen, with a couple of peasants picked up as guides at Tekû'a. The luggage was reduced to a minimum, and no trunks were allowed, each man having only such articles as could be carried in the bed-covers. The tents were also reduced to three in number, and the camp-chairs and other comforts were left in Jerusalem.

In the afternoon we reached Wâdy Hasâsch, "the valley of gravel," and found a triangular encampment of thirty black tents. The tribe was that of the T'aamirah, or "cultivating Arabs," so called because they have actually degraded themselves by sowing barley, which they sell in Bethlehem. They have a very bad name as thieves and murderers, but we found them extremely willing and civil, and the chief, 'Abd el Gâder (as they called him), was a capital fellow. The tribe is remarkable for wearing the turban, which none of the other tribes use, the heads of the Bedawin being usually either bare, or covered with the *kufeyeh*, or shawl. The T'aamirah also wear shoes, instead of sandals, and they are indeed of the same stock with the peasantry, and are not true Bedawin.

We now found that the storm which had driven us to Jerusalem in the winter had saved us from greater misfortunes. Even after the winter rains had fallen, we still found hardly any water in the desert, and there can have been none before the wet season, at the time of our first attempt to reach the desert; in addition to which, the climate had been so unhealthy during the past autumn, that if we had gone down into the desert at that season we should, in all probability, have had a repetition of our Jericho experience, under circumstances even more unfavourable.

On the 27th of February the Survey began, Sergeant Armstrong marching out with one Arab in the Engedi direction, while Corporal Brophy accompanied me northwards. The country was almost impassable, and our progress was painfully slow. In four and a half hours of hard riding we advanced only six miles, so deep were the valleys which we were obliged to cross. Our guides were disgusted, and 'Abd el Gâder was afraid of the high-fed and frolicksome mule which we gave him to ride, feeling sure, as he repeated with a resigned air, that it would end by breaking his head.

We gained a lofty peak, called Er Rucikbeh, where we put up the instrument, and got our observations finished, just as a haze or fog began to spread over the view. This afterwards cleared off, but threatened at first to develop into a simoon, or dust-storm, such as we had once before experienced in the Jericho plains in autumn.

The wonderful strength of the Arabs was here exemplified, for, at least one thousand feet below us, was an encampment, from which three men came running up to the top of the hill, and they never ceased to shout as they came, and mounted up with wonderful swiftness, though one of them was quite an old man.

The view from the height was most extraordinary; on every side were other ridges equally white, steep, and narrow; their sides were seamed by innumerable torrent-beds, their summits were sharp and ragged in outline. These ridges stood almost isolated, between broad flat valleys of soft white marl scattered with flints, and with a pebbly torrent-course in the middle. There was not a tree visible, scarcely even a thorny shrub; the whole was like the dry basin of a former sea, scoured by the rains, and washed down in places to the hard foundation of metamorphic limestone, which underlies the whole district, and forms precipices two thousand feet high over the shores of the Dead Sea.

The various observations which we were able to make as to the habits of the Arabs, will form part of a subsequent chapter; it is sufficient here to say that, though mere unlettered and ignorant savages, they have a system of patriarchal government, a code of laws, morals, and habits of hospitality and courtesy, which represent a rude kind of civilisation, surpassing in many respects that of the peasantry, whom they despise; but it is only by living long among these interesting nomadic tribes, that one can really understand their motives and ideas.

Fearful reports now reached us of the dangerous condition of the Engedi district, and it was said that Abu Dahuk, Chief of the Jâhalîn (or "ignorant") Arabs, had been defeated by the Dhullâm Arabs, whom we had already encountered at Tell el Milh, and that he had fled to the Hebron hills. I did not give credence to these reports, though they afterwards turned out to be partly true, suspecting that either the Arabs wanted to enhance the value of their services, or that the servants were frightened, and wanted to go back to the hills. I took the opportunity of expressing contempt for all the Arabs under the sun, and told my cowardly scribe that there was no *khauf* (or "fear") for Englishmen in any country.

The weather was very doubtful, and I therefore broke through our invariable rule and worked through the Sunday. We each took a separate route, and I went south in company with 'Abd el Gâder, a fine-looking, lean, eagle-nosed man, about thirty-five or forty, with a fierce moustache, and a short sword which he rubbed carefully with a piece of fat from his portion of luncheon meat.

The land was indeed a weary one as we toiled over the rolling hills and through the broad valleys; we saw a solitary fox, a covey of partridges, and some vultures, but for hours we never met with a human being, or came across a tent. The beautiful Retem broom was in blossom in the valleys, but the tawny hills were bare of everything except a few patches of the Belân, a thorny shrub of the rose tribe (Poterium spinosum).

Poor 'Abd el Gâder was dragged that day beyond Wâdy el Ghâr, which bounds the country of the T'aamirah, right into the lands of the K'aabneh, or "Worshippers of the Kaabah," a small tribe next to the Jâhalîn who hold the country as far as the Beersheba deserts. These last—the Jâhalîn—must derive their name from a remote period, as it is the title applied to the Arabs, who were "ignorant" of the religion of Islam. There is a fourth tribe called Rushâideh, now almost extinct, but once powerful in the neighbourhood of Engedi.

About noon we halted for lunch, under a blazing sun, in the middle of a plateau of glaring white soil. A distant hillock was visible, on which sat a solitary figure, singing a rude chant with considerable energy. Soon after, a most extraordinary person approached us; an elderly man, with grizzled beard and the true dusky complexion of the Bedawî, which differs from the mahogany colour of the peasants and of the T'aamirah; he had on a ragged indigo-coloured head-shawl, a sheepskin jacket, and a very short shirt; his well-braced calves and thighs were bare, and his feet, shod with sandals, were remarkable for the fine ankles. Over his shoulder was slung a brass-bound flint-lock gun of portentous length; and thus arrayed, he came jumping from rock to rock, like one of the wild goats of his own desert, leading with him a boy of about ten or twelve, who was clad simply in a shirt that once had been white.

This extraordinary figure came up close to the very feet of my guide, whom he knew, and saluted him in the usual curt, imperious manner, adopted by the Bedawin when treading on uncertain ground. Their creed is that a man should always appear terrible to his enemies, for which reason nothing more disconcerts them, when affecting a menacing frown, than a quiet smile or a question of a humorous nature; the champion at once feels himself ridiculous, and generally grins or looks foolish.

I was seated on the ground, eating an orange, and threw away the skin, which the old Bedawi at once seized and devoured. He then made signs to me to mount my horse, and also signs indicative of a wish to smoke, if I felt inclined to provide the tobacco. We went slowly back, as I now saw that we were in the territory of a strange tribe, and was doubtful how far my guide might be on good terms with them. As we came to the foot of a hill, two more Arabs appeared, starting from concealment; at first they seemed afraid, and then ran down full speed. One was a young man, with a long gun; the other was a boy with a club, which he whirled over his head with a threatening mien. 'Abd el Gâder gravely rebuked him, and he dropped the weapon, saluting in the gruffest voice he could assume, with the same short, sharp accent, which reminds one most of the snorting of a goat or sheep when it advances in alarm on a strange dog. Perhaps this demeanour is intended to show how brave and independent the Bedawî feels, while really hiding a considerable amount of inward trepidation.

The young man seized my bridle, but he let go on receiving a gentle kick from my offside boot, and fell in with the party behind, eagerly inquiring who I was. 'Abd el Gâder was not, I think, at his ease, but he showed great coolness, explaining that I was an English Consul, come to see the condition of the country. A Consul, it must be understood, represents the highest dignity amongst Europeans in the Bedawîn eyes, as a " Milord " does among the Lebanon mountaineers.

The immediate result of this announcement was a burst of eloquence from the Arabs. " Look at our country, O Consul!" they said; "it has no water, no vineyards, no corn; when will you come and give us water, and make us vineyards?" I replied with a comprehensive nod of the head and the remark that "God made the country for the Bedawî." These people seem to have a firmly-rooted conviction that Christians can command the rain, and that they had once made vineyards in this part of the wilderness.

The new-comers next descended to the more engrossing, if less poetic, topic of tobacco, but I pretended not to understand. These Arabs smoke "hunting-pipes" with a stem half an inch long, and generally fill them with dried stalks or wood-chips. They always ask either for tobacco or for gunpowder.

We reached a high, narrow saddle, when suddenly, from a hollow, six more men, fully armed, sprang up and joined the others, who were apparently the advanced scouts. I rode in front at a slow pace, and carefully refrained from looking round or showing any signs of uneasiness, as Bedawîn eyes are very sharp in watching for symptoms of alarm which may encourage them to bully. I confess that it is unpleasant to be followed by ten loaded guns, in the middle of a lonely desert, without a European to help in case of a fight, or any protection beyond the very doubtful one of a single Bedawî of another tribe.

The wild figures hovered round, half clad and

entirely savage, skipping like the wild goats of their own desert, and gesticulating energetically: and I could not but think of David's band of outlaws, who had once scoured this very wilderness, hiding in the hollows, or descending on the unwary sleepers by night. Powder and tobacco alone make the difference between the ancient and the modern nomads, and show that even the Bedawî is not untouched by modern civilisation.

At length we reached the boundary valley, and descended into it. Looking back, I saw the K'aabneh, perched on fragments of rock, watching to see that we really kept in the T'aamireh district; and, satisfied at last, they filed along a goat-track on the white cliff above us, and disappeared just as we stopped at a well. 'Abd el Gâder was much relieved, and he took care to tell me that his influence alone had prevented my being killed and robbed on the spot.

After dusk I was roused by a shot, and the cook rushed in to say that he had fired at some thieves approaching the mules. I chaffed him gently; but my servants were all much excited, and the Arab guards kept waking me with sudden sharp exclamations of "Ha, thief!" "Ha, man!" addressed to imaginary robbers, as though to intimate, "I see you, my friend, and am ready for you," but really intended to convince me that they were themselves awake. I carefully tied every loose article to my bed-head, in order to prevent the possibility of these trusty guardians stealing anything without producing a clatter of falling things.

On Monday, the 1st of March, we moved to Engedi, accompanied by 'Abd el Gâder and by six of his men. Our road was across rolling downs of white marl, only remarkable for the jerboa burrows. We passed by the graves of some of the Rushâideh Arabs, who had been killed, I believe, by the Egyptians, and our guides reverently kissed the tombstones, which were marked with the tribe Wusm, or sign. By one o'clock we reached the top of the cliffs over the spring, 2000 feet above the Dead Sea, where is a flat plateau, with cliffs on three sides, bounded by two magnificent gorges, which run down towards the shore; and on this plateau we camped.

The cliffs are vertical, but their feet are covered by a steep slope of soft debris. Both the gorges have springs in them, and both run with water in winter. The northern gorge is the finest, and as we looked down we could not but shudder when an Arab said quietly, "A man once fell from the top of this cliff."

The Arabs wished us to go down to the spring; but it would probably have cost us the loss of several of the pack animals if we had attempted to take them, loaded and fatigued as they were, down the winding track cut in the face of the precipice. I decided to camp above, and sent the beasts down unloaded to drink. They took an hour to go down, and another to come up, and all that time, as we watched from above, a stone might have been dropped on to their saddles. We afterwards found a hollow in the rocks above the cliffs with rain-water in it; and on this the whole party, with twenty-two animals, lived for two days, at the end of which time the water was exhausted.

That night we were entertained with a war-dance, which will be described in a later chapter—a wild scene, only partially visible in the darkness, by the light of the camp-fire.

Next morning I descended the pass to the warm spring of Engedi, 1340 feet beneath our camp; there is no scene more vividly impressed on my memory than that of this magnificently rocky and savage pass, and the view from the spring which is given in the illustration.

The spring itself, 83°F. in temperature, comes out from under a great boulder, and the water streams over a steep cliff, the course being marked by a fringe of vegetation beside the cascade. There is a little sloping plateau with remains of a square drystone platform, not unlike an altar; and round the spring there is a cane-brake and thicket of Solanum and prickly bushes, with the 'Osher trees, or "apples of Sodom," growing above, the fruit of which consists chiefly of skin and white pith, but is hollow within, while the leaves of the tree are thick and fleshy. Among these thickets the beautiful black grackles, with gold-tipped wings, with the bulbuls, and hopping thrushes, were the only living things visible.

The view extended across the calm blue sea to the great eastern precipices. The broad tongue of the Lisân ran out only some few feet above the water-level, and high above, the great Castle of Kerak, with its towers and bastions, stood distinct and white on its rocky scarps, taking one back in imagination to the middle ages.

On the south the scene was equally grand. The long western beach of the sea stretched away with a succession of little white capes running out into the blue water, and, above this, the great cliffs—bastion beyond bastion of castellated crags divided by great gorges, succeeded one another. A steep slope of debris lay at their feet, and beneath this was a second line of white terrace—the Siddim cliffs, which are shores of a former lake. A dark, square, rocky promontory was capped by a building conspicuous against the sky-line, being part of the fortress of Masada, and yet farther off the salt mountain of Usdûm, and the blue range of the Arabah closed the view, but were half hidden by the smoke of burning reeds in the marshes south of the lake.

Descending six hundred feet from the spring, by the ruins of former gardens, we rode northwards for about half a mile, and then, leaving our horses at a spot where the boulders were too rough to allow them a footing, we toiled along the shore for two and a half miles, in search of the sulphur springs discovered by Dr. Tristram. Scrambling over cliffs, or walking in the water round promontories, we reached the place; but the season had brought only a little rain to this part of the desert, and the springs were dry, being only recognisable by the strong local smell of the sulphur. Along this desolate shore we found the pickled bodies of fish from Jordan, and here and there a palm stem, carried over from the east, while in the hollows of the rocks we noticed the waves splashing up, leaving little pools which dried rapidly, and made a white bed of crystalline salt on the stones.

I must here take occasion to note the accuracy of the work done by Dr. Tristram. Wherever we came across his line of march, our observations fully confirmed those which he had made and I could not but admire the indomitable energy with which he had carried his expedition along the shores of the lake, in places where it seems almost impossible that animals could have found a footing.

On the morning of the 3rd of March, we were visited by a kind of simoon, a violent wind, accompanied by a dusty mist which hid the sea. Our tents were in the greatest danger of being blown over the cliff, and they soared up like balloons, being only kept back by turning out the whole party to hold the ropes.

I now saw reason to credit the stories of fighting having occurred farther south, and it seemed well to have some one with us who was known to the Jâhalin Arabs. I sent therefore to Hebron, and in the evening old Sheikh Hamzeh—the well-known guide whom Professor Palmer employed, and who accompanied Dr. Tristram—came into camp. Though over eighty years of age, he had walked all the way, seventeen miles, in about six hours.

Next morning we parted from our T'aamireh friends, for whom I had a great liking, and we marched south. None of the animals had been watered for about twelve hours, and the eagerness with which the horses rushed over slippery rocks to a pool left by the rains was surprising. A single Arab came down to the spot where I sat, with my Sergeant and the scribe. He addressed us very curtly, and wanted to know where our tents and luggage were. I replied, "Inside our horses," at which he stared, evidently not sure whether Frank magicians might not be able to make some such convenient arrangement.

Our new camp was on an open plateau, nine miles from Engedi, beside a rock-cut tank, full of water, and the water full of frogs—the only supply for drinking within several miles. This place is called Bir esh Sherky, "the Eastern well."

Rain fell during the night, but the morning was fine, and we set out to visit the magnificent fortress of Sebbeh, or Masada, the last Jewish stronghold after the destruction of Jerusalem by Titus. Old Hamzeh was mounted on a pony and rode gaily before us, flourishing his pipe, while his white beard floated in the wind, as he carolled a war-song in a very cracked voice.

We had five of the Jâhalin Arabs with us, whom we had picked up from the neighbourhood; they were the hardiest runners I have ever seen in any country, their muscles being strung like whipcord, and their lungs magnificent. Scantily clad, shod with sandals, and armed with long fowling-pieces, which were brass-bound, with flint locks, they trotted in front of the horses as we cantered.

After passing over undulating hills we reached the head of a gorge finer than any we had seen before, and crossing the shingly bed of the great valley, we climbed on to a white plain, at the end of which, eight miles from camp, we perceived an isolated square block of hill, with a flat plateau at the top, and vertical walls of rock all round. This crag has a great valley on either side, and a narrow plain beneath it on the east, reaching to the Dead Sea shore. As we descended into the northern gorge, we saw a large herd of what I at first took for gazelles, but as they cantered across the plain their great rounded horns showed them to be the Beden, or Ibex, the "wild goats" of the Bible, which abound among the precipices in this pathless waste.

The rock of Masada measures 350 yards east and west, by 690 yards north and south, and its cliffs are 1500 feet in height above the plain on the east. Two paths lead up to the plateau on the top, that on the east being a winding ascent, now almost impassable, but by which Captain Warren went up; this is apparently the path called the "Serpent" by Josephus. The second path, on the west, ascends from a narrow sloping bank of white marl, which is about 1000 feet high, and which Josephus calls the "White Promontory;" upon this rises the great ramp, about 300 feet high, which the Romans piled up against the rock during the siege, a work so laborious that it seems almost incredible that human efforts could have accomplished it, in so short a time. At the top of the ramp is the masonry wall which the besiegers built as a foundation for their engines, before discovering the great tragedy that had been enacted within the fortress, where the garrison had fallen by one another's swords (B. J. vii. 8, 4).

A fatiguing climb brought us to the plateau at the top. Here is a pointed archway, indicative of Crusading masons, and scored with the tribemarks of the Jâhalîn, and Rushâideh Arabs, which were on a former occasion mistaken by a distinguished Frenchman for planetary signs.

We fell to work at once with tape and compass to plan and describe the ruins. The buildings are principally on the north-west part of the rock, and they are of various dates. The most ancient appear to be the long rude walls, resembling the buildings at Herodium (Jebel Fureidis), but the majority of the masonry is to be ascribed to the Christians of the fifth or twelfth centuries. There is a chapel on the plateau, and also a cave, in which I found a curious inscription with crosses, which is, apparently, a new discovery. It is painted in red, and resembles some of the twelfth and thirteenth century inscriptions near Jericho.

The most extraordinary feature of this wonderful place has yet to be noticed. The Romans in their attack on Masada followed the same method which had reduced Jerusalem. They surrounded the unhappy Jews with a wall of circumvallation. Looking down from the summit, the ruins of this wall—a drystone parapet, running across the plain and up the southern hill slopes—could be distinctly traced.

Two large camps, also walled with stone, lay spread out behind this line on the west and east, and six smaller ones, like redoubts, on the low ground; the entire length of the wall was not less than 3000 yards, as measured on our plan, and the whole remains almost as it was left eighteen centuries ago, when the victorious army marched away to Italy, leaving behind, in this waterless wilderness, proofs of the genius of the great nation of engineers, which found no task beyond its power, and which, even here, eleven miles away from the nearest considerable spring, and twenty miles from any source of provisions, was capable of crushing the desperate resistance of a nation which had so long resisted the monarchs of Asia and Egypt.

At Cæsarea we had occasion to reflect on Josephus's exaggerated statements, but at Masada we cannot but admire the exactitude of his description. The wall of the citadel he makes to be seven furlongs in length, the actual measurement being 4880 feet. The length of thirty furlongs, which he states as that of the "Serpent" ascent, would give a gradient about equal to that of the great descent at Engedi. The remains of a building 200 feet square still lie close to the western ascent, where Josephus places Herod's palace. On the "White Promontory" Silva erected his mound, 200 cubits high, and on the top of the mound he built a stone wall, fifty cubits high, making a total of some 350 feet, which seems a very correct estimate of the height of the existing ramp and wall at the western ascent. Finally, Silva's camp was pitched in a convenient place, where the hills approached nearest to the rock of the fortress, and just at this point, opposite the western ascent, the ruins of the largest Roman camp still stand.

The silent record of the great struggle is the circle of stone which, guarded by Roman soldiers, shut out from the Sicarii all hope of escape; but though we know the history of the siege, no tradition exists of it among the Arabs. I pointed out the wall and camp to our guides, and received the usual reply: "They are ruined vineyards of the Christians."

For five hours we worked hard on the summit of the hill, and it was no easy task to drag the measuring line against the furious wind, which now began to rage, and over the fallen blocks of Herod's palace. I was disappointed in my attempt to reach the towers which lie half way down the cliff on the north. The rope-ladders were too short, and there was nothing to which we could fix them, while the fury of the wind would have rendered the descent over the crag most hazardous.

We rode back to Bîr esh Sherky much fatigued, but the great wind kept us awake all night, and rain again fell heavily on our unprotected beasts.

On Saturday the 6th of March, we moved on six and a half miles, to the main encampment of the Jâhalin in Wâdy Seiyâl. The wind was so strong, that in crossing the great ridges we were scarcely able to sit on our horses. We saw a large body of cavalry at one of the Arab encampments, sent by the Government to settle the recent quarrel with the Dhullâm. In the afternoon I looked down from a high ridge upon the main camp of Abu Dahûk, and sent our scribe to announce my arrival. I then rode up to the principal tent, and was invited to enter, but I noticed that the Arabs were extremely surly, owing no doubt to recent defeats.

"You have brought the T'aamireh here," said Abu Dahûk, a most villainous-looking young chief, half negro in features. "Is this their land?" I asked. "No, by the life of Allah," he said fiercely; "all the land to Engedi is ours."

I told him that I had lived three years in the Arab country, and knew their customs, "T'aamireh in T'aamireh country, Jâhalin in Jâhalin land" were, I said, my guides and friends. This speech was received with much satisfaction, and coffee was handed round. The tribe, however, impressed me very unfavourably, as dirty, and ill-mannered, in comparison with others.

In about an hour the rest of the party arrived, and the camp was set up, but the great wind still blew fiercely, and the rain began at night.

We passed a wretched Sunday in the wind and rain, the poor horses suffering from the cold, and standing over their fetlocks in mud. I was pestered with visits from the Arabs, who sat and blew down their empty pipes as a hint to me to fill them. At length Abu Dahûk asked point-blank for a pipeful, but I told him I could not fill a "finjan" (coffee-cup), in allusion to the enormous size of the pipe-bowls of the whole tribe.

In the afternoon I turned out the party in order to exercise the horses by riding them bareback. The Arabs admired this exhibition extremely, and brought out their guns and fired them off to give greater effect to the Fantazia.

Monday came and still the high wind blew, and the cold drizzle descended. Our stores had quite run out, and there was neither barley for the horses, nor food for the men; so I ordered a march to Hebron, sixteen miles distant, the Survey work being finished, excepting a piece which could be done on the way.

It was a memorable day. The tents were struck and packed wet, the stiff ropes were drawn tight with much difficulty, especially as the men's fingers were numbed with cold. The natives all crowded into the cook's tent, and I was obliged to drive them out with a whip, and to pull down the pole before I could get the loads packed.

At length, in a howling gale, and in face of a driving sleet, I began the march, on a horse whose legs were stiff with rheumatism, and its eyes closed up and swollen from the cold.

Poor old Hamzeh, curled up on a little pony, looked the picture of misery, though he still strove to be useful as a guide. The beasts groaned and the dogs whined; a mule fell, and was with difficulty reloaded; the wind blew the loads over to one side, and the beasts at times refused to face it. About noon I halted for a moment on the lee-side of the great tower of Kŭrmŭl, and took a bite at a piece of bread and goat's flesh; then on again we rode in the blinding sleet, following the track northwards over slippery rocks towards the distant city, now beginning to be visible.

Two of the dogs came with me, but two others, Tom and Jack, gave in and retreated to a cave, whence they were brought on the following day. Crossing the plateau we lost the way and floundered up to the girths in a quagmire; we had next to cross two valleys in which strong streams some three feet deep were rushing down. On reaching the town we were greeted only by the sour looks and curses of the Moslems who refused to direct us; and but for the Jews we might have been left in the rain all night.

I found the two non-commissioned officers whom I had sent on in front before striking the camp, and who had bravely worked in the remaining miles of Survey, seated over a charcoal brazier in the house of a Jew, and dressed in long skirts and white cotton stockings, their wet things being hung up to dry. I was soon dressed in similar garments, and hot coffee and wine restored me, but I never had been so cold in my life as during the long hours spent in that bitter wind and rain.

About eight in the evening the mules arrived, with poor old Hamzeh bound to his pony by a rope, having fallen off three times from cold and exhaustion.

Such was the conclusion of the Survey of the desert; in ten days of very hard work a party of three Englishmen had filled in 330 square miles, including visits to the various ruins in the district, and half a day spent at Masada. We had just finished the work when the great storm broke, and could now rest in a dry house with our beasts in a warm stable, and enjoy the reflection that this difficult piece of the Survey was happily accomplished.

GATH.

CHAPTER VI.

THE SHEPHELAH AND PHILISTIA.

THE difficulties and hardships of the desert being at an end, a pleasant time of good spring weather, in easy and interesting country, awaited us. The spring of 1875 will be the time to which I shall always look back as the pleasantest period I spent in Palestine.

We had reached Hebron on the night of the 8th of March, and the rain continued to keep us cooped up in one wretched room of the Jew's house for the whole of the next day, during which time I sent off in search of our dogs. On the following day the tents were erected on the green west of the town, and the luggage was brought out of old Hamzeh's house. A boy appeared soon after carrying our dog Jack under one arm, and Tom under the other, their faces most comically solemn and sad, as though they regretted having abandoned the party; they had been found in the cave into which they had retreated during the storm.

On the 11th of March we at last marched down from the hills to our new camp at Beit Jibrin. Past the "Oak of rest," and the Russian Hospice now building near it, we rode westwards to a narrow valley, wandering through vineyards and down rocky hillsides gay with flowers, and through hollows full of sprouting barley, and slopes covered with grey olives. The road led to the hill-town of Tuffûh (Beth Tappuah), thence down to the mud village of Idhnah (Dannah), and then northwest through an open corn valley by Deir Nakhâs which is perched on a hill; and finally we came to the camping-place by a long village, on low ground, surrounded by hills, which hide it completely, and by long olive-groves. West of the houses are the traces of the old fortifications (which King Fulco constructed in 1134 A.D.) extending some 2000 yards. To the south is a fortress, and about one mile south-east, up the hill, is the old Byzantine Church of St. Anne, which was repaired at a later period by the Crusaders.

Dr. Robinson was the first to show, by means of the distances to surrounding places, that Beit Jibrin is the ancient Eleutheropolis; but this name has disappeared, as is usually the case with foreign names for places in Palestine. The present name, Jibrîn, was thought by the Crusaders to have some connection with the angel Gabriel, and they seem to have erected a church to St. Gabriel, of which only the north aisle remains, though the site is still remembered by the peasants, who there venerate a piece of open ground, which probably marks the old nave, and is now dedicated to Neby Jibrîn, "the Prophet Gabriel." Here again we find the Moslems unconsciously worshipping at a Christian shrine.

The Gibilin of the Crusaders is the Beto Gabra of the fourth century, and the name can be traced yet farther back. The Talmudic scholars understood "the dew of heaven from above" (Gen xxvii. 39) to have some mysterious reference to Beth Gubrin, in Idumæa, and to its fertile neighbourhood; thus the present name is carried back to Jewish times, and there is no reason to suppose that the place ever had any other.

Beit Jibrîn is famous for its great caverns, hollowed out in the white soft rock on every side of the village. They have generally names of little importance, but one is called "Cavern of the Fenish" (or Philistines), and the ground near it is "the Garden of the Fenish." It is, perhaps, from these great caves, numbering eleven in all, that the place came to be considered as a former habitation of the Horites, or "cave-dwellers." Jerome states that Eleutheropolis, or "the City of Freemen," was once inhabited by the Horites, which he renders "freemen." This idea is derived, as are many of Jerome's more fantastic criticisms, straight from the Jews, for the same connection between these two names is to be found in the Talmud.

The question of the date of the great caverns is difficult. One of them has been enlarged, so as to cut into an old Jewish tomb, and it must therefore be comparatively recent. In another there are niches for funeral urns, which date back no doubt to Roman times. Others have inscriptions in Cufic on the walls, containing in one instance the name of Saladin. In one we discovered rudely-carved figures, perhaps intended to symbolise the Crucifixion, and there are many Latin crosses, and apses pointing east. One long tunnel with sculptured walls is called "the Horse's Cavern," but it seems to have been a chapel, fifty feet long and eighteen wide. Altogether there is not any evidence that the caverns, as they now exist, are older than the twelfth century, when the town was fortified, and there are indications that, if not originally excavated, they were at least enlarged in times subsequent to the Jewish epoch. There are, however, near Beit Jibrin, ancient tombs (one having thirty-four Kokim), and also cisterns and wine-presses, and a great vault containing 1774 niches for urns, showing the village to be a Jewish site; there are also domed caverns with flights of rock-cut steps, which seem to have been used for storing water. The site is extensive, and several days were occupied in its explora-

COLUMBARIA NEAR BEIT JIBRÍN.

tion; but it is not a naturally strong position, and we should not therefore expect it to represent any one of the great Palestine strongholds.

Our camp now resembled a ship after a storm, the wet clothing being hung on every rope to dry in the wind. It was a pleasant spot among the olives, west of the village, and we found the inhabitants and their gigantic Sheikh willing and civil, though they have a bad name. We were not, however, able to escape a disturbance in the neighbourhood.

On the 13th of March I rode to the white cliff called Tell es Safi, the site of the Crusading fortress of Blanche Garde, which was built in 1144 A.D., as an outpost for defence against the people of Ascalon. Of the fortress nothing remains beyond the rock scarps, which are only dimly traceable; but the position is one of immense natural strength, guarding the mouth of the Valley of Elah, and the situation is that in which Jerome describes the Philistine Gath. Identification is impossible without the recovery of the ancient name, but there is, I think, no place which has stronger claims than this site to be identified with Gath. It is now a mud village with olives beneath it; the cliff on which it is built is 300 feet high, and is burrowed with caves on the north; on the south a narrow saddle joins it to the ridge, but on every other side the "Shining Hill," as it is well called, is impregnable, and when protected by fortifications on the weaker side, it must have been a most important post.

Our instrument was set up on the roof of the little building dedicated to "St. George," marking perhaps the site of a Crusading chapel. The villagers crowded round, and were inclined to be insolent. As we descended the hill, one of them, a stalwart, powerful fellow, led down the Sergeant's horse, but refused to give it up without "bucksheesh." I suspected, from the various remarks I heard the others address to him, that he was the champion of the village. The remainder of the inhabitants sat watching on the hill-top, and there seemed every reason to expect a serious disturbance. The Sergeant endeavoured to shake off the hand which the champion kept on his rein, but the rascal at once took up a large stone and threatened him with it.

The man had no claim for payment, for a little boy had held the horse, and had been given a small coin. It was merely an attempt to bully; I therefore rode at him, upon which he turned at me with the stone and with violent language. I took out my pistol for the first and last time during the four years in Palestine, and put it to his head. Still he refused to drop the stone until he heard the click of the trigger as I raised it.

The champion dropped his missile at last, and turned a livid colour with fear, shame, and disappointment. "Go home, you scoundrel!" I said, "and to-morrow you shall sleep in prison at Hebron." It would have been very unwise to overlook this attack, but equally so to endeavour to make the man prisoner, so I rode off, leaving the champion of Gath disconcerted. Next evening he was brought in bound, by the soldiery from Beit

Jibrîn, and I passed him on to the Governor of Hebron, who was highly delighted, and begged us to make a prisoner of any one who even looked at us in a way we did not like. Such prisoners are a source of income to the Governors of towns.

The Sheikhs of Gath came humbly to ask "if the Gate of Mercy was not open?" but they refused to believe that I was chief of the expedition, because I had no beard. I referred them to Hebron; for mercy is a quality ill appreciated by Arabs. By this act of repression—the news of which spread with great rapidity—we secured perfect immunity from annoyance during the whole of our spring campaign.

On the evening of the 13th, Lieutenant Kitchener arrived, with Habib, the groom, the little dog Looloo, her new puppy, and the baggage. The camp was once more increased to six tents, and the meeting was most cheerful.

The equinoctial gales now came down on us, and delayed us for several days, doing much damage to the tents; our beasts were, however, stabled in the caverns, which are used by the natives for their goats and cows.

Beit Jibrîn had suffered severely from the fever of the last autumn. It was said that 500 people out of 1000 had died in the neighbourhood. The "cursed water" had appeared, by which title was intended a series of stagnant pools in the valley, which if not dry by autumn always foreboded fever in the village. I asked why the villagers did not drain them; the Sheikh replied, "It is from Allah." Such is the fatalistic indolence of the peasantry, which prevents any chance of progress or of civilisation so long as the hopelessness of the creed of Islam bars the way.

From Beit Jibrîn we visited a site which is of primary interest, as representing apparently the Cave of Adullam.

This famous hold, where David collected "every one that was in distress and every one that was in debt, and every one that was discontented," was, according to Josephus, at the city called Adullam (Ant. vi. 12, 3). This city was one of the group of fifteen (Josh. xv. 35) situate in the Shephelah or "lowlands." The towns next on the list, including Jarmuth (El Yermûk), Socoh (Shuweikeh), and others, lie north-east of Beit Jibrîn, and are close together. The term Shephelah is used in the Talmud to mean the low hills of soft limestone, which, as already explained, form a distinct district between the plain and the watershed mountains. The name Sifla, or Shephelah, still exists in four or five places within the region round Beit Jibrîn, and we can therefore have no doubt as to the position of that district, in which Adullam is to be sought.

M. Clermont Ganneau was the fortunate explorer who first recovered the name, and I was delighted to find that Corporal Brophy had also collected it from half a dozen different people, without knowing that there was any special importance attaching to it. The title being thus recovered, without any leading question having been asked, I set out to examine the site, the position of which agrees almost exactly with the distance given by Jerome, between Eleutheropolis and Adullam—ten Roman miles.

The Great Valley of Elah (Wâdy es Sunt) is the highway from Philistia to Hebron; it has its head not far from Terkûmieh, and runs down northwards, past Keilah and Hareth, dividing the low hills of the Shephelah from the rocky mountains of Judah; eight miles from the valley-head stands Shochoh, and Wâdy es Sunt is here a quarter of a mile across; just north of this ruin it turns round westward, and so runs, growing deeper and deeper, between the rocky hills covered with brushwood, becoming an open vale of rich corn-land, flanked by ancient fortresses, and finally debouching at the cliff of Tell es Sâfi.

About two and a half miles south of the great angle near Shochoh, there is a very large and ancient terebinth, one of the few old trees of the species, along the course of the valley, which took its Hebrew name of Elah from them. This terebinth is towards the west side of the vale, just where a small tributary ravine joins Wâdy es Sunt; and near it are two ancient wells, not unlike those at Beersheba, with stone water-troughs round them; south of the ravine is a high rounded hill, almost isolated by valleys, and covered with ruins, a natural fortress, not unlike the well-known Tells which occur lower down the valley of Elah.

This site seems to be ancient, not only because of the wells, but judging from the caves, the tombs, and the rock quarryings which exist near it. The hill is crowned with a little white-domed building, dedicated to "the notable chief" (Sheikh Madhkûr), who seems to have no other name. The ruins round it are named from the Sheikh.

But although to the site itself no name except Sheikh Madhkûr is applied, there are ruins below the hill and near the well, which are called 'Aid el Ma, or 'Aid el Miyeh, "Feast of the Water," or "Feast of the Hundred." Both pronunciations are recognised, and either is radically identical with the Hebrew Adullam. The 'Aid represents the Hebrew Ed, "monument," as perhaps also in the case of the Altar of Ed, noticed in a former chapter; and the Ma, "water," reminds one of Jerome's curious translation of the name Adullam—"Testimonium Aquæ, Monument of Water."

But if this ruined fortress be, as there seems no good reason to doubt it is, the royal city of Adullam, where, we should naturally ask, is the famous cave? The answer is easy, for the cave is on the hill.

We must not look for one of the greater caverns,

such as the Crusaders fixed upon in the romantic gorge east of Bethlehem, for such caverns are never inhabited in Palestine; we should expect, rather, a moderate-sized cave, or (considering the strength of the band) a succession of Mughâir, by which name the inhabited "hollow places" are known, in contradistinction to the 'Arkan, or larger caverns, in "cliffs."

The site at Adullam is ruinous, but not deserted. The sides of the tributary valley are lined with rows of caves, and these we found inhabited, and full of flocks and herds; but still more interesting was the discovery of a separate cave, on the hill itself, a low, smoke-blackened burrow, which was the home of a single family. We could not but suppose, as we entered this gloomy abode, that our feet were standing on the very footprints of the Shepherd-King, who here, encamped between the Philistines and the Jews, covered the line of advance on the cornfields of Keilah, and was but three miles distant from the thickets of Hareth.

No doubt many travellers will visit the famous site thus recovered, but I saw nothing more to describe than the bare chalky hill, with its black cave, its white dome, and scattered blocks of masonry, the ancient round, stone wells below, the magnificent old terebinth, and the cave stables in the opposite hillside.

The hill is about 500 feet high; it commands a fine view eastwards over the broad valley (up which the high-road to Hebron runs), its course dotted with terebinths and rich with corn; in the distance are high rocky mountains, dark with brushwood, and steeply sloping, with a small village, here and there, perched on a great knoll, and gleaming white.

There is ample room to have accommodated David's four hundred men in the caves, and they are, as we have seen, still inhabited. The meaning of the old name of the site is now quite lost, and there is a confused tradition of a feast of one hundred guests, by which it is generally explained.

It is interesting to observe that the scene of David's victory over Goliath is distant only eight miles from the cave at 'Aid el Ma. It was in the Valley of Elah, between Shochoh and Azekah, that the Philistines encamped in "Ephes Dammim," or "the Boundary of Blood." Saul, coming down by the highway from the Land of Benjamin, encamped by the valley (1 Sam. xvii. 2) on one of the low hills; and between the two hosts was the Gai or "ravine." Even of the name Ephes Dammim we have perhaps a trace in the modern Beit Fased, or "House of Bleeding," near Shochoh.

Two points required to be made clear as to the episode of David's battle with Goliath; one was the meaning of the expression Gai or "ravine;" the other was the source whence David took the "smooth stones." A visit to the spot explains both. In the middle of the broad open valley we found a deep trench with vertical sides, impassable except at certain places—a valley in a valley, and a natural barrier between the two hosts; the sides and bed of this trench are strewn with rounded and water-worn pebbles, which would have been well fitted for David's sling.

Here, then, we may picture to ourselves the two hosts, covering the low rocky hills opposite to each other, and half hidden among the lentisk bushes; between them was the rich expanse of ripening barley and the red banks of the torrent with its white shingly bed; behind all were the distant blue hill-walls of Judah, whence Saul had just come down. The mail-clad champion advanced from the west, through the low corn, with his mighty lance perhaps tufted with feathers, his brazen helmet shining in the sun; from the east, a ruddy boy, in his white shirt and sandals, armed with a goat's-hair sling, came down to the brook, and, according to the poetic fancy of the Rabbis, the pebbles were given voices, and cried : " By us shalt thou overcome the giant."

The champion fell from an unseen cause, and the wild Philistines fled to the mouth of the valley, where Gath stood towering on its white chalk cliff, a frontier fortress, the key to the high-road leading to the corn-lands of Judah, and to the vineyards of Hebron.

The Survey work round Beit Jibrin was unusually heavy, for, on an average, three or four ruined sites were found to every two square miles, and the number of names was very large. The storms also interrupted us, and thus it was only on the 1st of April, or three weeks from the date of our arrival in the district, that we could move on.

The spring flowers, including the delicate cyclamens, were now in full bloom, the hoopoes and storks had arrived, and Palestine was at its best. The work had extended over 180 square miles in the three weeks, and 424 names, only 50 of which were previously known, had been collected, including more than 200 ruins.

There was always some difficulty in ascertaining names; suspicion, ignorance, and fanatical feeling were against us, but we here found a new difficulty, for the peasantry were convinced that the Franks knew the old names better than they did themselves. One guide, pointing out the ruin of Horân, said that the real name was Korân. I asked why, and he answered that a European had told him. Thus, also, at Kefr Saba we were told that the Frank name was Antifatrûs; and at Adullam one man refused to tell me the name of the place, saying that the Franks knew it best.

I protest against the immorality of corrupting the native traditions, by relating to the peasantry the theories of modern writers, as authentic facts, for it destroys the last undoubted source of information as to ancient topography. The confusion caused by Crusading and early Christian traditions which have been engrafted in a precisely similar manner, forms already a most serious difficulty, and if in addition we are to have modern foreign theories disseminated among the peasantry, identification will be impossible. Throughout the course of the Survey, we never allowed the peasantry to suppose that we attached more value to one name which they gave, than to another, and we never asked leading questions or gave them any information as to ancient sites.

Our next camp was at the village of Mejdel, near the shore, just north of Ascalon, separated from Beit Jibrîn by nineteen miles of corn-land and sandy downs. The plain was dotted with brown mud villages, and was coloured with patches of purple lupines. We passed on our march through Keratiya, in which we probably recognise the name of the Philistine Cherethites, and where is a Crusading tower now known as Kŭl'at el Fenish, "Castle of the Philistines;" thence crossing over the sand-ridge we looked down on green hedgeless fields, brown ploughland, and beautiful olive-groves, and on the village of Mejdel, with its conspicuous minaret and tall palm-grove.

This place is the principal town between Gaza and Jaffa: it boasts of a bazaar and has a weekly market. The inhabitants are rich and well-disposed. There are sandy lanes, hedged with the prickly pear, round the town, and on the west a large cemetery near the sand-dunes. To the north, under a row of aged olive trees, we found a most pleasant camping-ground. We were also able to enjoy a daily bathe in the sea, which, however, nearly cost me my life on the 5th of April; for the surf was breaking, and a strong suckback of the waves carried me out into the broken water, whence I was rescued by Lieutenant Kitchener.

From this camp we made the large-scale Survey of Ascalon, and cleared up the curious question as to the two Episcopal towns of that name which existed in the fifth century, the one being apparently Ascalon by the sea, the second a ruined site called 'Askelôn in the hills near Beit Jibrin.

Ascalon, "the bride of Syria," is now entirely ruinous, and only the fragments of its great walls, built by the English, under Richard Lion-Heart, in 1191 A.D., remain, half buried by the great dunes of rolling sand, which are ever being blown up by the sea breeze from the south-west. The whole interior of the site is covered with rich soil, to a depth of about ten feet, and the natives find fragments of fine masonry, shafts, capitals, and other remains of the old city, by digging in this.

The walls inclose a half circle, or bow, as described by William of Tyre, the string being towards the sea, where are cliffs about fifty feet high, above the beach. The town measures one mile and three-quarters round, and three-eighths of a mile from east to west. The foundations of the five great towers, noticed by the chronicler of King Richard's expedition, are all discernible, with the land-gate, the sea-gate, the church, and some other ruins. The whole place is now full of gardens, containing palms, olives, apples, lemons, almonds, pomegranates, and tamarisks, irrigated by no less than forty wells of sweet water.

The walls are of small masonry, which is much less solid than the work of the Christian kings of Jerusalem, but the mortar is so hard that, in places, the stone has given way and cracked, while the mortar joints remain unbroken. A huge tower-foundation lies tilted up on one side, like a great cheese, close to the land-gate; it is twenty feet in diameter, and six feet thick.

The fruits here ripen a month earlier than in other parts of Palestine; and were it not that now, as in King Richard's time, Ascalon has no port, it would no doubt be a place of importance.

Of Herod's beautiful colonnades, nothing now remains. The Crusaders had little respect for antiquities, and the innumerable granite pillar-shafts, which are built horizontally into the walls, are no doubt those originally brought to the town by Herod.

The Jews held Ascalon to be no part of "the Land." Even as late as the twelfth century, three hundred Samaritans lived there. The famous Temple of Dercoto, in the town, is noticed in the Mishna, as well as the idol Serapia, which was here worshipped. A place called Yagur is also noticed in the Talmud as on the boundary of "the Land," apparently outside the walls of Ascalon; this, no doubt, is represented by the modern village of El Jûrah, on the north-east, beyond the fosse, among gardens and lanes which are half covered with sand.

It is indeed quite mournful to see how the dry blown sand, advancing, it is said, a yard every year, has climbed over the southern walls of the town, and has already quite destroyed the fruitful gardens on that side.

We heard a curious tradition at Ascalon. A tomb had been opened by the peasantry, near the ruin, some thirty years ago. Under a great slab, in the eastern cemetery, they found a perfectly preserved body, apparently embalmed, lying in its robes, with a sword by its side, and a ring on its finger. The dead eyes glared so fiercely on the intruders, that they let fall the slab, and as one of the party soon after died, they came to the conclusion that it was a Neby or "Prophet" whom they had disturbed, and the place has thus become surrounded with a mysterious sanctity.

Seven and a half miles north of Mejdel is the site of the famous city of Ashdod, now only a mud village of moderate size, on the eastern slope of a knoll which is covered with loose sandy soil and hedged in with prickly pear. On this knoll the old city no doubt stood, and though its elevation is not great, it commands the surrounding land, which accounts for the siege of twenty-nine years, by Psammetichus, that Ashdod underwent. On the south is a small white mosque, a water-wheel, and the fine Khân which has fallen into ruins within the last thirty years. There is a great mud-pond on the east, with palms near it, and to the south a marsh, fig gardens and numerous sycamore trees. The corn-lands are wide and fertile, but the place has no antiquities beyond a few bad coins and gems.

The ever-rolling sand-dunes have here encroached no less than three miles, and are lapping against the village. Riding due west from Ashdod we reached the shore, at a point which seems to have been rarely visited by former travellers. There are here extensive ruins of a town, stretching along the shore, and a square fort with round corner towers, probably of Crusading date. This is no doubt the ancient port of Ashdod, mentioned in the fifth century, and the place is still used as a landing by small boats.

The name which is given to this harbour as well as to the ports of Abu Zabûra, Yebna, and Ghûzzeh, is very interesting; they are each known as El Mineh, but the word is not Arabic. The Talmud speaks of the harbour of Cæsarea as

Liminch, and here we have the solution of the puzzle. The Jews were not a race of sailors; the only notices of the sea in the Bible, show the awe with which they regarded its rolling waves. They had no harbours along the coast, and apparently no word in their language for a port; thus they adopted a foreign epithet, and naturalised the Greek Limen, now further corrupted into the modern El Mînch.

One other great city occupied our attention from the Mejdel camp, namely Lachish, a place which seems to have been still known in the fourth century. We visited Umm Lags, the site proposed by Dr. Robinson, and could not but conclude that no ancient or important city ever stood there, nor has the name any radical similarity to that of Lachish. Much nearer indeed would be the title El Hesy, applying to a large ancient site with springs, near the foot of the hills, about in the proper position for Lachish. The modern name means "a water-pit," and, if it is a corruption of Lachish, it would afford a second instance of a change which is well known to have taken place in the case of Michmash—the K being changed to a guttural H. The distance from Beit Jibrîn to Tell el Hesy, is not much greater than that given by the Onomasticon for Lachish, while the proximity of Eglon ('Ajlân), and the position south of Beit Jibrîn, on a principal road, near the hills, and by one of the only springs in the plain, all seem to be points strongly confirming this view.

On the 15th of April we marched fourteen miles south to Gaza, over rolling corn-lands with patches of red sandy cliff, and by brown mud villages, with white Kubbehs, and large ponds in which the little red oxen were standing knee-deep. Riding up a low ridge, we came upon a great avenue of very ancient olives, which stretch south for four miles to the houses of Gaza.

This ancient city, the capital of Philistia, is very picturesquely situated, having a fine approach down the broad avenue from the north; and it rises on an isolated hill a hundred feet above the plain. On the higher part of the hill are the Governor's house, the principal mosque (an early Crusading church), and the bazaars. The green mounds traceable round this hillock are probably remains of the ancient walls of the city.

Gaza bristles with minarets, and has not less than twenty wells. The population is now eighteen thousand, including sixty or seventy houses of Greek Christians.

The Samaritans in the seventh century seem to have been numerous in Philistia, near Jaffa, Ascalon, and Gaza. Even as late as the commencement of the present century, they had a synagogue in this latter city, but are now no longer found there.

There are two large suburbs of mud cabins on

lower ground, to the east and north-east, making four quarters to the town in all. East of the Serai is the reputed tomb of Samson, whom the Moslems call 'Aly Merwân or "Aly the enslaved." On the north-west is the mosque of Hâshem, the father of the Prophet. The new mosque, built some forty years since, is full of marble fragments, from ancient buildings which were principally found near the sea-shore.

The town is not walled, and presents the appearance of a village grown to unusual size; the brown cabins rise on the hillside row above row, and the white domes and minarets, with numerous palms, give the place a truly Oriental appearance. The bazaars are large and are considered good.

Riding round the town to the east, I found the Moslem inhabitants celebrating a festival, in tents pitched in the cemeteries, where black-robed women, wearing the Egyptian veil, sat in circles, singing and clapping their hands to keep time. On the south-east of the city is a very conspicuous isolated hill called El Muntâr, "the watchtower," and on it another place sacred to 'Aly, a little white building, with three domes, surrounded with graves. This is traditionally the hill to which Samson carried the gates of Gaza, and a yearly festival of the Moslems is held here.

On the following day I rode out to a point north-east of Gaza, accompanied by Corporal Brophy and by a native soldier from the town.

The Teiâha Arabs were at war with the 'Azâzimeh, who had called in the Terabîn to assist them, and battles were being fought within a few miles of the city, quite unnoticed by the Turkish Governor.

We were riding across a heavy ploughed field, when I heard cries of "There they are!" and looking back I saw the main road occupied by a band of about twenty horsemen, half hidden by a swell of the ground. They were all well mounted, and armed with swords, guns, and pistols, and with great lances of cane with long iron heads and tufts of ostrich feathers. As I looked six spearmen started out and spurred full speed at our Bashi-Bazouk, who was some two hundred yards behind us. They came down like a whirlwind, shaking their lances horizontally, and kicking up a great cloud of dust. It was an awkward moment, for we were out-numbered, and flight or resistance would have been equally vain. I resolved to face it out, and turning back we also galloped up towards the six champions, who drew up round our soldier, and dug their spear-butts into the ground, then suddenly wheeled round and cantered back to the main body, which, to my great relief, filed slowly away eastwards. It appeared that they had mistaken us for Terabin Arabs, but, finding that we were English, and protected by the Gaza government, they had been afraid to interfere with us.

This little adventure gave us a good idea of the

tactics of the Bedawin in warfare. The military advantage of superior numbers is thoroughly recognised by these wary and pretentious warriors.

Space will not allow of an account of our explorations at Gerar, famous in the history of Isaac; of our visit to Deir-el-Belah, the Crusading Darum, fortified, in 1170, by King Amalrich; or of our inspection of the Protestant school for Moslem girls, established by an estimable and courageous English gentleman, for whom we felt much admiration. We spent a pleasant time at Gaza, and our party was increased by the arrival of Corporal Junor. We also rode up in one day from Gaza to Jerusalem, to attend the celebration of the Greek Easter.

News of a serious fight near Beersheba, in which 700 Arabs were killed and wounded, determined us to set our faces northwards, leaving the district north-west of Beersheba to be finished during the autumn of 1877. On the last day of April we left our Gaza camp, and marched back to Mejdel, and thence, on the following day, to Yebnah, the ancient Jamnia, famous as the seat of the Sanhedrim after the fall of Bether.

The great valley of Sorek, which rises north of Jerusalem, and runs down by Zoreah (Sŭr'ah) and Beth Shemesh ('Ain Shemes), reaches the sea north of Yebnah. It is here called "Reuben's River," from the little enclosure sacred to the

"Prophet Reuben," which, from the middle ages, has been a Moslem shrine for pilgrimage. The harbour north-west of Yebnah is known also as Minet Rubîn.

The district round Yebnah is full of sacred shrines. Neby Shît or Seth, Neby Yûnis or Jonah, and Neby Kunda, probably "the Chaldean," with many minor saints, have domes within a few miles of one another. The mosque of Yebnah, with its little minaret, was a Christian church, which was partly rebuilt and altered in 673 A.H. There are three other sacred places near it, one being a mosque dedicated to Abu Harîreh, Companion of the Prophet.

The town of Yebnah stands on an isolated hillock, with olives to the north, and it is supplied by wells with water-wheels, or Sâkia, as at Ashdod. There is nothing of great antiquity at the place, and even the walls of the Crusading fortress of Ibelin, built at Yebnah in 1144 A.D., have disappeared. The Crusaders considered Yebnah (or Jamnia) to be the site of Gath; but, as usual, their views are not supported by the facts of earlier history.

Three miles east of Jamnia the Valley of Sorek passes through a defile, having a hill on either side; on each hill a village stands above the rich corn-land, and each village is an ancient site. The southern—now Katrah—is supposed to be Gederoth; the northern, El Mŭghâr ("the Cave"), is the site which Captain Warren proposes for Makkedah.

This latter is a remarkable place, and one of the most conspicuous sites in the plain. A promontory of brown sandy rock juts out southwards, and at the end is the village climbing up the hillside. The huts are of mud, and stand in many cases in front of caves; there are also small excavations on the north-east, and remains of an old Jewish tomb, with Kokim. From the caves the modern name is derived, and it is worthy of notice that this is the only village in the Philistine plain at which we found such caves. The proximity of Gederoth (Katrah) and Naamah (Na'aneh) to El Mŭghâr also increases the probability that Captain Warren's identification of El Mŭghâr with Makkedah is correct, for those places were near Makkedah (Josh. xv. 41).

North-east of Makkedah, Ekron still stands, on low rising ground—a mud hamlet, with gardens fenced with prickly pears. There is nothing ancient here, any more than at Ashdod or Jamnia, but one point may be mentioned which is of some interest. Ekron means "barren," yet the town stood in the rich Philistine plain. The reason is, that north of the Sorek Valley there is a long sandy swell reaching to the sea-coast—an uncultivated district, now called Deirân, the Arabic name being equivalent to its old title, Daroma; Ekron stands close to this dry, barren spur, and above the fertile corn-lands in the valley.

Our last Philistine camp was at the edge of the low hills, in a fig-garden, just south of Dhenebbeh. We reached it on the 8th of May, and left on the 15th, on which day we completed one thousand square miles, which had been surveyed in eleven weeks, since the 25th of February—the most rapid piece of work during the whole course of the Survey.

The village of Dhenebbeh lies south of Wâdy Sûrâr, the old valley of Sorek. The view up this valley, looking eastward, is picturesque. The broad vale, half a mile across, is full of corn, and in the middle runs the white shingly bed of the winter torrent. Low white hills flank it on either side, and the high rugged chain of the mountains of Judah form a picturesque background. On the south, among the olives, is the ruin of Beth Shemesh, to which place the lowing kine dragged the rude cart through the barley-fields. On the north, a little white building with a dome is dedicated to Sheikh Samat, and stands close to Zoreah.

Such is a slight sketch of the Philistine campaign, the full details of which must be left to be enumerated in the memoir of the map, of which they form a large section. We must hasten on now to other questions of greater interest and importance.

VOL. IL

The Sea of Galilee.

CHAPTER VII.

GALILEE.

The Philistine campaign was followed by three weeks' rest at Jerusalem during the east winds of May. On the 8th of June we once more marched out with our whole expedition, intending to finish the northern district, of 1000 square miles, within the year, if possible.

Our first halt was at the "Robbers' Spring;" our second at Shechem, whence we revisited Gerizim on the 9th, and saw once more the old Samaritan Manuscripts. On the 11th we passed through Samaria, and over the hills of Manasseh, reaching Sileh, on the edge of the Great Plain, by a march of twenty miles. The dogs suffered much from heat and thirst, and little Jack drank so much on arriving at Siloh, that he became swollen and unable to move, until I had given him a good glass of raw whisky.

On the 12th we still marched north, by Lejjûn and Keimûn, across the Kishon, through the oak woods, and, crossing the perennial stream of Wâdy el Melek, we reached Shefa 'Amr in the afternoon, and here commenced the Survey of Galilee.

One of the principal pieces of work to be done was the running of a line of levels from the Mediterranean to the Sea of Galilee, for which purpose the British Association had voted £100. The line which I chose, and which was approved, was the shortest possible, and Wâdy el Melek afforded us a most convenient line of ascent to the Buttauf Plain, whence we were to descend to Tiberias. Under my direction, nineteen miles were run in 1875, and in 1877 Lieutenant Kitchener finished the remaining seventeen miles on the low ground, which could not be entered in summer. By this means the level of the Sea of Galilee, variously computed at from 300 to 600 feet below the Mediterranean, has been fixed as 682·5 feet.

The history of the Shefa 'Amr camp was not marked by any special incidents, beyond a quarrel at the spring, which threatened to be serious, but which was converted, by immediate action, into a good lesson to the Moslems which secured us peace. Our most valuable discoveries in this part of the country included the probable site of a synagogue, and the recovery of Osheh, a town known to have been close to Shefa 'Amr (or Shafram) and one of the places where the Sanhedrim sat for many years; it seems undoubtedly to be the present ruin of Húsheh. We also found a very remarkable tomb at Shefa 'Amr, profusely covered with sculpture, and with a Greek inscription and crosses. Outside the door are sculptured lions, a grape-vine with birds in the branches, and other designs. It appears to be a Christian sepulchre, probably of the fourth or fifth century, but perhaps earlier. The façade is shown in the frontispiece of this volume.

On the last day of June we marched east to the miserable little hamlet of El B'aineh, which, with two others, stands on the north slopes of Jebel Tór'an, an isolated block of mountain rising out of the plateau of the Buttauf. Here we found the inhabitants all fever-stricken from the malarious exhalations of the great swamp, which even as late as July extended over half the plain. The place was evidently unhealthy, and we were tortured by the armies of huge musquitoes rendering sleep impossible at night. The levelling operations required us to camp in the plain, but we hastened on the work as much as possible, looking forward to a retreat into the mountains of Upper Galilee, which, being 4000 feet above the sea, would be cool and pleasant, and, as we hoped, safe from the scourge of cholera, which had already devastated Damascus, and was creeping slowly south.

The view from the summit of Tôr'an is interesting and extensive. The Sea of Galilee is visible, and we were able to fix the direction of many points along its shore.

On the south, separated from Tôr'an by a second plain, lay the low bare range of the Nazareth hills, Neby S'ain, and Gath Hepher with the tomb of Jonah, being visible, while rather farther east Kefr Kenna stood among its olive-groves and gardens of pomegranates.

Tabor, crowned with two monasteries, was also plainly visible, east of the Nazareth range, the slopes partly hidden by oak-groves. Through a gap, between it and the western hills, the outline of Gilboa and part of Jebel ed Duhy could be seen. The plain of Esdraelon was hidden, but the cone of Sheikh Iskander was visible to the south-west.

To the west the view extended over the low wooded hills to the long range of Carmel, which was visible, from the Peak of Sacrifice to the white monastery where, on a little spit, stands the German wind-mill, which showed up quite black against the gleaming sea.

The brown and fertile plain of the Buttauf, in the basaltic soil of which tobacco, corn, maize, sesame, cotton, and every species of vegetable grow luxuriantly, lay at our feet. The high blunt top of Jebel Deidebeh ("mountain of the watch-tower"), crowned with its ring of thicket, rose behind, shutting out the view. Beyond this was the chain of hills running eastwards, with rolling grey uplands dotted with olives, while farther still, some ten or twelve miles away, rose the mountain-wall of Upper Galilee, culminating in Jebel Jermûk, a bare craggy ridge which closed the view to the north. Turning yet farther east, the large town of Safed shone white on the mountain side, divided into two quarters, with a double-pointed summit behind them. Beyond all, dark and dreamlike, the great Hermon, "Sheikh of the mountains," was seen streaked with silver lines of snow.

But the view due east of Tôr'an was yet more interesting. A yellow plateau shelves down from the foot of the mountains of Upper Galilee and runs into little tongues and promontories, separated by tiny bays, along the north-western shores of the Sea of Galilee: only in one part of this line is there a cliff, just where the little fertile plain of Gennesaret terminates at Khân Minieh; the rest is shelving ground almost to the water's edge.

The deep chasm running down from Safed, and known as "the Valley of Doves" (W. el Hamâm).

debouches into the green oasis of the Ghûweir, or plain of Gennesaret. East of the sea the long flat plateau of Bashan stretches from the precipices which enclose the lake, and reaches away to the volcanic cones and dreary lava-fields which are backed by the peaks of Jebel ed Drûz.

Tiberias was hidden below the cliffs, and only about half the blue and limpid lake was seen behind them; most conspicuous on this line are the Horns of Hattin, so fatal to the Christian kingdom in 1187, and here also, as on the east, a broad plateau runs almost to the top of the precipices.

It is wonderful to reflect how numerous are the ancient towns which encircled this little lake; speaking of the west side alone, they number more than twenty. Hidden by the cliffs we have Tiberias, or Rakkath, and Hammath (El Hummâm), Tarichæa (Kerek), Sinnabris (Sennâbreh), and Magdala (Mejdel), with Kedish, the probable site of the Kadesh of Barak.

On the western plateau stand Adamah (Admah), Adami (Ed Damieh), Bitzaanaim (Bessûm), Lasharon (Sarôna), Shihon (Sh'aîn), and other sites of Biblical interest. Arbela, with the synagogue of Rabbi Nitai (200 B.C.), Hattîn (the ancient Zer), Yemma (the Talmudic Caphar Yama), Kefr Sabt (Caphar Sobthi), Seiyâdeh (the Talmudic Ziadethah), Tell M'aûn (Beth Maon), Sha'arah (Beth Sharaim), and several other towns of later times swell the long list of cities. The district is full of sacred places: Rabbi Akiba, Rabbi Meir, and the great Maimonides, were buried near Tiberias, and the supposed tombs of Jethro and Habakkuk are still shown on the hills above.

One site alone is conspicuous by its absence—the tomb of Nahum, which was known to the Jews in the fourteenth century, but is apparently now lost for ever. This loss is a subject of real regret, for could we light upon the tomb of Nahum, we could perhaps settle for ever the position of Capernaum, "the village of Nahum."

The various scholars and explorers who have written since Robinson are divided into two parties one placing Capernaum at the ruins near Khân Minich, the other selecting the large site at Tell Hûm. The places are only two and a half miles apart, but modern disputants are not content with such wide limits. There is a point which strikes one as curious in the controversy. In all the arguments usually brought forward, no reference is made to the information which can be deduced from Jewish sources dating later than Bible times. To this information I would call attention.

Identification, properly so called, is impossible when the old name is lost; but in the case of Capernaum traces of the name may perhaps be recovered still. It is generally granted that the Talmudic Caphar Nahum, or "Village of Nahum," was probably identical with the New Testament Capernaum, and it is on this supposition that the only philological claim of Tell Hûm is based; but the loss implied of an important radical at the commencement of the name Hûm, if it be supposed to be a corruption of Nahum, is a change of which we have scarcely any instance; moreover, Hûm in Hebrew means "black," and still retains its original signification in Arabic. Tell Hûm was so named, no doubt, from the black basalt which covers the site. If we are to seek for an ancient corresponding title, I would suggest Caphar Ahim, a town mentioned in the Talmud with Chorazin, and famous for its wheat, as being probably the ancient name of the ruined town at Tell Hûm.

An investigation of the name Minich is more satisfactory. In Hebrew it is derived from a root meaning "lot," or "chance." In Aramaic it has an identical meaning, and the Talmud often mentions the Minai, or "Diviners," under which title were included not only every kind of sorcerer and enchanter, but also the early Jewish converts to Christianity.

Now this word Minai is intimately connected with Capernaum. In the Talmud there is a curious passage (to be found in Buxtorf's great Lexicon) where a certain faction, called Huta, are defined as "sons of Caphar Nahum;" and these Huta, we find from another passage, were none other than the Minai.

It is evident that the Jews looked on Capernaum as the head-quarters of the Christians, whom they contemptuously styled "sorcerers," and the importance thus attached by them to that town, as a Christian centre, is in accordance with the expression in the Gospel, where Capernaum is called Our Lord's "own city" (Matt. ix. 1).

The Talmudic doctors speak, then, of Capernaum as the city of Minai, and as such it continued to be regarded by the Jews down to the fourteenth century. In 1334 A.D. Isaac Chelo travelled from Tiberias to Caphar Anan (Kefr 'Anân), presumably by the direct road passing near the "Round Fountain." He was shown on his way the ruins of Caphar Nahum, and in them the tomb of Nahum, and he remarks incidentally as to the place, "here formerly dwelt the Minai." It is evident that he cannot be supposed, without twisting the narrative, to refer to any place so far from his route as is Tell Hûm. The site at Minieh would have been within a mile and a half of his road, and the name is apparently connected with Capernaum by his valuable note about the Minai.

The same connection is traced in 1616 A.D., when Quaresmius speaks of Capernaum as shown at a place called Minieh, and thus we are able to trace back an apparently unbroken Jewish tradition connecting Capernaum with the "Village of the Minai," and with the ruined site of Minieh.

In addition to the Jewish tradition connecting Minieh with Capernaum, there is a second indication which favours that identification. Josephus speaks of the fountain which watered the plain of Gennesaret, and which was called Capharnaum. It contained a fish named Coracinus, which was also found in the Nile. There are two springs to which this account has been supposed to apply, the one two and a half miles south of Minieh, the other scarcely three quarters of a mile east of the same site. The first irrigates a great part of the plain of Gennesaret; the Coracinus has been found in it, and the waters are clear and fresh; this is called 'Ain-el-Madowerah, "the round spring." The second is called 'Ain Tâbghah, a name apparently not Arabic, but of Hebrew origin, and meaning "immersion." Not only is the origin of this name contrary to the theory of the spring having been originally called Capharnaum in Hebrew, but Dr. Tristram points out that the water being warm, brackish, and muddy, is unfit for the Coracinus, which has never as yet been found in it.

'Ain Tâbghah is not in the plain of Gennesaret. It is a spring surrounded by an octagonal reservoir, which was built up to its present height by one of the sons of the famous Dhahr-el-'Amr in the last century, and the water is thus dammed up to about fifty-two feet above the lake. An aqueduct leads from the level of the reservoir to the cliff at Minieh, where is a rock-cut channel three feet deep and broad, resembling more the great rock-cutting of the Roman road at Abila, than any of the rock-cut aqueducts of the country. The water was conducted through this channel to the neighbourhood of the Khân, or just to the edge of the plain of Gennesaret. It is important to notice that the spring can only have watered the neighbourhood of Minieh after the reservoir had been built, and that it must ever since then have been unfitted for the presence of the Coracinus.

But even if we are prepared to consider this artificial irrigation to be as old as the time of Josephus, and the Tâbghah spring to be the fountain of Capharnaum, it is still the Minieh site which is thus indicated as representing that town, for the distance from the spring to Tell Hûm is nearly two miles, while to Minieh it is scarcely three quarters of a mile. Tell Hûm, in short, is wanting in the very important requisite of a spring irrigating the plain of Gennesaret.

In favour of the Minieh site we have then Jewish tradition, and the existence of springs more or less fulfilling the description of Josephus; but it must not be denied that in favour of Tell Hûm we have a Christian tradition from the fourth century downwards.

Jerome places Capernaum two miles from Chorazin. If by the latter place he means the ruin of Kerâzeh, the measurement is exactly that to Tell Hûm; if he refers to a site of Chorazin east of the river Jordan, the result is still the same, as in neither case could Minieh be intended.

The account of Theodorus (530 A.D.) is more explicit, and seems indeed almost conclusive as to the site of his Capernaum. Two miles from Magdala he places the Seven Fountains, where the miracle of feeding the five thousand was traditionally held to have taken place; these, as will presently appear, were probably close to Minieh; and two miles from the fountains was Capernaum, whence it was six miles to Bethsaida, on the road to Banias. These measurements seem to point to Tell Hûm as the sixth-century Capernaum.

Antoninus Martyr (600 A.D.) speaks of the great basilica in Capernaum, which it is only natural to identify with the synagogue of Tell Hûm, which seems probably (by comparison with those at Meirûn) to be the work of Simeon Bar Jochai, the Cabbalist, who lived about 120 A.D.

Arculphus (700 A.D.) visited the fountain where the five thousand were fed, and from the hill near it he saw Capernaum at no great distance on a narrow tract between the lake and the northern hills. His account thus agrees with that of Theodorus, though in itself so indefinite, that it has been brought as evidence in favour of both the sites advocated for Capernaum.

Sæwulf (1103 A.D.) proceeded along the shore for six miles, going north-east from Tiberias, to the mountain where the five thousand were fed, then called Mensa, or "table," which had a church of St. Peter at its feet. It is evident, from the measurements, that this hill was in the neighbourhood of Minieh, where Theodorus also seems to place the scene of the miracle, as above noticed.

John of Würtzburg (about 1160 A.D.) speaks of the mountain called Mensa, with a fountain a mile distant, and Capernaum two miles away.

Fetellus (1150 A.D.) is yet more explicit. Capernaum, he says, is at the head of the lake, two miles from the descent of the mountain, and apparently three from the fountain where the five thousand were fed, which fountain would probably be 'Ain-et-Tîn, a large source, west of Minieh, and not far from the hill which Sæwulf points out as being the Mensa.

The whole of this topography is summed up by Marino Sanuto, whose valuable chart of Palestine shows us the position of the various traditional sites of the fourteenth century. On this chart the Mensa is shown in a position which is unmistakable. The valleys which run down to the Plain of Gennesaret are drawn with some fidelity, and the Mensa is placed north of them; at the border of the lake, Bethsaida is shown, about in the position of Minieh, and Capernaum near that of Tell Hûm; in the letterpress the account is equally clear, Capernaum being placed at the north-east corner of the lake, and Bethsaida just where the lake begins to curve round southward.

Christian tradition points, then, to Tell Hûm as being Capernaum, but Jewish hatred has preserved the Jewish site under the opprobrious epithet of Minieh; the question is simply whether —setting aside the important testimony of Josephus—Jewish or Christian tradition is to be accepted. A single instance will be sufficient to show the comparative value of the two. Jerome speaks of Ajalon, for example, as three miles northeast of Bethel, just where the ruin of 'Alya now stands; he very honestly adds, however, that the Jews pointed out another site at a village called Alus, which, from his description, may be proved to be the modern Yalo. Recent writers have shown that Jerome was wrong and the Jews right; and yet, further, Jerome's site cannot possibly be reconciled with the position in which he himself correctly places Beth Horon. This is but one instance out of many in which Jerome blunders when differing from the Jews, and no impartial reader can study the Onomasticon with Jerome's translation, without seeing that in the fourth century the topography of Palestine was only imperfectly understood.

It may be safely said that Christian tradition, though affording often valuable indications, cannot be taken as authoritative, for the chances are equal that it is correct or the reverse. When, as in the cases of the Temple, of the Place of Stoning, of Joseph's Tomb, and of Jacob's Well, it agrees with Jewish tradition, the sites thus preserved invariably appear to be authentic, and fulfil the required indications found in the Bible; but when these two traditions are discordant, the Christian ceases to be of much value, for it is evident that the traditions of the Jews, handed down unbroken, by an indigenous population which was never driven from the country, must take precedence of the foreign ecclesiastical traditions of comparatively later times, which can so often be proved self-inconsistent, or founded on a fallacy.

It is a wonderful reflection that to Jewish hatred we perhaps owe our only means of fixing one of the most interesting sites in Palestine, and that through the opprobrious epithet of Minai or "Sorcerers," the position of Christ's own city is handed down to the Christians of the nineteenth century.

With these remarks I may close the description of the sacred places of the Holy Land, and conclude this chapter with a short account of the attack on my party, which so nearly prevented the fruits of our labours from being ever summarised in the present volumes.

On Saturday the 10th of July, 1875, we left the fever-stricken village of El B'aineh, and marched to Safed. The party consisted of five Europeans and ten natives, of whom two were suffering with fever. The march was long and arduous, and the final ascent of 2000 feet, leading to the town, which lies in a saddle of the high mountains of Upper Galilee, and looks down on the lake, was very fatiguing to our animals.

We chose a camping-ground north of Safed, close to the Moslem quarter, at the head of the valley which runs by 'Ain ez Zeitûn and divides the city from the Jermûk mountain; here we pitched our tents, and enjoyed the cool fresh breezes, and the shade of the olives. I sent my letter of recommendation to the Governor of the town, and asked for three or four soldiers as camp guards, and for a couple of Bashi-Bazouks to accompany us as usual on our rides.

The tents were about half set up, and I was resting on my bed in my shirt-sleeves and slippers, when I heard angry voices in altercation—a sound not unusual in camp when bargains were being struck. I looked out, and to my astonishment saw a Sheikh, evidently a man of good position, and well dressed, engaged in throwing stones at Habib, who, with his hands spread out, was calling the bystanders to witness the treatment he underwent. Habib was a hot-headed fellow enough, but he had received much schooling in our service, and certainly on this occasion he kept his temper. I advanced towards the group much astonished, but intent only on demanding an explanation. The Sheikh, however, seemed to have lost his senses; he was a thin, pale man, rather above the middle height, and his face was distorted with passion; he strode up to me in an excited manner, and before a word or gesture on my part could have given offence, he seized me by the throat with both hands, and shook me roughly, with a voluble outpouring of words which were quite unintelligible.

My first feeling was that of extreme astonishment. For nearly four years I had been accustomed to be treated with respect by even the highest officials in the country, and my presence had always been sufficient to put a stop to the hottest quarrels among natives. I could not but think that the Sheikh must be out of his mind. My second thought was that to put up with such an insult would be to lose my influence with natives for ever, and I therefore knocked the Sheikh down. This strong hint was not, however, enough for him, and he got up and again attacked me, advancing with one arm behind him—a method of fighting the object of which I could not understand, but, being naturally enraged at his disgraceful conduct, I hit out with each fist, and again knocked him off his legs. As he fell his intentions became clear, for in his hand was a hanjar, or knife, with a blade a foot long, which in another moment would have been sheathed in me, if I had not used the means of defence most natural to an Englishman.

By this time the news of the insult received by the "Kabtàn" had spread in the camp, and my Maronites came running up, quite beside themselves with rage, and for the moment they were unmanageable; they seized the Sheikh, and before I could interfere, my tall muleteer had taken his knife away and had bound the arms of the stupefied chief behind his back. The action was a foolish one, and I should certainly not have authorised it. The Sheikh cried out at once, "Where are my people?" and fierce recriminations commenced between the Maronites and the Moslem bystanders. We were thus, without a moment's notice, plunged into one of those fanatical riots which it had been my constant effort to avoid, and on the brink of which I had so often before found myself, but had always hitherto been able to calm down.

The ominous murmur of the crowd which thickened every moment was followed by a shower of stones, showing that immediate and energetic action alone could save our little band. Our servants were running to the tents for their arms: for we had three shot-guns, a rifle, and eight revolvers ready for use. I had the Sheikh immediately released, and sent Habib at once to the Governor. I watched his unsuccessful attempt to pass through the crowd, who pushed him back, and taking advantage of the general diversion of attention thus created in one direction, I sent our long-legged muleteer round the other side of the hill, bidding him run full speed to the Governor's house.

The temper of the native servants was our greatest danger, for they were thoroughly exasperated, and being all strong plucky fellows they were eager for the fray. I pointed out to Lieutenant Kitchener the gun which our groom was vainly endeavouring to load, and begged him to prevent the use of firearms by our men, while I went to the front to endeavour to pacify the crowd. The obedience to orders which we finally succeeded in enforcing on our Maronites saved us, and it was the result of the steady discipline of the four years, which had brought even the roughest of our camp-followers in some degree into military habits.

The crowd now numbered about three hundred persons, many of whom were armed, and all the more violent engaged in hurling stones at our heads; blocks of every size came whizzing through the air in a thick shower. Lieutenant Kitchener was struck by them more than once, and a muleteer was knocked over. I advanced towards the crowd and endeavoured to calm them, but their numbers gave them courage, and I soon became a mark for the stones, which fell all round without, however, touching me.

The cries which Christians in Palestine have good reason to dread, associated as they are with memories of massacre, were now raised by the mob — "Allah! Allah!" the shout which has since then been heard so often in Bulgaria, and

"Dîn! Dîn! Dîn Muhammed!" the cry of the Damascus massacres.

At this juncture our little cook-boy became hysterical from fright, and rushed into the crowd with his arms flung into the air. He was hustled roughly, and I ran after him and caught him by the tail of his long baggy trousers, and dragged him back, telling him to go to the tents, where I now endeavoured to rally the whole party, being most energetically assisted by Lieutenant Kitchener.

I began to have hopes of separating the two sides, and a momentary lull was caused by the accidental appearance of a "policeman," who, however, soon made himself scarce; but just at this moment a number of fully-armed men came running down the hillside, all relatives or retainers of the Sheikh, who, as we afterwards found, was no less a person than 'Aly Agha 'Allân, a near relation of 'Abd el Kâder himself.

I advanced at once to meet these assailants, and singled out two men, one a white-bearded elder with a battle-axe, the other a tall man with a club. They addressed me with many curses, and the old man thrust the battle-axe against my ribs; but it was a wonderful instance of the influence which a European may always possess over Arabs, that they allowed me to take them by the arms and turn them round, and that on my telling them to go home, with a slight push in that direction, they actually retreated some little way.

Meantime a most extraordinary figure appeared, a black man with pistols in his belt, brandishing a scimitar over his head, and bellowing like a bull. He was the Agha's slave, and was bent on revenge; seeing him so near, and seeing also a gun pointed at my head, I retreated to the tents. I could not help laughing, even at so serious a juncture, when I found myself supported by Sergeant Armstrong, who stood at "the charge" armed with the legs of the camera-obscura!

I now saw that Lieutenant Kitchener was opposing another group to my right front, and went forward to him, when I was at once greeted with a blow on the forehead, from a club with nails in it, which brought the blood in a stream down my face. The man who wielded it, raised it once more, in order to bring it down on the top of my skull, but luckily I was too quick for him, and ducked my head close to his chest. The blow fell short upon my neck, but even then it stunned me for the moment, and I staggered. Had the club come down as intended, it would no doubt have killed me.

Lieutenant Kitchener at once stepped up to defend me, and parried another blow which smashed his hunting-crop, and maimed his arm; we both recovered together, and repaid the blows with our steel-headed whips. The club-man disappeared, and was afterwards falsely represented to have been killed.

My whip flew out of my hand, and left me unarmed ; I saw too that the crowd was gradually hemming in our camp, and there was no sign of coming help. I stood by the tent, quite at a loss what to do, when a gun was put into my hands, and just then a man with a huge stone ran forward at me. I raised the gun, and covered his face, but I felt unable to draw the trigger. It was fortunately unnecessary to do so, for he at once turned tail and fled.

We had now for about half an hour kept back the crowd from our tents without firing a shot, but matters were growing very serious, and there seemed little chance of our escaping the furious mob, who only wanted a leader to encourage them in attacking our little band, now crowded near the tents, and nearly all wounded with stones or clubs.

"There is nothing for it but to bolt," I said.

And so we bolted over thistles and stone-walls to a hillside some hundred yards away. I found that Lieutenant Kitchener was missing, and again we ran back to look for him. To my great relief he was seen a little farther down the hill, having escaped very narrowly from the scimitar of the negro slave already noticed.

We stood on the hillside in suspense and anxiety, but were much surprised to hear no longer the cries of the crowd. In a few moments our scattered servants came to look for us, and we found that the Governor had sent a body of soldiers, who arrived happily almost at the very moment of our retreat; our resistance was thus just sufficiently prolonged to save our lives and property.

We came back to camp, and, soon after, the Kady, the Commandant of the garrison, and the Jewish Consular agent for England appeared. I at once produced the Firman, and in the presence of these dignitaries we had an official report of our wounds and bruises made out. Of the great crowd not an individual now remained in sight; they had melted away as quickly as they had gathered, concealing their guns and clubs under their cloaks as they slunk off.

Not a member of our party had escaped injury. Daud, our valiant groom, had a gash extending across his head; Habib had been hit in the wind with a stone; the cook had been severely bruised and beaten, and a muleteer had been much injured with stones; fortunately there were no gunshot wounds, though at least three shots had been fired, one of which was directed at Lieutenant Kitchener.

Darkness came over the camp during the inquiry, and we held a council as to our next proceedings, determining to march at once to the coast, as it would be unsafe to attempt to continue our work until the assailants had been punished. We held our ground, however, for the night, in spite of the threat of 'Aly Agha that he would return and cut our throats. We nevertheless kept a patrol during the dark hours with guns loaded with ball cartridge, and were thus ready for a renewal of the attack.

Next morning we marched out in good order at daybreak, with four mounted guards, and reached Mejdel Kerûm the same evening. I shall not easily forget that march; my head was so stiff with the swelling of my neck, that I could not move it, and my feet were quite full of the long thistle-thorns, which ran in after I had lost my slippers. Lieutenant Kitchener's arm and side were equally painful, and several of our servants lay helpless on their mules and donkeys. On the following morning I rode hastily to Acre, and laid the affair before the Pacha, telegraphing to Constantinople at the same time.

Such was the attack at Safed. It was due to the insolence of one man, accustomed to overbear and bully the few Christians who pass through the town, and to the fanaticism of the Moslem population, which had always been a source of danger to us, as the reader will already have seen. The success of our defence was due to the obedience of the party, and to our refraining from the use of our firearms; but above all to the providential intervention of the soldiers for whom I had sent, and who arrived just when we were on the point of being overwhelmed by numbers.

A delicate task now lay before us—to convert the defeat into a victory by obtaining the punishment of the offenders; but on the 13th of July the strain proved too much for my health. Excitement, fatigue, pain, and anxiety, added to the malarious poison imbibed in the swamps of the Buttauf, brought on a severe attack of fever, which soon affected my brain, and for twenty-four hours Dr. Varten did not, I believe, expect me to recover. Lieutenant Kitchener also soon succumbed, and the rest followed. Thus we all lay in our beds in the Carmel convent, where we were most kindly treated; and on Sergeant Armstrong devolved the duty of nursing us, which he most efficiently performed.

As soon as we recovered, we began to endeavour to obtain justice. But here a new difficulty arose; the cholera was raging over the whole of the north of Palestine, and at Beirût the Consul-General, Mr. Eldridge, was ill. Thus the Vice-Consul could not come down to attend the trial at Acre, while the various representatives whom he chose each in turn excused himself, and the native *personnel* of the Consulate fled from their posts. There was a great deal of scheming on the part of the offenders, with intent to pervert the course of justice, and we were obliged meantime to break up the expedition, the men being recalled to England by the Committee of the Palestine Exploration Fund.

I must not omit to express my gratitude to the Committee, for the confidence they showed by leaving the affair entirely in my hands, and by promptly supporting all that I did; any other course would certainly have so hampered us as to make it impossible to steer a way through the many difficulties connected with the trial; nor am I less sensible of the ability and firmness displayed by Mr. Consul Moore, who was at last sent to our assistance, to try the case, as joint Commissioner, with a courteous Turkish official.

Through Mr. Moore's exertions, we were at length able to obtain justice. 'Aly Agha was sentenced to nine months' imprisonment; his slave, who was proved to have used various weapons, to two years of hard labour; and several other offenders to shorter terms. The sum of £270 was also paid, as a fine, to the Committee of the Palestine Exploration Fund.

And thus at length we found ourselves free to leave Haifa, and to return to England, looking forward to rest, and a better climate, to restore our injured health. We left the German hotel, where we had lived together for so many weeks after breaking up the expedition, and were driven down in a German cart to Tantûra, where we slept in a mud hut. Next morning we started on a ride of forty miles, to Jaffa; but our strength had been so reduced by the fever, that it proved almost too much for us. When at length, thoroughly worn out, we reached the sand-hills near the town, we were stopped by certain Quarantine officials, who, being unable to read our pass, wanted to keep us prisoners in a miserable tent, probably in the hope of extorting money. Our Bashi-Bazouk engaged in a quarrel with them, and meantime we slipped away and galloped on; but Lieutenant Kitchener could no longer sit on his horse, and fell off upon the sand. Leaving him at the edge of the orange-gardens, I galloped off to bring assistance, and returned to find him gone; my anxiety was not, however, of long duration, for he had crept through the garden, and I soon found him in bed in the hotel. Such was our last ride together in Palestine.

On the 1st of October, 1875, I saw the shore of the Holy Land disappear into the sea. The triumphal entry which I had promised myself into Safed was made by Lieutenant Kitchener alone, in the spring of 1877; the Governor of the place went out to meet him, and the repentant Agha, having undergone his term of imprisonment, came to the tent to express contrition. The colony of the Algerines is now, I believe, almost ruined; for they had to pay large sums besides the fines above mentioned, and their prestige was quite destroyed by the execution of the sentences against them.

Thus I hope that the affair has in the end proved a salutary lesson, and has shown the natives of Palestine that English subjects cannot be insolently treated with impunity.

In conclusion, I may note that immediately after our return Corporal Armstrong was promoted, on my recommendation, to his present rank of Sergeant for good conduct at Safed.

A DERWISH.

CHAPTER VIII.

THE ORIGIN OF THE FELLAHIN.

THE history of the Survey has been brought down to the end of the 1875 campaign. During 1876 the whole party was employed in preparing the results for publication, a work frequently interrupted by recurring attacks of fever. In January,

1877, Lieutenant Kitchener once more took the field, but my health did not allow of my return to Palestine. When I left the country 4700 square miles had been completed, and Upper Galilee remained to be surveyed. This has now been most successfully accomplished, and 1300 square miles have been added to the map, making 6000 in all; thus the work extends from Dan to Beersheba, and from Jordan to the Mediterranean—a complete survey of Palestine west of Jordan.

The remaining chapters of this work are devoted to a sketch of the inhabitants of the country, and to notes on the present condition of Palestine and on its possible future, being the result of four years of observation and special inquiry.

I am fully aware of the difficulty of giving a thoroughly accurate account of the natives of the Holy Land. Four years is not a sufficient time to allow of such an intimate knowledge of their character, thoughts, and customs being obtained as should justify an account resembling that which Lane has given of Egypt, for the Moslems are very reserved in their intercourse with Christian strangers, and it is most difficult to obtain their confidence. There are several Europeans who have lived so long in Palestine as to be far more competent than I can claim to be, to write about the native population; but in one respect we enjoyed unusual advantages; for we lived almost exclusively in the villages, and amongst the peasantry, and we thus had opportunities of studying their life and character which have not fallen to the lot of previous travellers or explorers, few of whom have passed more than a single season in the country.

In considering the character and manners of the natives of Palestine, there is one circumstance which must always be kept in sight—we are dealing with a Semitic, not with an Aryan, people, and they must be judged from a Semitic point of view. The faults and virtues of the Semitic races are so distinct and peculiar, that it is not easy for a European to judge of them fairly; their ideas of right and wrong, of the beautiful and the praiseworthy, of religion and morality, are essentially different to our own.

In religion, above all, this difference is remarkable, and for two reasons. In the first place, the Semitic character is eminently conservative, while the Aryan is liberal; hence authority is to the Semitic people the foundation of faith, while reason claims to have its voice heard among the Aryans. The incredibility of any account is not weighed for a moment in the East, so long as the authority on which it rests is unimpeachable; thus a Moslem sermon consists in tracing back from mouth to mouth up to the lips of the Prophet the precept which the preacher enforces. How different in principle is this way of regarding religion, when contrasted with the logic of a

European preacher appealing to an educated audience!

In the second place, a peculiarity of the Semitic people seems to be the absence of the æsthetic faculty; they have no art, no sculpture, no poetry, that we should recognise as such; their religion forbids them to picture the human form, and the most prized of their art productions are only specimens of caligraphy profusely ornamented. A Moslem will not willingly look at a picture, and probably holds it upside down if he does. Even the famous "Thousand Nights and a Night" are of Persian, and therefore of Aryan, not Semitic origin.

This peculiarity has a most important influence on the religion of the Semitic people. The poetic fancy of the Greek led him to clothe in symbolic language his keen sense of the beauties of the world around him. The return of sunrise, and of spring, the fierce heat of the summer, and the deadly shadow of winter, alike furnished him with an ever-recurring series of subjects for poetic imagination; and from the love and worship of nature arose the myth, while from the myth we trace the folk-lore of the peasantry, and the nursery tales of modern times.

It seems not too much to say that this poetic love of nature is foreign to the Semitic mind. The worship of a personal God is the one great truth which presents itself to this people; natural phenomena are regarded only as the creations of His hands, and not as being themselves individual divinities; and the dictum of the great French scholar is not to be forgotten, "The Semites have no mythology." Hence also arise the palpable absurdities which result from attempts to treat the history of the Old Testament as if it were of mythological origin.

Where there is no nature-worship there can be no mythology, where there is no mythology no "folk-lore" can be produced, and thus we arrive at the same conclusion which was gradually forced on me, that it would be vain to expect to recover amongst the peasantry in Palestine such stories as Grimm collected among the German peasants, or any remnants of an indigenous mythological system.

The inhabitants of the country, excepting the European colonists and residents, are all alike of Semitic origin, including the Jews, the Syrians, and the Arabs, while the foreign residents are principally German, with the Turks and the mongrel Levantines. Of these nationalities the three first are the most interesting, and the Syrians, by which title, for want of a better, I denote the peasantry, are by far the most worthy of minute study and description.

In order to obtain some knowledge of the native peasantry, it is necessary to examine their character, language, and religion, which are the three fundamental questions regarding any nation. We may thus be able to conjecture their origin, and to account for their peculiarities. To these three subjects the present chapter is devoted.

The character of the peasantry is a curious mixture of virtues and vices, exaggerated by the entire absence of education. Among their finer qualities may be noticed their great patience and power of endurance, their sobriety, their good-nature, and kindness to animals, their strong sense of religion, and of submission to the Divine Will, their personal courage, which is often remarkable, and their great natural intelligence and quickness of perception, with their power of adapting themselves to novel situations; their docility under recognised leaders is also remarkable, as is also the natural dignity, courtesy, and modesty of their behaviour in those parts of the country where they are unspoilt by the influence of the worst class of tourists.

Their vices, on the other hand, are often most repulsive, and their uncleanness and brutal immorality are well known, though not subjects for discussion. Their love of money is evidenced by their ordinary conversation; for a passing group, when casually overheard, is almost invariably talking of piastres. Insolence of demeanour to strangers whom they suppose to be unable to assist themselves, is also common, but this is due perhaps in part to oppression and religious hatred, though also, in great measure, to that exclusiveness of feeling which restricts all ideas of benevolence to the small circle of the community or family. The worst vice of all is their universal untruthfulness; and the shamelessness of the peasantry in this respect is evidenced by their proverb, "A lie is the salt of a man." A successful liar is spoken of as *shâter ketîr*, or "very clever," and nothing is more respected than the capacity for cheating every one. May not this be considered as a characteristic of the Semitic people from the days of Jacob downwards?

Though liars by nature, and often forced to lie by the oppression of an unjust government, the peasantry are able to appreciate truthfulness in other nations. There is an expression which is common amongst them, and of which we have reason to be proud; for in striking a bargain they will promise by the *Kelim Ingleez*, or "Englishman's word," as equivalent to saying that they will faithfully perform their undertakings. This reputation for trustworthiness is well supported by many an Englishman in the country, and we never lost an opportunity of reminding the peasantry that an Englishman's word was his bond.

These traits of the national character are all characteristic of Semitic origin, and are not less distinctive of the Jews; high religious zeal, endurance, intelligence, energy, and courage of a peculiar kind, are qualities eminently remarkable in the Jewish character, and, on the other hand, love of money, craft, exclusiveness, and lying, are vices which have always been chargeable against that nation.

With qualities such as those above enumerated the native peasantry are capable, under a wise government, of becoming a fine people: the present rule of the Turks discourages them in every way; their natural quickness is uncherished by education, their industry is rendered useless by unjust taxation and robbery, their worst vices are unchecked, and they have become broken-spirited and hopeless, under an oppression of which no idea can be formed in England; their only object is therefore to drag on their miserable lives with as little trouble as possible.

One trait remains to be noticed as forming a serious drawback in any attempt to improve the condition of the people. This again is a Semitic characteristic, namely, unbounded personal conceit and vanity—a peculiarity of the people which is most striking and disagreeable to any one dealing with them.

A Syrian believes himself to be far more capable of conducting the most difficult affairs than a European specially educated; and the peasantry—perhaps not well impressed by the behaviour of tourists ignorant of the language—are generally convinced that the Franks are far less clever than themselves, while the marvels of civilisation are commonly attributed to a knowledge of magic which the Franks are universally believed to possess.

Such childish ideas are no doubt due to the want of any education; but education does not always improve the Syrian, but rather renders him more insufferable, and in speaking of politics, or any other branch of ordinary conversation, the Syrian townsman exhibits, with ludicrous self-complacency, the meagre information which, in his eyes, is enough to fit him for delivering an authoritative opinion on the destinies of nations, or on deep scientific subjects.

This self-conceit is not less noticeable in religion; spiritual pride, and the conviction that they alone are fitted to understand the true faith, make the conversion of this nation to Christianity practically an impossibility, and incline them to accept without question the studious misrepresentations which are disseminated by their religious teachers.

Such conceit is also eminently characteristic of the Jews. Among the Rabbinical writers it reaches a pitch which is little short of insanity, and the lesson of humility taught in the parable of the Publican and the Pharisee might well be inculcated daily on Jew and Syrian alike.

Among minor traits, the want of appreciation of humour is the most remarkable, and it is no doubt connected with the above-mentioned self-conceit. The Eastern people are by nature grave and dignified, and they have but little sense of the ludicrous. Thus what is known amongst us as "chaff" is never heard in conversation among natives of Palestine, and their only attempts at witticisms are feeble puns. This again may be said to be a peculiarity of the Jews, puns being common in Hebrew writings.

In order to trace the origin of any people it is necessary, as Max Müller tells us, to know the language they speak, and to trace its history. The examination of the peasant language in Palestine is therefore of the highest interest.

The Syrians speak a dialect of Arabic, which ranks between the purer Egyptian and the very corrupt Mughrabee language, in the scale which has for a standard the Arabic of the Bedawîn of Arabia. The main characteristics of pronunciation are as follows :

The letter Jîm is pronounced like J in joy, not hard, like G, which is the Hebrew pronunciation of the letter still used in Egypt. The Dhal is confused in pronunciation with the Zain, with which it has a common origin in Hebrew. The Tha and the Sin are in the same way both pronounced like S, and both represent the Hebrew Sin. The Kaf is almost always pronounced Chaf; the Kof is sounded like hard G, or like Gof, as among the Bedawîn, and sometimes it is yet further changed into J or Jof, while among the people near Jerusalem, as well as in Damascus, it is hardly sounded at all, being represented by a catch in the breath, like the letter Hamzah. The Lam and Nun are confounded, and used for one another, especially at the end of words, where the L is almost always changed to N. Further peculiarities to be noted are, the addition of *sh* to negatives, as *ma fish* ("there is not,") for *ma fi*, the broad pronunciation of the vowels (the Wow being often sounded where it does not really exist), and the unnecessary use of diminutives or double diminutives. Lastly, the Alef is prefixed to words of which it forms no radical part, as in the cases Ajdûr for Jedûr, Abzîk for Bezîk, etc.

Now these peculiarities, in almost every case, serve to connect the peasant dialect with the old Aramaic, which Jerome tells us was the language of the natives of Palestine in the fourth century. The addition of unnecessary vowels is remarkable in Talmudic writings, and, as has been shown above, the Fellahîn, in their vulgar pronunciation, preserve the most archaic sound of certain letters which were (according to Gesenius and scholars of equal authority) originally indistinguishable from others, but which in the polite pronunciation of the townsmen have now quite distinct sounds. Thus, for instance, in the modern Idhen we should scarcely recognise the Hebrew Uzen, "an ear," but when this word is pronounced by a peasant in Palestine it resumes its old sound of Uzen.

Nor is it from pronunciation alone that we are able to judge of the character of the language; words in common use are equally instructive. Thus, for instance, almost all the words used in the Bible to express such natural features as rocks, torrents, pools, springs, etc., etc., are still in use in the peasant language quite unchanged, not only in connection with ancient sites, but in the common nomenclature of the country. A few words do, indeed, appear to have lost their original meaning, as in the cases of the Hebrew Tireh, " a fenced city;" Birch, " a fortress;" and Râmeh, " a hill," names still commonly applied to villages, but the meaning of which appears not to be understood by the peasantry; these cases seem, however, to be exceptions, which prove the rule that Aramaic, and even Hebrew words—not now used in the Arabic language—are of common occurrence among the peasantry, their original signification being still understood.

There are also words apparently peculiar to the peasant dialect, such as 'Arâk, for a " cavern " or " cliff," which is not found in any dictionary. Space will not allow of a further disquisition on this subject, but it might easily be shown how simple an explanation of local names is often afforded by translating them, when not otherwise intelligible, as though of Aramaic origin. On the whole, the language appears to bear so strong an affinity to that which we know to have been commonly spoken in the country as late as the fourth century, that the peasantry may, without exaggeration, be said to speak Aramaic rather than Arabic, or at least a dialect formed by the influence of the language of their Arab conquerors on the original Aramaic tongue.

One of the most valuable results of this inquiry is, that a philological reason is thus afforded for the general preservation of the names of ancient sites in Palestine, which has always been considered extraordinary, and perhaps doubtful. The language being unchanged, it is evidently natural that local names should be also unchanged, the original meaning being understood by the peasantry in most cases. Many instances of this might be brought forward, and the alteration which has occurred in the nomenclature of the country, as a whole, seems wonderfully small, almost every important site retaining its Biblical name. The investigation of the language appears to me to raise the study of identification from an empirical pursuit of fancied resemblances to the level of a science governed by recognised laws of change and modification, laws which must be observed strictly in all cases of really satisfactory identification.

If we may judge the origin of any people by language, then by their dialect, the descent of the Fellahîn, or "tillers," may be traced from older inhabitants of Palestine, and perhaps from the pre-Israelite population, which—despite the fierce onslaught of the first Jewish conquerors under Joshua—was, as we may gather from the Bible, never entirely outrooted, but remained in the land (in much the same position as that which the Saxons occupied under their Norman rulers) as a distinct people, though members of the same great family (the Semitic race), regarded as inferior to the Jewish dominant race, "hewers of wood," "drawers of water," "the beasts of the people." It was precisely to this class that the educated Jews of the second century of our era assigned the Aramaic language; the holy Hebrew of the Sacred Books being confined to the priests, to whom alone, after the return from the Captivity, that more ancient tongue appears to have been intelligible.

It is interesting to inquire whether foreign influence is traceable in the peasant language. Foreign words do indeed occur, such as "Burj" for a tower, or "burg," and El Minch for a harbour, which has already been explained to be a corruption of the Greek Limen; but these words, with many Crusading names of places which are attached to mediæval, or later sites, cannot properly be said to be commonly used in the language; in fact, it is extraordinary to note how very small the influence of foreign conquerors, Greek, Roman, or

Frank, seems to have been on the language. The pretentious titles, Eleutheropolis, Nicopolis, Scythopolis, etc., have quite disappeared, and the old native names of these cities, Beth Gubrin, Emmaus, Bethshean, etc., are those now known, with the important exception of Nâblus, the modern name for Neapolis, the ancient Shechem —a change which may perhaps be traced to Jewish hatred of the name of Shechem.

Their language, then, seems to show that the Fellahîn are a people well worthy of study, because apparently of a very ancient stock, which is still preserved comparatively pure; and we may therefore naturally expect their religion, habits, and customs to have an interesting bearing on the graphic accounts of peasant life which are found in the Bible.

By their religious peculiarities, still further light is thrown on the history of the modern Fellahîn.

The professed religion of the country is Islam, the simple creed of "one God, and one messenger of God;" yet you may live for months in the out-of-the-way parts of Palestine without seeing a mosque, or hearing the call of the Muedhen to prayer. Still the people are not without a religion which shapes every action of their daily life, a religion of most complex growth, requiring the utmost patience to enable us to trace it to its various original sources.

In almost every village in the country a small

building surmounted by a white-washed dome is observable, being the sacred chapel of the place; it is variously called Kubbeh, "dome;" Mazâr, "shrine;" or Mukâm, "station," the latter being a Hebrew word used in the Bible for the "places" of the Canaanites, which Israel was commanded to destroy " upon the high mountains, and upon the hills, and under every green tree" (Deut. xii. 2).

Just as in the time of Moses, so now, the position chosen for the Mukâm is generally conspicuous. On the top of a peak, or on the back of a ridge, the little white dome gleams brightly in the sun; under the boughs of the spreading oak or terebinth, beside the solitary palm, or among the aged lotus-trees at a spring, one lights constantly on the low building, standing isolated or surrounded by the shallow graves of a small cemetery. The trees beside the Mukâms are always considered sacred, and every bough which falls is treasured within the sacred building.

The Mukâms are of very various degrees of importance; sometimes, as at Neby Jibrin, there is only a plot of bare ground, with a few stones walling it in; or again, as at the Mosque of Abu Harireh, (a Companion of the Prophet), near Yebnah, the building has architectural pretensions, with inscriptions and ornamental stone-work. The typical Mukâm is, however, a little building of modern masonry, some ten feet square, with a round dome, carefully white-washed, and a Mihrab or prayer-niche on the south wall. The walls round the door, and the lintel-stone are generally adorned with daubs of orange-coloured henna, and a pitcher for water is placed beside the threshold to refresh the pilgrim. There is generally a small cenotaph within, directed with the head to the west, the body beneath being supposed to lie on its right side facing Mecca. A few old mats sometimes cover the floor, and a plough, or other object of value, is often found stored inside the Mukâm, where it is quite safe from the most daring thief, as none would venture to incur the displeasure of the saint in whose shrine the property has thus been deposited on trust.

This Mukâm represents the real religion of the peasant. It is sacred as the place where some saint is supposed once to have "stood" (the name signifying "standing-place"), or else it is consecrated by some other connection with his history. It is the central point from which the influence of the saint is supposed to radiate, extending in the case of a powerful Sheikh to a distance of perhaps twenty miles all round. If propitious, the Sheikh bestows good luck, health, and general blessings on his worshippers; if enraged, he will inflict palpable blows, distraction of mind, or even death. If a man seems at all queer in his manner, his fellow-villagers will say, "Oh, the Sheikh has struck him!" and it is said that a peasant will rather confess a murder, taking his chance of escape, than forswear himself on the shrine of a reputed Sheikh, with the certainty of being killed by spiritual agencies.

The *cultus* of the Mukâm is simple. There is always a guardian of the building; sometimes it is the civil Sheikh, or elder of the village, sometimes it is a Derwîsh, who lives near, but there is always some one to fill the water-pitcher, and to take care of the place. The greatest respect is shown to the chapel, where the invisible presence of the saint is supposed always to abide. The peasant removes his shoes before entering, and takes care not to tread on the threshold; he uses the formula, "Your leave, O blessed one," as he approaches, and he avoids any action which might give offence to the *numen* of the place.

When sickness prevails in a village, votive offerings are brought to the Mukâm, and I have often seen a little earthenware lamp brought down by some poor wife or mother, whose husband or child was sick.

A vow to the saint is paid by a sacrifice called Kôd, or "requital," a sheep being killed close to the Mukâm, and eaten at a feast in honour of the beneficent Sheikh.

At the festival of Bairam, processions are often made to these shrines; and at the more famous Mukâms—such as Neby Mûsa, near the Dead Sea, or Neby Rubîn, south of Jaffa—hundreds of pilgrims gather round the little building. In

1874 I saw one of these ceremonies at the village of Dhâheríyeh. The chief men of the place assembled in the morning, clad in their best dresses, with spotless turbans and new cloaks, each with his pipe (a luxury forbidden during Ramadân) in his mouth. They marched, chanting, through the village in a compact body, with the Sheikh in front, and they visited two little domed buildings in succession. They did not enter the chamber, though one man looked in through the window, but in conclusion, eight elders, closely packed in a circle, with their arms on one another's shoulders, swayed slowly backwards and forwards, in a weird and solemn dance resembling an incantation. It was thus, perhaps, that David danced before the ark.

The worship of local personal divinities by the peasantry reminds one strongly of the ancient *cultus* of the Canaanite tribes, which seems never to have been stamped out during the period recorded in the Bible; and the veneration of sacred trees and sacred hill-tops, which seems thus handed down, is also specially denounced in the Mishna. The Mukâm worship thus forms one more striking point of resemblance between the modern Fellahin and the original inhabitants of Palestine.

A very curious circumstance with regard to the Mukâms comes to light on careful examination. It is striking to find that the saint or prophet has often a name unmistakably Christian; Bulus

(Paul), Budrus (Peter), Metta (Matthew), are instances. In almost all the great Crusading towns El Khŭdr will be found to have a chapel, now venerated by the Moslems; and El Khŭdr is St. George, as can easily be shown, as, for example, at Darum, where he is also called by the latter name. The plain fact of the matter is, that the peasantry have adopted Christian sacred sites, and have received Christian saints into their Pantheon. This can be proved by innumerable instances, of which the following are among the most striking.

In 1631 A.D., a little chapel was erected by the monks near a cave at the foot of Carmel, and called by them "the School of the Prophets." In 1635 A.D., a Moslem Derwish took possession of the building, and the Mohammedans still hold it. This place is regarded as sacred by the Moslem peasantry, though the shrine is well known to be of Christian origin.

In 1187 A.D., a chapel of St. John stood near the caves of certain hermits, which were opposite Castel Pelegrino, now 'Athlit. A glance at the Survey shows caves still existing east of that fortress, and near them is a little Mukâm of the Prophet Ahia, which is the native name of John the Baptist. Here, then, the Moslems have again adopted a Christian shrine.

In 1432 A.D., Bertrandon de la Brocquière was shown a mountain between Gaza and Hebron, called the "Penance Mountain of St. John." A hill called "the place of separation of Ahia" is still shown by the peasantry in that direction.

Nor is it Christian tradition alone which is thus absorbed. Jacob Shelleby, the Samaritan, complained to me that the Moslems had robbed the Samaritans of the "Mosque of the Pillar," which the latter now believe to have been the scene of Joshua's "pillar by the oak," near Shechem, just as they robbed the Christians of the little chapel of the Hizn Y'akûb, also close to Nâblus.

It might, perhaps, be argued that the reason of this adoption of Christian sites by Moslems is to be sought in a common origin of Christian and native tradition, and that the adoption proves the sites to be authentic. It is easier to advance this theory than to disprove it; yet the tomb of Samuel is now fixed by a tradition, which was not generally accepted until after the twelfth century, and the venerated tomb of Moses, which is connected with the site of an old monastery, is now shown *west* of Jordan, in plain contradiction to Scripture. Surely these, at least, are not genuine sites; but above all, the tradition still preserved by the Bedawîn which connects the "high mountain" of Our Lord's Temptation with a hill 500 feet below the level of the Mediterranean (see Chap. I. vol. ii.) cannot be regarded as anything but a monkish legend.

Stories may be collected among the peasantry which are evidently garbled versions of Scriptural episodes. The actors are sometimes local worthies, such as Sheikh Samat, whose tomb seems to be the supposed sepulchre of Samson, which was shown by the Jews in the fourteenth century; in other cases they are the companions of the Prophet, and especially Imâm 'Aly, while the enemies of the Faithful are represented as Christians.

It has been thought by some that these tales are really ancient and of value; but I believe that a much more probable origin is to be found in the teachings of mediæval monks. In more than one case the sites connected with these stories were also recognised in the middle ages; as, for instance, the so-called tomb of Samson—not in Zoreah, but in Gaza—now called by the Moslems "Aly the Enslaved," and corresponding to the mediæval tomb of Samson also at one time shown in Gaza. The site of the Tomb of David in Jerusalem can also be traced to a Christian tradition of late date, and so with many others too numerous to mention; and there is, as far as I have been able to find, no proof that any of these garbled versions of Bible events are genuinely ancient or derived from native tradition. Even the legend of the Fenish, or Philistines, which seems to be the most probably genuine tradition yet collected, is of dubious origin, for the peasants say that the Fenish were Christians, and the sites connected with the name are invariably Crusading towns or fortresses.

The very general preservation of mediæval and

Byzantine sacred places among the peasantry is evidence of the great influence which the monks in the middle ages must have possessed. Jerome speaks of the "great number of the brethren" living in Palestine in his days, and the ruins found in every part of the country show that from the fifth to the thirteenth centuries it must have literally swarmed with monks and hermits. The peasantry seem to retain almost an affectionate memory of the convents; the titles "Monastery of Good Luck," "Charitable Convent," etc., show the appreciation in which these institutions were formerly held; and perhaps the sincere efforts of many good men to convert the heathen may still be traced in the blind veneration which is bestowed by Moslems, who "know not what they worship," on sanctuaries which were, as their modern names show, originally dedicated to the patron saints of the now despised and hated Christians, who once ruled the land.

The Mukâms may be divided into the following six groups. First, there are the places sacred to well-known Scriptural characters, the sites being generally derived from Jewish tradition, and apparently authentic—as, for instance, the tombs of Abraham, Isaac, Jacob, Joseph, Eleazar, and Phinehas. Noah also has many Mukâms in Palestine; and to one, at least, is attached a curious tradition of the Flood, which is supposed to have welled up from a spring near the sacred place. Seth, Shem and Ham have also Mukâms in Philistia, and the twelve patriarchs have places sacred to them, with the exception of Gad, Issachar, Asher, and Naphtali. The tomb of Joshua seems also to be preserved, as noticed in a former chapter.

The second class of Mukâms is that of sacred places derived from Christian tradition, which, as above shown, is a very large one.

The third includes many saints who cannot easily be identified, as the Prophets Kamil, 'Anîn, Baliân, and Nurân, with many others. In this class many *pairs* of saints may be included, as "the Sheikh of the Olive" and his mother; Sheikh Waheb ("the devoted") with his sister S'adeh, and many others, survivals perhaps of the old Phœnician duads and triads: to this class we may add a number of female saints who have descriptive names.

The fourth class consists of well-known historical characters now held in high veneration, including the various Companions of the Prophet, and many yet more modern personages, such as Sheikh Shibleh and Sheikh Abu Ghôsh, who were famous bandits in 1700 and 1813 respectively.

The fifth class of Sheikhs, consisting of those with descriptive titles, is, perhaps, in some respects the most important; for from these we learn most of the common ideas of the peasantry as to their saints. Thus we have among them Sheikhs called the Persian, the Median, the Æthiopian, the rain-giver, the healer, the inspired, the madman, the idiot, the protector, the just, the wise, the serpent-charmer, the pilgrim, and the champion, with a host of others, showing how varied are the supposed characters and powers of these invisible guardians.

The sixth class includes those Sheikhs with common names, such as Abraham, David, Joseph, Mohammed, etc., which as a rule, are of but little importance.

We have, then, in this great Pantheon of local deities, a jumble of traditions, Jewish, Christian and Moslem, showing the various influences which have successively acted on the peasantry. There are, indeed, indications of possibly ancient traditions, but the large majority at least of those current among the peasantry are probably traceable to monkish origin, and in many cases are evidently not older than the middle ages.

The stories usually related of the Sheikhs are neither interesting in themselves, nor do they apparently conceal any mythological meaning. One saint flew through the air after death in her coffin; a second prayed with his cloak spread on the sea; the bones of a third were collected by his dog, and carried to a mountain-top where they still lie buried; a fourth called the remains of his camel, which had been partly eaten by infidels from a dust-heap, the camel answering his appeal with an audible voice, and gathering its scattered limbs and bones to form a living beast again. In the main the stories are childish, and resemble those current among the Italian peasantry of the present day in connection with Christian saints.

These traditions are not easily collected, partly because of the distrust which the peasants show towards strangers, partly from their fear of the displeasure of the saint, partly because such stories are considered rather the women's business; in many cases the real history is, however, evidently forgotten, and the peasant answers that it is "from ancient times," and that he worships because his father and grandfather did so before him. Such forgetfulness or ignorance as to the origin of certain Mukâms is universal among the peasantry, and I have been assured by those best acquainted with the natives that it is genuine.

There is a difference in intelligence between inhabitants of different districts, and in different grades of peasant society, but even the least ignorant know scarcely anything, while the cowherds and goatherds are very little better than brute beasts. There was something almost pathetic in the childish confidence which the poor peasants seemed to repose in the wisdom and power of the English. Habib told one man that the English would some day take the country, and that then the poor would be made rich; and his listener actually believed that, because he was the poorest, he would be made king of the district. Another Fellah said he had heard that the French had bought the sea; a third thought that we were going to take away the ground in boxes.

Most of the peasantry believed we were seeking for hid treasure, which by incantation would be wafted to England; and some supposed that we were parcelling out the land, and erecting cairns on the high mountains where the chief men would build their houses. Sometimes they dug for gold under our cairns; often they pulled them down, and had in consequence to be imprisoned. A shepherd in Galilee saw us levelling, and had a vague idea we were making a railway. "Will you let the sea into Jordan?" he asked; "or will the steamships go on wheels?" Such are a few instances of common Fellah ideas. The peasantry could hardly believe that in England there were no Arabs living in tents, and no camels; and they supposed that though Christians might be more numerous there than among themselves, still the majority of the population in every European country must be Moslem.

Belief in the supernatural powers of certain persons of superior sanctity is not confined, among the peasantry, to the dead. Many living saints are also recognised in Palestine. Thus we heard of a man who fell into a well, and called on a famous living Wely or "favourite of God" at Jaffa; a hand, he said, pulled him out, and on going to the house of the Wely, the latter declared he had heard him some ten miles off, and had assisted him. The peasants are naturally prone to believe the marvellous, and such stories are devoutly credited.

The most peculiar class of men in the country is that of the Derwîshes, or sacred personages, who wander from village to village, performing tricks, living on alms, and enjoying certain social and domestic privileges, which very often lead to scandalous scenes. Some of these men are mad, some are fanatics, but the majority are, I imagine, rogues. They are reverenced not only by the peasantry, but also sometimes by the governing class. I have seen the Kady of Nazareth ostentatiously preparing food for a miserable and filthy beggar, who sat in the justice hall, and was consulted as if he had been inspired.

A Derwîsh of peculiar eminence is often dressed in good clothes, with a spotless turban, and is preceded by a banner-bearer, and followed by a band, with drum, cymbal, and tambourine. In one case at Kannir, the banner-bearer was a negro, who worked himself into a sort of fury, foamed at the mouth, and charged at us with the sharp spearhead of the flag. As a rule, however, the saint is half naked, and perhaps blind, and holds a tin pot or plate for alms. One of this class, a fine old mendicant from Mecca, with a shock head of uncut locks, came, spear in hand, to our Jeb'a camp and offered, for a fee, to "pray for the column (or cairn) in the day of our journeying." Another ran before us for a mile or more (as Elijah went before Ahab's chariot), shouting loudly as he ran.

It is natural to reflect whether the social position of the Prophets among the Jews may not have resembled that of the Derwishes. Revered by the people, but hated by the ruling class when their influence was directed against the king, or the court religion, the Prophets, though solitary, poor, and unaided, became powerful in times of religious revival, when they suddenly assumed the position of leaders, and became persons of political importance, just as a Derwish might do even now in times of fanatical excitement.

The Derwishes belong to regular tribes with recognised chiefs: thus there are the Raf'ai or "snake-charmers," who draw out serpents from their holes, and who are regularly initiated by their Sheikh, who is a disciple of the "Saint of God, Raf'ai," who came from Egypt. There are many others, including those who perform strange feats—eating scorpions, or sticking sharp swords into their cheeks or eyes. By Europeans in Palestine the Derwishes are generally regarded as impostors.

The peasantry have numerous superstitions: they believe in incantations, in charms, in divination by sand and other means, and in the evil eye, their children being purposely left dirty, or even besmirched, to avoid the consequences of an envious look. The belief in evil spirits is also general. These include, first the Jan, or powerful demon, good or bad, the latter kind having for bodies the tall smoke-pillars of the whirlwind, so commonly seen in summer; secondly, the 'Afrît, who is seemingly equivalent to a ghost; thirdly, the Ghoul, or Hag of the cemetery, which feeds on the dead : a place haunted by one of these demons is carefully avoided, or at least never approached without the most polite salutations, intended to appease the unseen spirit; fourthly, there are the Kerâd or "goblins," whose name is akin to the Arabic word for a monkey; lastly, there is the Shaitân or Satan, a name often applied to human beings of an evil disposition.

Among the peculiar religious institutions of the country are the sacred trees, which are generally oaks, or terebinths, with names taken from some Sheikh to whom they belong. They are covered all over with rags tied to the branches, which are considered acceptable offerings.

On most of the great roads piles of stones will be found, erected at some commanding point, and consisting of little columns a foot high, made up of perhaps a dozen pieces of rock one above another. They are called Meshâhed or "monuments," and they mark the spot whence some famous sanctuary is first seen by the pilgrim.

Last of all the Shûsheh should be mentioned,

the one long tuft of hair left at the back of the shaven head, by which the Moslems believe that the angel Gabriel will bear them to heaven. This fashion of wearing the hair is traced back to primitive times, and is thought to be connected with the worship of Thammuz.

The great fasts of the Moslem religion are most rigorously observed by the more pious among the peasantry. During the month of Ramadân many of them will travel or toil all day without drinking, eating, or smoking, and some even keep ten days more than the prescribed number, as a work of supererogation. Bairam, with its feast of flesh, which is perhaps the only meat tasted by the Fellah during the year, is but a slight recompense for this self-denial, which is yet more trying in a hot and wearisome climate.

Such are the blind and confused religious views of the so-called Moslem peasantry. It cannot but be evident to any observer who stays long in the country, that the fatalism of the creed has a most unhappy influence on the people. Christian villages thrive and grow, while the Moslem ones fall into decay; and this difference, though due perhaps in part to the foreign protection which the native Christians enjoy, is yet unmistakably connected with the listlessness of those who believe that no exertions of their own can make them richer or better, that an iron destiny decides all things, without reference to any personal quality higher than that of submission to fate, and that God will help those who have lost the will to help themselves.

The above notes are necessarily much condensed. But the general result seems to point to an almost unmixed Aramean stock as that from which the peasants of Palestine have most probably sprung. The native divisions of the population are curious and instructive, namely, the various Beni or "Sons" in different districts; thus, for instance, the greater part of Samaria is called " the country of the two tribes," alluding perhaps to Ephraim and Manasseh. The peasantry are very stationary, and the majority of the villagers have scarcely ever travelled more than ten miles away from home; yet migrations of the various Beni are traditionally said to have occurred in former times, and they would be perhaps worth tracing.

It appears in short that in the Fellahîn, as descendants of the old inhabitants of Palestine, we find a people whose habits and customs are well worthy of study, because we should naturally expect them to throw much light on the Bible narrative. These habits and customs will now be briefly described.

COSTUMES.

CHAPTER IX.

LIFE AND HABITS OF THE FELLAHÎN.

In the last chapter the Fellahîn have been considered in their religious aspect, and matters connected with the possible origin of their race have been discussed; but we have now to sketch their manners and customs.

The wonderful account given by Lane of the

life of townsmen in Egypt, would apply almost equally well to the middle classes in Damascus and Jerusalem; but the life and manners of the peasantry are far more valuable in illustration of the Bible narrative than are those of the townsmen; and for this reason the present sketch, however imperfect, will, I hope, prove of some value, by drawing attention to a people who have been as yet but little studied, and who are often confounded with the Bedawîn, or with the governing nation—the Turks—of whom, perhaps, scarcely a hundred are to be found in Palestine.

The notes which follow are necessarily slight, not for want of further material, but on account of space, and they are confined to the main points which seem most interesting. To draw comparison with Biblical incidents will be unnecessary, for the accounts will speak for themselves to all who are familiar with the sacred records.

A Fellah village consists of from twenty to a hundred cabins, huddled together, generally on rising ground and near water. In the hills the village is built principally of stone, the materials being collected from ancient ruins, and hardly ever, I believe, fresh quarried; in the south the roofs have stone domes, in the north they are of brushwood, supported on logs or beams as rafters, and covered with mud, which requires to be rolled every year. The interiors generally contain no furniture beyond bedding, mats, and cooking utensils; the house has no chimney, and the smoke of the wood fire goes out at the wooden door, or by the unglazed windows. Among the better class of the peasantry a few carpets will be found in use; and a raised diwân, as described in the account of our feast at Jeb'a, occupies part of the room. The village generally has one high house, of two storeys, in its middle, where the Sheikh or hereditary chief lives; booths are erected in summer on the roofs of the houses, where the inmates sleep at night; on the outskirts of the village are orchards of fig or pomegranate, with hedges of prickly pear, and perhaps fine olive-groves; close by is the Mukâm, with its white dome, and round it the shallow graves with rough headstones, between which the purple iris (or lily of Palestine) grows very commonly, while in the better built tombs a little hollow for rain water is scooped in the covering slab of stone, as an act of charity, towards thirsty birds.

In the plains the only difference in the villages is, that the cabins are built of sun-dried brick, and roofed with mud. The bricks are made in spring by bringing down water into ditches dug in the clay, where chopped straw is mixed in with the mud; thence the soft mixture is carried in bowls to a row of wooden moulds or frames, each about ten inches long by three inches across; these are laid out on flat ground and are squeezed full, the clay being then left to harden in the sun. The houses thus built require to be patched every year, and the old roofs are covered in spring with grass self-sown, which withers as soon as the sun becomes strong (Ps. cxxix. 6).

The population of a village averages about four hundred, ranging from thirty or forty, up to a thousand in the well-built Galilean towns. The men are employed in agriculture, the boys tend the flocks, the women cook and fetch water. The first scene on approaching a village is that at the well or spring, to which lithe damsels and portly matrons, scantily clad, bring down the great black or brown jars, returning rapidly with the load of water poised on a pad on the head. The screaming, scolding, and chatter of these crowds of women passes all description; if of one of them the traveller asks for the Sheikh, he still receives the old answer, "Behold, he is before you" (1 Sam. ix. 12).

On entering the village the Ghŭfr or "watchman" (2 Sam. xviii. 24) is next met, and the stranger is brought to the guest-house, where he is served with coffee, and entertained at the public expense, a small gratuity being given to the Ghŭfr on leaving. The visitor will be struck above all with the power exercised by the Sheikh, or by the elders, and with the respect for age, and for etiquette, leaving the impression of a patriarchal form of society, which really exists among the villagers.

The food of the peasants is almost entirely

vegetable, consisting of unleavened bread dipped in oil, of rice, olives, grape-treacle (Dibs), clarified butter (Semn), and eggs, besides gourds, melons, marrows, and cucumbers; in times of scarcity the Khobbeizeh, or mallow, cooked in sour milk or oil, forms an important element. Meat they hardly ever touch, save at the great feast, or at the Kod sacrifices; and their drinks consist simply of water and coffee, both of which they imbibe in enormous quantities. To this diet the beauty of their white teeth, the toughness of their constitutions, the rapidity with which their wounds heal are no doubt traceable, while the prominent stomachs of the children are due to drinking too much water. Coffee with lemon-juice is also commonly used as a remedy for dysentery.

The costume of the Fellahîn differs in various parts of Palestine, resembling that of the Egyptians in the south, and that of the Lebanon mountaineers in the north, while in Samaria it is more distinctive. The dress of Christians is also entirely different from that of the Moslems.

The typical male peasant dress in Palestine consists of five articles only. On the head is the turban, consisting of a woollen or silk shawl, wound round a red cap (Tarbûsh) with a blue tassel, inside which cap is a second, or perhaps two, felt caps (Libdeh), and within these again is a white cotton skull-cap stitched all over (Takîyeh). The colour of the turban shawl among the richer, or more pious, is white; a Sherif or descendant of the Prophet wears a green Mukleh, or large turban, and the Samaritan colour for the turban is crimson. In the south of Palestine the commonest kind is striped with yellow and chocolate. This respected head-dress, which is never willingly taken off in public, is drawn down behind the ears, thus causing them to grow out at right angles, or even to become doubled down.

The body is covered with a long shirt, which is made extremely full, with sleeves down to the knees; this dress is confined by a broad leather belt (Matt. iii. 4), to which a clasp-knife is often hung. The shirt reaches to the ankles, but during a journey the peasant girds up his loins (1 Kings xviii. 46), bringing the hem of the shirt between his legs up to his belt, and thus leaving the legs bare to the mid thigh. The sleeves are often used as receptacles for money, which is knotted up in a corner, while valuable papers are kept inside the Libdeh, and bread or other provisions are thrust between the shirt and the skin, above the belt. The sleeves are often tied together with a cord between the shoulders, leaving the arms bare. The shirt is open in front from the neck to the waist.

The fourth article is the 'Abba—a cloak coarsely woven of wool; those made of better materials are black, with coloured binding, and in summer a very light thin white cloak is used in riding; but the typical 'Abba is striped white and brown (or indigo) in broad vertical stripes; it is cut square, with holes for the arms, and is shaped to the neck behind, being a comfortable, but not an elegant, garment.

The feet are shod with leather shoes, which are generally red, with pointed toes, and a long pointed flap behind. Horsemen, however, wear the red boot to the knee, with a tassel in front.

The richer peasants wear, in addition to other garments, the Kumbâz, or cotton gown, striped in red and purple, or in yellow and white, with narrow vertical stripes; and they even have the Jubbeh, or short cloth jacket: both of these articles are worn by the townsmen.

The Kufeiyeh, or shawl head-dress of the Bedawîn, is worn by the boys and herdsmen in many parts. The shape of the turban also differs in various districts, being very high in the centre of the country, and large in the south. The shawl is sometimes twisted, sometimes laid in flat folds. The enormous turbans once worn are now scarcely seen, though a few old men among the peasant Sheikhs will put them on for great ceremonies.

The dress of the women is, as might be expected, far more varied. In Philistia it resembles that of Egypt—a full blue robe, sweeping the ground, a black head-shawl, and a face-veil hanging from the eyes to the waist, supported by a wooden or metal cylinder, which acts as a clasp, fixing the face-veil to the head-veil. These face-veils are ornamented with a fringe of silver or gold coins. In Gaza and Ashdod the women wear a sort of visor, covering the nose, mouth, and chin, and made of white stuff, ornamented with gold coins.

In the Jerusalem and Hebron hills the dress is less complicated, and strikes one as probably unchanged since the earliest times, for it could not well be simpler. The blue shirt is not quite so full as that of the men, but it is rather longer, and the sleeves are pointed. No face-veil is worn, but a heavy white head-veil comes down to the waist, and the requirements of modesty are supposed to be fully met by drawing this over the mouth, or, if the woman's hands are engaged, by holding the corner in the teeth.

As the traveller advances northwards, through Samaria and Lower Galilee, he meets with another distinct costume: a dress with tight sleeves and fitting the figure, descends half way below the knees; a chemise is worn under it, having sleeves full at the wrist, and a pair of blue cotton drawers or trousers—peg-topped in shape, tight at the ankle, and fuller above—appear under the dress, which is generally of striped stuff, purple (or pink) and white. A heavy sash is wound round the waist, and a coif or kerchief is tied over the head, while the hair is cut in a thick fringe above the eyebrows. This is the dress of the girls, and that of the matrons sometimes differs only in the headgear, though many of them wear the full white shirt, as in the south, with a black cloak drawn over the head.

The women's head-dress in Samaria has never, apparently, been very accurately described, but it is of peculiar interest. It is a sort of bonnet, with a horse-shoe shape in front, and on the front are sewn silver coins, lapping over one another, and making a crescent-shaped tire round the forehead and down to the ears. This tire is bound by a handkerchief round the head. It is apparently heavy, and a woman will carry her dowry of perhaps £5 round her face. Seen in profile, it makes the forehead appear high and the back of the head depressed. A crimson face-veil is attached to it, covering the mouth, chin, and breast. There can be little doubt that in these head-dresses we find still in use the "round tires like the moon," against which the prophet inveighs (Isaiah iii. 18). This costume is the one shown in the illustration.

The women have fine eyes, and the use of *kohel* —a mixture of soot and other substances—skilfully applied to the lashes has certainly a good effect; but the little daubs of indigo or soot, rubbed into punctures which are made by a bunch of needles, forming regularly tattooed patterns on the face, breast, feet, and hands, have anything but a pleasing appearance. A single mark between the eyes is usual, and looks not unlike a patch (Lev. xix. 28).

The use of henna is common to men and women alike. Henna is a sign of rejoicing, and is not worn in mourning. At a marriage, the tails of the horses and the doors of the house are coloured with it, as well as the faces and hands of the guests. Women colour the nails, the finger-joints, and the palms of the hands. A little henna has rather a pretty effect, being a sort of orange-red in colour.

Bracelets and anklets are worn, the commonest being of coloured glass such as is manufactured at Hebron, or of bad silver; various charms and amulets for protection against the evil eye are also carried.

The dress of the Christians in Palestine differs from that of the Moslems. The former wear a shirt with tight sleeves, a waistcoat of a flowered or embroidered pattern, a shawl neatly wound round the waist, trousers, of blue cotton or of cloth, reaching to the ankles, and of the baggy description commonly shown in sketches; and lastly, they wear a short cloth jacket with tight sleeves, open in front, called Jubbeh, which, as above noticed, is sometimes worn by the richer Moslem Sheikhs, and by the townsmen. The Christians wear the Kufeiyeh in travelling, or the Tarbûsh, with the inner caps, but without the roll of silk or stuff which forms the turban.

The ordinary dress of Christian women is very picturesque; their dark curly hair is confined by a little kerchief folded diagonally with the peak behind. Their jackets of striped or flowered stuff fit tightly to the figure, and show the shirt in front; and they wear the Shintiyàn, or trousers, made as full as a petticoat, tied below the knee, and falling in plaits round the ankle—an extremely graceful and pleasing dress.

The above description of Christian costume applies chiefly to the Galilean district, for the Christians are most numerous in Upper Galilee. In Nazareth, where the peasantry are rich, the white Izâr, or enveloping mantle of linen, coming over the head and swelling out like a balloon round the figure, is worn by the women; but this is, properly speaking, the dress of townsfolk, not of the agricultural classes.

The Bethlehem costume is unique. The men, though Christian, appear to wear the turban, and also the Kumbâz, or striped dressing-gown of cotton, which is generally adopted by the upper classes. The dress of the women consists of the full shirt with pointed sleeves, but it is made, like Joseph's coat, of many colours, and has broad squares of yellow or red let in to the breast or sleeves, giving a most striking brilliancy of colour. The girls wear a white veil, the matrons an extraordinary cylinder of felt, not unlike a Greek priest's cap, generally sewn over with coins, and partly covered by the white veil. This dress is figured in many works (as in the illustrated edition of

Farrar's "Life of Christ"), and needs no further description. A string of coins often hangs from the bonnet under the chin, and more than one poor woman has been murdered for the sake of her head-dress.

There is a class of the peasantry of whom a few words must now be said, namely, the lepers. The common diseases of the country are ophthalmia, dysentery, and fever, with liver complaints; but on the whole the peasantry are healthy, strongly-built, and of great strength and endurance. They drive the lepers from their villages, and oblige them to resort to the miserable communities which live, supported by charity, on the outskirts of great towns. Loathed and neglected, they drag on a miserable existence, and propagate a diseased race—a reproach to the Government, which does nothing to assist or control them.

The following notes are obtained from the best possible authority—namely, from Dr. Chaplin, at Jerusalem:

Leprosy appears to be a mysterious disease, the cause of which doctors do not know. It is not peculiar to one nation—Norwegians, Italians, Spaniards, Hindoos, suffer from it, as well as Syrians. It is not caused by food, not seemingly due to climate, and temperature has no connection with it. It is doubtful whether it is contagious or hereditary. One curious fact is that townsmen do not suffer from it, though the lepers live close to the towns. From almost every village a few lepers come to the towns, and notably from the Christian village of Râm-Allah.

The ordinary tubercular leprosy is due to the presence of *bacteria* in the tubercles, and the disease works out from within, not inwards from without. It appears not to be the same disease described in Leviticus, though the white leprosy—a spot deeper than the skin, with white hairs (Levit. xiii. 3)—is still found in Palestine. The name leprosy is derived from El Burs, a shortened form of the Hebrew term used for the disease.

No cure is as yet known for tubercular leprosy, for the reason of the presence of the microscopic parasites is not yet discovered. The prevention of this plague, which is now rather on the increase in Palestine, seems to be possible, if habits of greater cleanliness and morality, with more comfort and better food, could be introduced among the peasantry, and if at the same time strict laws were enforced for secluding the lepers in asylums.

This dreadful plague does not become manifest before the age of twelve, nor later than forty-five. The patients suffer pain at first, and, in later stages, much distress; their physical strength and animal life dies out, and they are, in their own words, "like oxen," without feeling or intellectual power, scarcely conscious of the outer world; their voices become changed to a feeble whine, husky and querulous; their joints and features waste away, and swelling and black discolouration ensue. The flesh decays, until the appearance of an advanced case is ghastly in the extreme; and a raw wound may be burnt with an iron in their bodies, producing only a slightly pleasing sensation. They die finally of leprosy.

The lepers at Jerusalem live in huts near the south-west corner of the town, inside the wall, and marry lepers, and the disease which reappears in their children thus becomes hereditary.

Turning from this repulsive subject to that of the daily life of the peasantry, we may next notice their marriages, funerals and amusements.

The distinctive physiognomy of each village is extremely striking. In one the people will be good-looking, in another ugly; in each case there is a strong family likeness between the various inhabitants of any one place, which is apparently due to constant intermarriage between the peasants of the same village.

The principal ceremonies connected with weddings are the processions of the bride and bridegroom through the street, accompanied by their friends. The procession of the dower is also accompanied by a band of women, singing, clapping the hands, and uttering shrill cries; but the bride's fortune among the peasantry is necessarily small, and, as in Italy, a single chest on a mule conveys the whole trousseau.

At Nazareth, in 1872, we witnessed two of these wedding processions, or Zeffehs—one Moslem, one Christian.

First came a group of women clapping their hands in time, and uttering the Zaghârit, or shrill ululations, commonly used as a mark either of joy or of sorrow. Most of them wore over their heads the black cloak with an embroidered border; their palms were dyed with henna, and they had the moon-shaped tire as above described, and tight-fitting bodices of silk, gleaming with red, green, yellow, blue, and purple, in stripes and patches. One woman carried a basket of flowers on her head, with a bottle of wine and a cake. The bride followed, closely veiled, dressed in glorious array, mounted on a horse, and supported by three of her female relatives, while two other women held the bridle.

Presently the Zeffeh of the bridegroom passed in turn, consisting of some two hundred of his friends. They were in white, with 'Abbas and with silk Kufeiyehs, or turbans. Many were armed with old brass-bound guns, which they let off at intervals. The shouting crowd went before the bridegroom to the market-place, and there a ring of some hundred and fifty men was formed; they were jammed close together, shoulder to shoulder, clapping their hands and shouting "Alla-lá!" at the top of their voices, their bodies swaying in time, while the best-man, in a green dress, hopped round on one leg, and another man, in a black and purple head-dress, which was tied beneath the chin, his cheeks being reddened with henna, and the sleeves of his shirt rolled up, sprinkled rose-water over the whole circle. A gun was let off, and a sort of proclamation was made, after which the clapping was resumed at a furious pace, the best-man becoming almost frantic.

The procession moved on, and the bridegroom appeared on a horse, with a red saddle and a pad behind; in his hand was a nosegay, and over his head an umbrella. He smoked a cigarette, and a small boy in green was mounted behind him. The women of his family followed, and pairs of guests danced a sort of Mazurka step beside him. But amid all this ceremonial rejoicing there was no real gaiety, no one had a smile on his face, but all was conducted with oppressive decorum.

On the second occasion—that of the Moslem Zeffeh—the women were preceded by a band of tambourines and kettle-drums, the latter fastened on a boy's back, and beaten by a man who occasionally hit the drum-bearer instead of the drum. The bride wore a pink veil above the Izâr, and a black face-veil, and she was supported by two women, also veiled. The bridegroom was followed by a man carrying a rush-bottomed chair, on which he sat during the dancing. There were two sword-dancers on this occasion, who went through the usual tame performance, which is more effectively executed by the Bedawin, as will be seen in the next chapter. I was told that the words of the chorus were "Ya 'Aini! Ya 'Aini!"—" O my eye!"—a term of endearment.

The ordinary village Zeffeh resembles those above described, but the dresses are not often so gay as those at Nazareth.

Of the native children there is little to be said; they receive, as a rule, no education, and are neither disciplined nor cared for, the affection of the parents being apparently in most cases small. They learn to curse almost as soon as to speak; and I have seen a boy of six or seven throwing stones at his father with the most vile language. They have none of the gaiety of children; but are as solemn as their elders. To animals they are cruel, and to one another mischievous and tyrannical. As the boys grow older, they are sent out to keep sheep, goats, or cows, and they acquire a wonderfully accurate knowledge of the country round the villages; thus the goat-herds are the great authorities as to the names of ruins or springs.

I have only once seen children in Palestine playing at any game; this was near Samaria, and the sport appeared to be a sort of hockey; but as a rule they seem to do nothing but mischief.

The shepherd-boys, however, have a kind of game called Mankalah, which Lane has already described as played in Egypt, and the holes which they make in the rocks for this purpose are often found on the hillsides, and might considerably puzzle archæologists.

The adults appear to have no amusements; they say themselves, with terrible truth, that they have "no leisure in their hearts for mirth," being hopeless and spiritless under their hard bondage of oppression, usury, and violence.

The ordinary amusements of the townsmen are

MALE DANCERS.

the public readings of romances, the dances of the Egyptian 'Almehs, and games of chess and draughts. Gambling, though considered disgraceful, still is common in towns where low cafés and restaurants exist, but none of these amusements are known in the villages. Once in the Jordan

Valley we came across a party of Egyptian dancing girls, journeying from Damascus to their native land, and once in the Lebanon we witnessed the weird performance of some male dancers in female dress, castanets on their fingers, and skirts round their waists, as shown in the illustration from a sketch made on the spot; but these performances are very rare, and confined to the wealthier towns, as are also the tricks of conjurers and clowns.

The only sport which may be witnessed among the peasants is the mock tournament of the Jerid, a combat between two bodies of horsemen, who throw darts or sticks at one another. But the riding is, as a rule, so bad that it has but little interest to an Englishman, accustomed to see better horsemanship. There are often men who ride in front of these cavalcades as clowns; they are called Sutàr, and are dressed in caps to which fox-tails are suspended; the clown, indeed, seems to be the only ideal of comedy which Syrian minds can conceive, their general views of festivity being rather inclined to pomp than to real gaiety.

The last ceremonials to be noticed are those connected with death. Among the Fellahin they are very simple. The body is buried almost as soon as the breath has left it. Thus, I have seen a boy killed by falling from an olive, and buried within a quarter of an hour. The graves are so shallow that the hyænas often dig up the corpses, and they are only marked by a few stones. The bier, covered with a green cloth, and with the turban placed on it, is followed by the women with shrill shrieks (Zaghârit), and in one instance, near Ascalon, each woman held a handkerchief in her hand, and waved it at the bier as she followed.

Turning next to the ordinary occupations of the Fellahîn, we find them to be an agricultural and pastoral people.

The land tenure in Palestine is of three kinds: crown-land; Wakûf, or glebe-land, belonging to mosques and other institutions of a religious character; and lastly, Mulk, or freehold. The first two kinds are farmed to the highest bidder, and the rental obtained is called Miri. The Mulk-land is of four kinds: first, land inherited since the time of the Moslem conquest; secondly, land legally bestowed from the crown-lands; thirdly, land so bestowed in return for tribute; lastly, tithed lands of which not more than half the produce is due to Government. The Mulk-land is held by private individuals.

The lands belong to the villages which they surround, and are reckoned by the Feddân, a very indefinite measure, being the amount which a yoke of oxen can plough. In the hills it ranges from thirty-six to forty acres, and in the plains from twenty-eight to thirty-six, the soil being richer and heavier. The corn-seed per Feddân is from twenty-five to sixty kilos (Constantinople measure), and the yield per Feddân is about two hundred bushels of wheat, or fifty of barley.

The limits of the lands are marked by valleys, by ridges, and by large stones, by which also the sub-divisions of the land among the villagers are shown. It is most interesting to note that the word Tahum, used in Hebrew to signify the "limits" of the Levitical cities (Numb. xxxv.), is still employed in the same sense by the peasantry, and in one case a great stone, marking the present boundary of the lands of Es Semû'a (Eshtemoa), which was a Levitical city, is just about the proper distance of 3000 cubits from the village, and is called Hajr et Takhâin, also probably a corruption of Tahum.

There is a custom regarding the land which seems of antiquity—namely, the Shkârah, or land which is cultivated by the villagers for any one of their number who is unable to till it himself; thus there is the Shkâret el Imâm, or "glebe of the religious minister," and Shkâret en Nejjâr, or "carpenter's portion," which is cultivated for the village carpenter in return for his services.

The possessions of a village vary from ten to a hundred Feddâns; thus at Abu Shûsheh, for instance, 5000 acres of arable land are held by a place containing some 400 inhabitants.

The ordinary crops are barley and wheat, and in addition to these, millet, sesame, Indian corn, melons, tobacco and cotton, are the summer crops;

while lentils, beans, and chick-peas, with other vegetables, are grown in winter. Indigo grows wild, and is occasionally cultivated in the Jordan Valley. The land is never allowed to lie fallow, unless through want of labour to cultivate. A rotation of crops is observed, but manure is rarely used. To the list of productions must be added the beautiful and extensive groves of olives, especially noticeable in the low hills, with the vineyards, on the high ridges as at Hebron, where the grape is swelled by the autumn mists, and the fig-gardens, which flourish especially in the Christian district of Jufna and Bir er Zeit. Pomegranates, apricots, walnuts, plums, apples, mulberries, pears, quinces, oranges, lemons, and bananas, may be noticed among the fruit-trees which are found in the gardens near springs. The irrigation of the vegetable gardens by means of small ditches trodden by the foot, is another instance of the survival of a Jewish method of cultivation (Deut. xi. 10).

The first agricultural operation is that of ploughing, which is commenced in autumn at the time of the first rains, and again continued in spring for the later crops. The first period is about the end of November, the second in March and April.

The plough is of the most primitive kind, very small, with a coulter like an arrow-head, and a single handle like that of a spade, with a cross piece, which is held by one hand, while in the other the ploughman has a stick with a nail at the end, used as a goad. To this pointed spade (as the plough may be called) is attached a long pole, which connects it with the heavy yoke of the cattle. The furrow is extremely shallow, and the instrument, indeed, only scratches the upper soil, leaving virgin earth untouched below. There are generally two ploughs which follow one another, the first perhaps harnessed to a single camel, the second to two small oxen, or to an ox with an ass (Deut. xxii. 10).

The sower follows the plough, and scatters his seed, not only into the good soil of the furrows, but partly among the thistles and artichokes which grow rank in the unturned soil, partly on the beaten path beside the field, partly among the rocks and stones which crop up in patches amid the arable ground (Matt. xiii. 3—8).

The barley harvest begins in the plains in April, and continues in the hills as late as June. The stalk of the corn is very short, and the stubble is left comparatively very long. The men sit on their haunches to reap, the sickle (Seif) being not unlike our own. The handfuls thus cut are tied round with a stalk, forming little shocks, and these are stacked in bundles, and then loaded in nets on camels, and carried to the threshing-floors (Beiyâdir or Jurûn) at the villages. An ancient custom—to which the peasantry can assign no origin—is observed in reaping; the corner of the field is left unreaped, and this is given to the "widows and the fatherless;" this corner is called Jerû'ah, and in the same way a bunch of wheat is left on the ground to be gleaned by the poor and helpless (Lev. xix. 9, 10). These gleanings are threshed by the women separately (Ruth ii. 15—17).

The threshing-floor is a broad flat space, on open ground, generally high; sometimes the floor is on a flat rocky hill-top, and occasionally it is in an open valley, down which there is a current of air; but it is always situated where most wind can be found, because at the threshing season high winds never occur, and the grain is safely stored before the autumn storms commence. The size of the floor varies, from a few yards to an area of perhaps fifty yards square, and rich villages have sometimes two such floors. The grain is thrown down and trampled by cattle, or by horses, attached to a heavy wooden sledge made of two boards and curved up in front. A boy stands or sits on this, and drives the horse. A number of recesses are sunk in the under side of the sledge, and into these small rough pieces of hard basalt (Hajr es Sôda) are let, which, acting like teeth, tear the corn. This instrument is called Môrej, and is supposed to be that mentioned by Isaiah (xli. 15) as "having teeth." The name is the same as the Hebrew Moreg, and the name Jurn, applied commonly to the threshing-floor, is the Hebrew Goran.

In other cases two or four oxen are yoked together and driven round the threshing-floor. I have seen them muzzled, though this is rare (Deut. xxv. 4).

The threshed grain is collected on the floor in a conical heap (Sóbeh), and is winnowed by tossing it with a wooden shovel, or with a three-pronged wooden fork. The wind scatters the chaff, and the grain falls round the heap, and it is afterwards sifted.

The corn is stored in underground granaries, which are carefully concealed, and form traps for the unwary horseman. These granaries (Metâmir) are often under the protection of the Mukâm, and are therefore excavated near that building. They are circular wells, some four or five feet deep, and the mouths are closed with clay like that used for the house-roofs.

The olive crop seems to require but little attention from the peasants; the land is ploughed twice or thrice each year, but the trees are neither manured nor pruned, and hence they only bear the full crop every other year. In October the fruit is ripe, and the trees are beaten with long poles, or shaken—much to their injury, and the fallen fruit is gleaned. It is said that the plague of locusts has more than once proved a subsequent blessing, because the olive-trees were eaten down and thus pruned, and yielded a plentiful harvest in the following year. The oil is pressed in two kinds of mills; one called M'aserah, from its "squeezing;" the other Matrûf, with a cylinder of stone placed vertically in a cylindrical stone case, and revolving in it, iron bars being fitted like spokes into the cylinder.

The olive grows slowly, and there is no doubt that many of the trees round Shechem and Gaza are of great age. At Gaza the natives say that not a single olive-tree has been planted since the Moslem conquest of the land; and indeed, traditionally, they refer the oldest of the trees in the great avenue to the time of Alexander the Great. The name Rûmi, or "Greek," sometimes applied to the olives, appears to be connected with this tradition. It seems possible that the first statement, that olives have not been planted at Gaza since the Moslem conquest, may be true, for the tree rarely dies, but when the trunk decays, fresh stems spring from the roots, and a group of olives takes the place of a single tree. The old olives are surrounded by an army of suckers (the "olive branches" of Scripture—Ps. cxxviii. 3), and these, as the parent stem decays, grow strong and tall in its room, so that the grove perpetuates itself without any trouble on the part of the owners.

The olive-tree is the glory of Palestine, and one of the chief sources of wealth to the peasantry; the cool and grateful shade endears it to the traveller, and many a time have our tents been protected in stormy weather by the broad boles. The shade of the fig-tree is considered unhealthy by the Syrians, as producing ophthalmia, but that of the olive is a favourite shelter.

The pastoral employments of the Fellahîn occupy a good part of their attention; the young men, as in Jacob's time, are the shepherds and cowherds, and are often found far from home. In spring the rich pastures of the plains, and of the Jordan Valley attract the flocks, which are driven down to temporary settlements known as 'Azbât. An arrangement is sometimes made with a Bedawin tribe to protect the flocks, and in other parts there are lands in the desert recognised as belonging to the villagers. The sheepcotes are generally caves (1 Sam. xxiv. 3) along the edge of the Judean desert, and in these the boys sleep with their charges at night, especially during the lambing season, which occurs early in spring.

The diminutive size of the oxen is striking, and the dry climate seems to dwarf most of the domestic animals, sheep, goats, and horses being all small. There are two breeds of goats; the one, long-haired and white, with enormous horns, is seen rarely; the other is the ordinary black or piebald breed, with shorter hair. The sheep are less numerous, and are generally driven with the goats. In the plains, however, they are better able to find food; and in Philistia especially, the fat-tailed Syrian breed affords excellent mutton. The way of fattening sheep for a feast is curious. A child will sit with its arm round the animal's neck and feed it with mulberry leaves from a bag, almost pushing them down its throat. The name given to the fatted sheep is Kharûf.

Scarcely less important to the villagers than the flocks are the camels, which supply the place of carts and wagons. These animals give but little trouble, as they pick up any thorny shrub for food. In spring they are clipped, and covered with tar and oil, as a protection against insects. Their black appearance, after the tarring, is ludicrous, and their odour is then even more offensive than usual.

Such, slightly sketched, are the occupations and daily pursuits of the Fellahîn. It is almost unnecessary to point out how every act of their lives, not less than every word of their mouths, contains some echo of the old Bible times. Their peculiar habits are handed down from so remote a period that they themselves—being accustomed, with the ordinary conservatism of Orientals, to tread, without a thought of change, in their fathers' steps, have forgotten the origin of many of their customs. They can only say: "It is from ancient times;" "It always was done so;" "Our fathers did thus." And as in their worship so in everything else, they repeat mechanically the actions of their predecessors.

Their ordinary expressions are so like those used in the Bible, that one seems to step back out of the present century to the days of Abraham, when one lives in the more remote villages, far away from hotels and dragomans. "As the Lord liveth" is still a common oath, and the villagers address the stranger as "my father," or "my brother," and salute him with the words, "Peace be unto thee."

It is easy to look alone on either the dark or the bright side of the peasant character; the lights and shades are strongly marked, and a partial experience would probably lead to a one-sided estimate, according to the temperament of the observer; but the truth seems to be, that a people with naturally fine qualities have been degraded, and entirely ruined, by an unjust and incapable government.

The whole of Syria is under the Wâly of Damascus, and Palestine is under the Mutaserifs of Acre and Jerusalem, who are appointed by that Wâly. These provinces are again subdivided, and Kaimakâms or lieutenant-governors, are placed in such towns as Jaffa, Ramleh, Jenin, etc. The change of the Wâly generally results in the entire change of all these various authorities, and the Wâly is replaced perhaps once in six months, perhaps oftener. Thus even if a capable and just man be appointed, he has no time to carry out any plans he may form, and his successor probably reverses everything that he has done. The stipends paid are also so inadequate, that it is impossible for any of the governors, or sub-governors, to live on them alone. The consequence almost invariably is that the governor " eats," as the peasantry call it; sometimes he eats little, sometimes much; but there is only one man—Midhat Pacha—against whom one never heard this accusation made. The rulers have no interest in the prosperity of the country, or in improving the condition of those they rule; their only idea is to enrich themselves, and to lay up for that rainy day which must come when the Wâly is changed, unless they can induce his successor to keep them in their posts.

Not the least corrupt of these dignitaries is the Kâdy, but with this difference—the Pacha or Kaimakâm is often a soldier, and affects no special piety or principle, regarding the state of affairs with jovial cynicism; but the Kâdy is a religious character, a judge whose statute-book is the Koran, who has been a Sokhtah (or, as we say, Softa), an "inquirer," taught in the school of the 'Ulema at Constantinople. He wears a white turban, and says his prayers regularly; he has paid a high price for his appointment, and expects some return for his capital. Thus the land is cursed not only with tyrannous governors, but with corrupt and unjust judges.

The system of government is simple. The only duties are to collect the taxes, and to put down riots, which constantly occur. The crown-lands are farmed to the highest bidder, who, I believe, occasionally under-farms the taxes. Soldiers are sent to collect the money, and the crop is assessed before reaping. This is one of the most crying evils in the land. In order to save the over-ripe grain, the peasant is often obliged to give away half of it, as a bribe to those whose duty it is to assess the tax, and who deliberately delay so doing until the last moment.

The tax on the Mulk-lands has been definitely fixed, without regard to the difference of the harvests in good and bad years; this again is a crying evil, and leads to the ruin of many a village. At Kurâwa, in 1873, the people told me, with tears in their eyes, that the olive crop had been so poor that the value was not as much as the amount of the tax about to be collected.

The taxes are brought into the towns by the Bashi-Bazouks; sometimes the Kaimakâm will himself make a tour to collect them, and he, with all his followers, is received as an honoured guest, and fed and housed at the village expense. The soldiers also live at free quarters, and exact money under a variety of pretexts from the luckless villagers, who have no man to speak for them.

There is a third evil, almost as fatal to the prosperity of the land—the conscription, which often carries off the flower of the bread-winning population. The number taken from a village varies, and as a punishment, the whole male population is sometimes marched off in irons to the headquarters. Few of the poor fellows, who are thus torn away from the weeping women, ever see again the dark olives and the shining dome of their own hamlet, or come back to plough their yellow fields, and tend the red oxen or the black goats in their far-off native land. Hurried away to Europe, or to Armenia, they lead a miserable life, receiving but little pay, and bullied by ignorant officers. There is no sadder sight than that of the recruits leaving a village in Palestine.

Under such a government it can scarcely be a matter of surprise that the Fellahin are lazy, thriftless, and sullen. They have no inducement to industry, and, indeed, as one of the better class said to me, " What is the use of my trying to get money, when the soldiers and the Kaimakâm would eat it all." There is only one way of becoming rich in this unhappy land, namely by extortion. If in the time of Christ the country suffered as much as it does now, from unjust judges and tyrannical rulers, what wonder that to be rich was thought synonymous with being wicked, or that it should be Lazarus only who was considered fit for Abraham's bosom?

The improvidence of the Fellahin is very great, and is due principally to a feeling of uncertainty as to their immediate future. Living is cheap enough, and I have heard of a family of five who spent only twenty-five pounds in a year. But the peasantry are eaten up by usury; their very clothes are bought with money borrowed at forty or fifty per cent.; and a company which would lend money at twenty per cent. would be a boon to the villagers, if it could induce the government to assist it in collecting the interest.

The self-government of the peasants is a reproof to their foreign rulers. Naturally a docile people, they obey their Sheikhs and elders implicitly, and have notions of equity, as well as of charity and mutual helpfulness among neighbours. Their moral code is theoretically strict, especially as regards the women. In the bottom of a valley west of Beit 'Atâb, is a curious cavern with a stalagmitic gallery round it, which is called Mughâret Umm et Tûeimîn—"cavern of the two side galleries." At the end of it is a great well-shaft in the rock, some sixty feet deep. It is said that a woman pronounced guilty by the elders is brought to the cave and cast down this horrible well. A similar cave exists in the Anti-Libanus, and a similar use is there made of it. In spite of this, the stories told by lepers and others make it clear that the Fellahin are as immoral as they well can be.

The above sketch is intended rather to draw attention to a people well worthy of study than to form an exhaustive account of their manners and customs. In language, in dress, in religion, and in customs, they represent in the nineteenth century a living picture of that peasantry amongst whom Christ went about doing good; and, indeed, the resemblance is equally striking when they are compared with the earlier inhabitants of the land, from the days of Samuel downwards; and the parallel is so remarkable that it seems justifiable to dub the Fellahin by the simple title of "modern Canaanites."

A BEDAWI WOMAN.

CHAPTER X.

THE BEDAWÎN.

THE last two chapters have been devoted to the settled population of the villages in Palestine, the antiquity of the race being evidenced by the language and customs. The peasantry must not be confounded with the Bedawin or nomadic tribes, living in the uncultivated districts; for the two nations are quite separate branches of the Semitic people, and they themselves acknowledge the distinction. The Bedawi speaks with the greatest contempt of the Fellâh, and rarely, if ever, do intermarriages occur, as both sides would consider themselves degraded by the alliance. The Fellahîn call the nomadic people Arabs, and the nomads call themselves Bedawîn, both names being derived from their place of abode—the wild lands of the broad southern and eastern plateaux.

The narrow peninsula of cultivated hills, in which the settled population lives, is surrounded by the broad sea of desert, over which the Arab delights to roam. Thus from the great Moab plateau and from the mountains of Gilead, from the southern Desert of the Wanderings, and from the western plain of Sharon, the wave of nomadic life is constantly lapping against the mountains of the Fellahîn. This wave has its ebb and flow, which even in the last five years has been very marked. In time of peace the Government is strong, and the Arabs are driven back to the deserts; but in time of war the outlying encampments of the great eastern and southern tribes, encroach upon the village lands, and the armed horsemen extort blackmail from the border towns and hamlets. On the whole, however, the settled people seem to be gaining ground, and especially in Lower Galilee; in the Sharon Plain the Bedawîn are mere shadows of their forefathers, only a few miserable tents of degraded Arabs, whom the peasants call "cousins of the gipsies," being left to represent the once powerful tribes which, under Akil Agha, were the terror of Palestine. These small encampments, surrounded as they are in Philistia by the arable land, resemble the pools left by the retreating tide on the shore of the sea, which, unless the wave return, must gradually disappear.

The time-honoured conflict between two races is noticed, as it is almost unnecessary to observe, in the Bible records. The Arabs are mentioned in the Old Testament (Neh. iv. 7), and the hosts of Midian, with their countless camels, were no doubt the ancestors of the modern Bedawin. The nomadic people are most interesting to the student of the earlier Jewish history, before the consolidation of the nation in Samuel's time; for if among the peasantry we find a vivid picture of the life and customs of the later period, it is from the Bedawin that we learn most that can throw light on the Patriarchal times, and on the life of Abraham and of his immediate descendants.

A study of the Arabs is carried on under difficulties west of Jordan. The great tribes are found either east of the river, or in the desert of the Tih, and in order to form a really good estimate of Arab character, it would be necessary to live in these remote districts for many years, following the migrations of one of the great tribes. The Arabs of the Jordan Valley are probably not of pure blood, and seem in some cases to have been mixed up with negroes, flying to the deserts from Damascus and other towns. The tribes are very small and scattered; many are offshoots of the Sugr and 'Anezeh nations, whose countless tents stretch away far into the Eastern desert; others have migrated from the north, and one tribe—the T'aamireh—is of Fellâh origin, though now nomadic.

The migrations of the western tribes do not extend over large tracts, but are confined to small districts marked by recognised boundaries. Thus Wâdy Fûsâil is the border between the Mes'aid and the K'abneh Arabs, and the Plains of Jericho belong to the Abu Nŭseir. In the Desert of Judah, the two most powerful tribes are the T'aamireh, who wear turbans and sow corn, and the Jâhalîn; south of these are the Dhullâm, and south of Beersheba the 'Azâzimeh. West of this last great tribe, are the Tiyâhah round Gaza; and the Terabin extend towards Egypt. The Arab clans in Philistia and Sharon are too numerous and insignificant to require notice; and in Galilee also there is a large number of very small tribes. The above-enumerated are the most important Bedawin divisions west of Jordan; but the Sugr, from the east, occupy in spring the whole of the valley of Jezreel, and in times of disturbance they enter the Plain of Esdraelon.

Within the assigned limits, the migrations of a

tribe over some 200 to 400 square miles are regulated by the temperature of the seasons, and by the pasturage and water supply. Ranging from one spring to another, and from the sheltered valleys visited in winter to the favourite camps on breezy slopes in summer, the nomads seem to resemble the Jews at the period when, for forty years, they lived in the wilderness—not, as we often imagine, travelling steadily in one line, but rather inhabiting the small area of the Sinaitic peninsula, till the time for a further migration arrived.

The camps are scarcely ever placed in the immediate neighbourhood of water, but the Arab women go perhaps a mile away from the tents, and bring the needful supply in the black skins (Ghirbeh), carrying them on their backs or on diminutive donkeys. I have often asked the Arabs why they did not pitch close to the water, but never got a satisfactory answer. They have probably learnt from experience that the low ground near water is often malarious, and the great requisites for a camp seem to be shelter and concealment. The situations are not always, however, wisely chosen; for, in more than one instance, a sudden thunderstorm in the hills has brought a flood down the great valleys, in the bottom of which the smaller groups of tents are often found, and the water has carried away and drowned the whole settlement, together with its flocks.

The scantiness of pasture and of water supply, obliges the Arabs to divide themselves into numerous small camps, dotted over their territory. The Sheikh of the tribe, with his family, generally collects the largest encampment round his tent, and this forms the rendezvous of the rest. Among the Arabs of the Judean desert the largest number of tents in one camp is about thirty, and these contain some thirty families, or over a hundred persons. The total numbers of a large tribe like the T'aamireh are about 1000 persons, or 300 tents, but the average is about 100 families.

The tents are arranged in different ways. Among the Sugr a large encampment was set out in parallel lines some fifty yards apart, the tents in each row being close together, end to end. Among the T'aamireh and Jâhalîn the usual form is a rectangle. The average length of the tent is some twenty to twenty-five feet, but the small ones will sometimes be only ten feet long, and the larger forty feet. The distance between two tents in a line is about four feet. Thus a camp of twenty tents occupied a space of two hundred feet by seventy feet. In another case the form was a triangle, the reason of this arrangement being that the flocks are driven into the enclosure at night, and thus protected from the attacks of robbers or prevented from straying by themselves.

The Arab tent is extremely unlike the usual representations, in which it is shown either as a sort of hut or as a bell-tent, instead of a long black "house of hair," with a low sloping roof and open front. It has, however, been carefully described by Burckhardt, and there is little to add to his account. The canvas of the roof and side walls is of goat's hair, black, with occasionally stripes of white running horizontally (Cant. i. 5). The pieces of stuff are about two feet wide, and thirty to fifty feet long. The tent has generally nine poles ('Awamîd), arranged three and three, those in the centre being the longest; thus the tent has a low ridge both ways in order to run the rain off. The cloths at the side can be easily removed as the sun or wind requires, one side being always left open. The tents are supported by cords and by pegs (Autâd), which are driven with a mallet (Judg. iv. 21). The average height of a tent is about seven feet.

Frail and cold as these habitations might be thought to prove in winter, they are really far more comfortable than would be expected. Being so low, the wind does not blow them over, and they are, moreover, most skilfully pitched, generally below a steep bank or low swell. Even in heavy storms I have found the interiors dry, and the heavy canvas does not let the rain through. The Arabs, however, suffer very much from rheumatism in winter. In summer they occasionally inhabit reed huts ('Arish), which are cooler than the tents.

The language of the Bedawîn differs from that of the peasantry, being nearer to that of the Arab tribes from the neighbourhood of Mecca, and thus to literary Arabic. Their names for natural objects are not always the same employed by the Fellahîn, and they are seemingly less ancient, though this difference is also partly due to the different character of the ground in the districts which the nomads inhabit. The old names are not preserved among the Arabs as they are among the peasantry, but descriptive titles have, as a rule, replaced the former nomenclature. These facts tend rather to confirm the views already expressed as to the antiquity of the Fellâh race, contrasted with the more modern settlers who have encroached on their territory.

The Bedawîn have, in addition to their ordinary language, a kind of slang, which they use among themselves, and which we were quite unable to understand. The corrupt pronunciation of ordinary words also renders it very difficult for any one accustomed to the peculiarities of the Fellâh dialect to comprehend the Arabs.

The character of the Bedawîn is not so easy to penetrate as at first appears. They are a crafty and reserved people, with strong ideas of policy and prudence. Nothing is more disagreeable to an Arab than to be made to look foolish, and they are careful not to put themselves in a false position. They also conceal under an affectation of carelessness and indifference a very keen perception of what is going on. I have often watched a Bedawi walking by my side, and noticed how carefully he scanned every pebble in the road, and how the slightest sign of life—a bird, a gazelle, or a distant figure—attracted his attention at once, long before I had observed anything. Their sight is generally very clear and good, and their agility and endurance are astonishing.

A traveller visiting a camp might easily imagine his hosts to be too lazy to move; but if he wakes from a doze, he will be astonished to see these grave, solemn figures, skipping like squirrels or creeping like cats, inspecting perhaps his property, or endeavouring to make sure that he is asleep. This sudden change of demeanour is quite in accord with the Arab character, and the skill with which they conceal their intentions and thoughts makes them very dangerous enemies.

The creed of a Bedawi is that a man should be terrible to his enemies, and the assumed sternness of their faces is sometimes rather ludicrous. In making an attack they will be careful to ascertain first that they are really in a safe majority, and if they are outnumbered, they hide in the undulations of the ground, in a manner which would excite the admiration of any military man.

The Bedawîn are very trustworthy; they keep their promises honourably, and their law of hospitality is strictly and chivalrously observed. The murder of a guest who has eaten salt in their camp is, I believe, almost unknown, and they have a righteous horror of shedding blood, as the blood feud must go on until some heavy indemnity has been paid. The life of any European is thus probably quite as safe among the Arabs as in London.

Among those tribes which live beyond the corrupting influences of townsmen, the character of the Bedawîn is said to be very noble; their chivalrous and courteous demeanour, and their generosity, are praised alike. Unfortunately, the tribes with which we lived are settled on the border-land, and have been much spoilt by intercourse with greedy peasants. We found them generally very avaricious, though in some cases their ideas concerning money were amusing from their simplicity.

With their friends, the behaviour of the Arabs is kindly and unaffected; and especially among the Abu Nuseir we met several specimens of what we should call "good fellows" in England. The hostility usually shown to strangers is due to the unceremonious way in which travellers will enter their country, without conforming to any of their ideas of courtesy and etiquette.

There is no greater mistake than to regard the Arabs as barbarous or uncivilised. They have a peculiar civilisation of their own, which is suited to their wants, and a system of government with recognised laws, which are strictly enforced. Their life is, in fact, a perfect picture of a patriarchal system, suited to a people who are not numerous, nor engaged in any very complex transactions; they acknowledge certain leaders, generally hereditary, but who are only obeyed because they have obtained for themselves a reputation for wisdom in council, and prowess in the field. These chiefs direct the policy of their tribe in its relations with other Arabs, or with the Turkish nominal Governors, and their tact and ability are often remarkable. The main duties of the elders are the arrangement of marriages, and of treaties with other tribes, and the settlement of disputes, which are submitted to them and regularly tried. The Sheikh has the power of life and death, of peace and war, and unless he disgraces his tribe by a blunder, he is pretty sure of prompt and general obedience.

The costume of the Bedawin is so simple, that it may probably have remained unchanged since the days of Abraham. They wear the same shirt which has already been described as used by the peasantry, and generally they wear also the 'Abba; but their head-dress is the Kufeiyeh, except among the T'aamireh, who, as before stated, are not true Bedawin. The Kufeiyeh is a shawl made of silk or cotton, with tassels on two edges; it is about a yard square, and is folded diagonally, and placed on the head with the point of the triangle behind.

A cord of hair or rope is wound twice round the forehead and head, coming down behind the ears almost to the nape of the neck, and this holds the shawl in place; the cord is called the Aghâl, and is commonly black.

The head-dress thus formed is extremely comfortable, and for four years we scarcely wore any other. The poorer Arabs wear only the shawl and cord; the richer have felt and cotton caps inside it. The Kufeiyeh is the best possible protection from the sun, for the tight cord over the temples is a preventive against sunstroke, and the ends of the shawl can be drawn over the face and tucked into the Aghâl, thus shielding the eyes from the mid-day glare.

Another distinctive article of Bedawîn dress is the sandal, which also requires special description. It is a skeleton shoe with a light leather sole, which is supported by a string of hide, passing beneath the ankle and above the heel, and then brought round between the great toe and the second toe, where it is attached to the sole; this string is then drawn tight, and fixed with a leather button. The sole is further connected with the string by two straps on either side, and the whole structure fits almost as tight to the foot as a shoe. Such, no doubt, was the sandal mentioned in the Bible, and not the complicated cross-gartering which is commonly represented in pictures of Old Testament incidents.

In winter the Arabs also wear, under the 'Abba and over the shirt, a sheep-skin jacket, the woolly side in, the outside tanned a sort of brick-red colour. This garment looks very comfortable; but the bare legs and scanty skirts of the Bedawîn give them a most miserable appearance in the cold weather.

The weapons of the Arabs are different from those of their forefathers; and in the adoption of gunpowder and tobacco, we find evidence that they are not incapable of making use, as far as is convenient to themselves, of the newest inventions of civilisation. Even in the Jordan Valley I have seen French cigarette-papers used; for this more convenient method of smoking has in the sea-side towns quite taken the place of the old-fashioned pipes, and is making rapid progress among the peasantry also.

The Arabs carry the sword, gun, and lance (Rumh), the last being mentioned in Scripture. The sword (Seif) has a short and straight blade, resembling a large knife. The gun (Barûd) is of great length—often five feet from muzzle to stock—and is bound with brass; the stock is very much lighter than with us; anything is used to load the piece, and very indifferent powder is employed. The lock is, I believe, invariably a flint one. The powder is carried in a ram's horn, which is attached to the leather belt.

The bow, javelin, buckler, and shield seem to

be now obsolete, though mentioned by travellers of the fifteenth century as still in use among the Arabs. The introduction of firearms is no doubt the reason of the disappearance of these weapons.

The helmet and coat of mail are still found among the tribes east of Jordan; the first being a light iron cap (Kub'ah), with a spike on the top, and a thin plate to protect the nose; the latter, a garment, with sleeves, which descends to the knees, or rather lower; these coats are of links closely woven, and are of considerable weight.

The Arabs seclude their women more than is the custom among the peasantry, and they are carefully veiled in presence of a stranger. Each tent has its Harim, or women's partition, and this, no doubt, is what is alluded to in the passage where Isaac is said to have brought Rebekah into his mother Sarah's tent (Gen. xxiv. 67). The women, however, enjoy greater consideration than among the Fellahin, and an old woman is sometimes admitted into the council, and becomes a power in the state—a privilege which has as yet only been claimed by a small minority in our own country.

The dress of the Arab women is remarkably becoming, and their appearance is imposing, as they sweep over the grass, in long trailing garments with ample hanging sleeves; their faces are swathed in a shawl head-dress, generally of dark colour, which is bound over the mouth, and leaves the nose and eyes exposed; their black curly locks are also hidden, except in the case of young girls. The under-dress is indigo-coloured; the upper, which is very wide, with large sleeves and open in front, is generally of a dull olive-green; thus the general effect of their costume is very dark, and their faces are discoloured by extensive tattooing and by the blue paint on the under lip, which is dyed all over to give greater brilliance to the appearance of the teeth. It is curious to note that the women, as a rule, are ugly, while the men are handsome.

When going to fetch water, the women wear only the under-dress, which they tuck and tie up until they present most comical figures. A great part of their lives seems to be spent in going to and fro between the tent and the spring, with their little black donkeys, or in sitting squatted on the edge of the stream, beating the clothes which require washing (and generally require it very much) with a stone.

The women are all cooks, and their cookery is excellent in its way. They grind the corn in a stone hand-mill; and make thin cakes of unleavened bread; and butter and cheese by shaking the milk in a skin which is hung up on sticks. Even on their raids the Arabs take with them one or two young women to cook for the party.

The occupations of the men in time of peace are mainly pastoral. The wealth of the Arabs consists in their horses, flocks, herds, and camels. Among the Abu Nuseir, a regular trade in beasts goes on, and they act apparently as agents for selling the animals of other tribes. The immense number of the animals which are pastured in the apparently barren and waterless waste is astonishing. I have seen the plains of Beersheba swarming with camels, and the Plain of Esdraelon has sometimes been quite covered with the flocks and herds of the Sugr.

The eastern Arabs pride themselves on their horses, but west of Jordan there are scarcely any. The mares are hardly ever sold, and often belong to more than one owner. Thus it is possible to buy the "head" of a mare, which means to own it, subject to the rearing of a colt for each of the owners of the "body" and "tail," who claim the young ones at a certain age. The Arab horses are small and light; the better class walk very slowly, and they can neither jump nor trot, but their powers of endurance and their hardihood are immense, and their speed at a gallop is generally fair; they are rarely vicious, and their paces are pleasant when they are properly trained.

The Arabs scarcely ever attack a neighbouring tribe, but they prefer to journey a distance of several days before committing any outrage, and they retreat as rapidly as they came when once the booty is captured. These marauding excursions are called Ghazû, and are the main events of their lives; the whole of their affected listlessness is then laid aside, and each Ghâzi, or "champion," vies with the others in his feats of daring and activity. The appearance of a party of the Bedawîn horsemen, charging with long lances trembling in their hands and held horizontally over the head, is extremely picturesque and imposing.

The Arab, in time of peace, does not require much amusement; he is content to sit quiet, smoking and drinking coffee. Among the more degraded, however, the Egyptian dancing-girls are sometimes welcomed, and all the tribes indulge occasionally in what is termed a Fantazîa, a word apparently of Italian origin, and introduced by the Franks.

These Fantazîas we often saw, but perhaps the most effective was that executed in our honour at Engedi. A single Arab faced four others, and held a sword over his head in both hands. The performance began by an extemporary song from the sword-bearer in honour of the Kabtân and his party, the other four Arabs clapping their hands in regular time. Suddenly this ceased, and they advanced towards the swordsman, uttering in a sort of growl, the word, "Sŭ-hûbb, Sŭ-hûbb," repeated many times. The swordsman also advanced, and then recoiled, and the four, closely packed shoulder to shoulder, began to clap their hands, and crouched as if about to spring. The swordsman then crouched down and writhed to and fro, almost kneeling, as if in mortal combat. After a few moments he sprang up as though victorious, and began his song again, while the four, as if enchanted, stood erect, clapping their hands and swaying their bodies backwards and forwards. The growling and struggling were again repeated, and the dance seemed to be intended to represent the combat of a single hero against many foes.

The night was dark, and the wild scene was only dimly visible by the fitful blaze of a fire of thorns, which sometimes flared up and showed the eager excited faces and lank wiry figures, giving them the appearance rather of wizards engaged in some terrible incantation, than of ordinary sword-dancers. Finally, the triumphant hero sung the praise of the "Konsul Kabtàn," and alluded delicately to the probable "bucksheesh." The other four here joined very heartily in the chorus.

It was remarkable that the Sheikh of the tribe could be seen, a few yards off, engaged in prayer during the greater part of the time that this strange dance was going on. His attention appeared to be in no way distracted by the noise, and there was nothing, in Arab estimation, incongruous in the two occupations which were being thus carried on at the same time.

Such is the simple life of the Arab tribes. Except in the use of tobacco and gunpowder, these people seem unchanged since the days of Abraham. It was thus no doubt that that Patriarch travelled to and fro with his flocks, herds, and servants; thus he made war and entered into treaties with the surrounding tribes. The wells which he dug, and which had to be re-opened by Isaac, were perhaps similar to the Hŭfeiyir, or "pits," which the Arabs now dig in the beds of great valleys, as for instance at Gerar and Beersheba.

The Bedawîn are very religious, and observe the appointed hours of prayer much more devoutly than most of the Fellahîn; if water is obtainable, they wash their hands, arms, legs, and faces before praying, and we were often considerably hindered in our Survey work by the inconvenient piety of the Arab guides. It is said that the Arabs east of Jordan are pagans, and that moon-worship and yet more curious rites exist among them. These practices date from the times of "ignorance," before the proclamation of El Islâm, but I have never seen anything of the kind among the tribes with whom we lived.

The Arabs have many traditions, chiefly relating to their own origin and to the descent of their clans. As they despise writing, regarding both this and the cultivation of the ground as degrading, and only fit for peasants, these traditions are handed down from mouth to mouth; the stories naturally become more marvellous every time that they are repeated, and in some cases they present extraordinary confusions, as at Jericho, where the Imâm 'Aly, Companion of the Prophet, is said to have fought a battle with Abu 'Obeideh ibn el Jerrâh, who was a well-known Moslem general of the time of Omar, and the conqueror of Jerusalem.

I have already alluded to the curious fact that Christian legends of the middle ages are current among the Abu Nuseir Arabs round Jericho, the case of the "high mountain" of the Temptation being the chief instance. There is also a legend well known in the Jordan Valley and in Galilee, of a famous chief named Zîr. He is said to be the maker of certain curious pits dug in a line near 'Ain Fŭsâil, and connected with an old aqueduct. The same legend is connected with pits found east of Jordan, possibly intended for the same use, which was apparently the collection of water. Zîr also found his way to the Nazareth hills, and the acacia-trees near Semûnieh are said to have grown from his tent-pegs.

The Bedawîn reverence the tombs of their own ancestors, and, in some cases, of those of other tribes. The Abu Nuseir are descended from a tribe which had a peculiar reputation for sanctity, and which was free to roam among the rest as a company of Derwishes. Some of these Arabs were, by mistake, killed by the Egyptian Government, and their graves are shown in a valley called the "Holy Valley," near Mar Sâba. Any Arab entering this valley makes use of the expression, "Your leave,

O blessed ones," and kisses the tombstones on passing. A second place of the kind exists not far north of Engedi, where are the graves of certain of the Rushâideh tribe, who were massacred by Ibrahim Pacha. On passing this spot our guides kissed the rude headstones very reverently.

There are many grave-yards in the desert, generally near sacred places or large trees, or on the top of the larger Tells. In one or two instances a white-washed tomb is built, in the middle of the cemetery, over the body of some noted Sheikh, and necklaces, or the furniture of a horse, are hung as gifts upon it. The Arabs often bring the dead bodies from a considerable distance in order to inter them in the cemetery of the tribe.

There is one habit of the Bedawin which has given rise to misconceptions, and is worthy of notice. The camels and other property are marked by a recognised tribe-mark called Wusm. Each tribe, and each division of a tribe, has its mark, and some are curious. The Rushâideh mark is a circle with a cross—resembling the astronomical sign for Mars. The Jâhalin have a T, a cross, or a C with a dot in the centre. The Tiyahah have two parallel strokes, the Dhullâm have three, and the K'abneh a double cross. These marks are found on the flanks of the camels, on the gravestones, and on ruined buildings. Thus at Masada the gateway is covered with the Rushâideh and

Jâhalîn marks, the reason being that the Arabs believe that a hidden treasure exists there, and they therefore assert their ownership by putting the tribe-mark on the place.

Two traditions are very commonly repeated among the Bedawîn. The first is that hidden treasure exists in certain places, and can be discovered by the use of incantations. There is some foundation for this expectation of finding treasure, for it seems to have been common to bury money in old times, as indeed it still is; and the hoards are found from time to time. A quantity of gold Alexanders were lately found in the neighbourhood of Tyre, and a number of shekels were discovered near Jericho in the winter of 1873, and were brought to us in Jerusalem; these were subsequently pronounced genuine in Europe. In Haifa also a treasure of Byzantine coins was found under the sill of a doorway in the gardens. The Arabs have exaggerated ideas on this subject, and they suppose treasures to lie hidden in every ruin.

The second common idea is that the desert was formerly cultivated and full of water. All over the plateau west of the Dead Sea ruins are shown which are said to be remains of former vineyards, and even the Roman camps at Masada are so called. This idea is also perhaps founded on fact: "the vineyards of Engedi," mentioned by Solomon, have entirely disappeared together with its palms, and the palms of Jericho have left only two survivors. The Crusaders cultivated sugar in three places along the Jordan Valley, yet only the ruins of their mills and aqueducts are now left, with the semi-fossilised stalks of the sugar-canes near Beisân. But although the country is thus shown to have been at one time more productive, still no such entire change as the Arabs suppose is likely to have taken place, for the desert is called desert in the Bible, and the Dead Sea plateau is the old Jeshimon or "solitude."

The preceding pages will, I hope, serve to show how broad is the distinction between the peasantry and the nomadic people, and how interesting is the study of both the races as throwing light on the Bible narrative. We must now pass on to consider briefly the other inhabitants of the Holy Land.

CHAPTER XI.

JEWS, RUSSIANS, AND GERMANS.

The Jews in Palestine inhabit only the larger towns, where they are engaged in trade and in money transactions. The greater number live in the four holy cities—Jerusalem, Tiberias, Safed, and Hebron; but many are found also in the coast towns of Gaza, Jaffa, Haifa, Acre, Tyre, and Sidon. The number of Jews in Jerusalem was estimated by the Consular reports in 1872 to be 8000, but it has considerably increased since then, owing to the arrival of a large body of Russian and Polish Jews, who fled, it is said, from the conscription in those countries. Whatever be the cause, the fact is undisputed, that the Jews are steadily gathering in Palestine. In Jerusalem they have been encouraged by the munificence of Sir Moses Montefiore, and have formed a sort of building-club for the purpose of erecting houses to the west of the town.

The following facts relating to the Jews are obtained from the best authority—namely, from

Dr. Chaplin, the physician of the Jewish hospital in Jerusalem.

The largest section of the Jews in Jerusalem is that of the Ashkenazim, which comprises the fair-haired sallow German Jews, with the Polish, and the gigantic Russian Jews. The Ashkenazim are subdivided into national communities, and also into religious sects, all of the "high church" order, including the Parushim (or Pharisees), the Chasidim (or Assideans of the Book of Maccabees), the Chabad, and the Varshi. These four sects agree in recognising, in various degrees, the authority of the Talmudic law, and the traditions of the elders.

Next in order come the Sephardim, or Spanish Jews, who still wear the black turban originally imposed on them by the laws of the mad Caliph Hâkem; they include also the Mughrabee Jews, who speak Arabic. In their physique, and the dignity of their appearance, the Sephardim are far superior to their European co-religionists; they also belong to the extreme party of the Chasidim and Varshi, in whose synagogues they will pray when not near to one of their own.

The old Sadducean party is now represented only by the Karaites, or "low church" Jews, who discard the authority of the Mishnic or Oral law, and do not admit the authority of the Talmudic commentators. In Jerusalem they have but one small synagogue, and their number in the city is probably not above a hundred; the greater part of the Karaites are now found in Baghdad, Arabia, and Russia.

Many of the Jews are shopkeepers, others are money-changers, and a few are craftsmen and farmers; but a great number live on the Halûkah, or alms, collected from their brethren in Europe to support the poor in Jerusalem. Many are under the protection of the foreign Consulates, and they have of late years gained considerable immunity from Moslem persecution.

The Jews always live in a distinct quarter. The Jewish quarter in Jerusalem in the middle ages was, however, that now occupied by the Moslems. Their streets are not remarkable for cleanliness; thus at Tiberias the "king of the fleas" is said to hold his court, and if one half the stories which have been related to me by trustworthy witnesses were admitted, the Ashkenazim must be the dirtiest people on the face of the earth.

The good qualities of the Jews are numerous: they are energetic and able, very courteous to strangers, and charitable to one another; but they are fanatical to the last degree, and Palestine under Jewish government would probably be closed against outer influence even more effectually than it is under the Turks.

The Jewish costume is more curious than picturesque; their weedy figures are clad in the

Kumbaz or striped cotton gown, under which they wear a shirt, and white drawers, with cotton stockings. On their feet they have low leather shoes, on their heads a soft felt hat. On feast days they appear in a fur cap, just like that commonly represented in Rembrandt's pictures— no doubt the Jewish dress of his own days; and their gaberdines are also edged with fur. The Spanish Jews wear a dress not unlike that of the better class of Moslems, and are indeed only distinguished by their black turbans. The Jewish women wear sometimes the native dress with the Izar, sometimes European print gowns, with gaudy Manchester shawls over their heads. The men of the Pharisees and other high-church sects, are also distinguished by the love-lock, a long lank curl which hangs down in front of the ear beside the cheek, and is, to the eyes of an European, one of the ugliest and most unmanly fashions which could be invented.

The position of Jewish women is not enviable; they are divorced on the smallest pretext, even for cooking a dinner badly, and they live in constant anxiety. One Jew, whom I met at intervals, had three wives in the course of as many years, and this is, I believe, no uncommon occurrence. The women are extremely superstitious, and I have been told of their mixing their own nail-parings, or locks of hair, in their husbands' food in order to secure their affections.

The Jews venerate the tombs of many of their ancestors. Thus at Tiberias the tomb of the great Moses ben Maimon, or Rambam, commonly known as Maimonides, is shown; at Meirûn in Galilee the sepulchre of Simeon bar Jochai, the builder of twenty-five synagogues, is yearly the scene of a curious festival; at Shechem the Jews visit Joseph's tomb, and make sacrifices of gold-lace, shawls, and other articles, as they do also at Meirûn; in Jerusalem the sepulchre of Simon the Just is also the scene of an annual feast.

The Jewish attitude in prayer is one of the most extraordinary peculiarities of the nation. The prescribed key, for intonation of the prayers, is high and nasal, and they sway their bodies backwards and forwards, with much energy, as they sing. The scene thus presented in a synagogue is almost ludicrous, and no one ignorant of the language, would give the worshippers credit for their beautiful and affecting liturgy, which has influenced our own far more than we are ourselves, as a rule, aware.

And now turning from the native population to the foreign element in the country, a few words may be devoted first to the Russian Pilgrims.

The reasons which induce the Russian Government to promote pilgrimages to Palestine are best known to themselves; the fact remains that the pilgrims receive Government help. The great hospice on the west side of Jerusalem, capable of accommodating 1000 persons, was founded in 1860, and includes the Russian cathedral; at Easter this large building is quite full, and the town swarms with Russian men and women. The strength and endurance of these peasants is wonderful: old women of sixty or seventy trudge on foot from Jaffa to Jerusalem, a distance of thirty-five miles by road; they undergo the fatigues of the crowded Easter ceremonies, and then walk down again to the coast. The savings of a whole life are sometimes expended on such a pilgrimage, and the only reward is the bunch of wax candles which, together perhaps with a coarse lithograph of some saint, the pilgrim brings back to his native village, where he enjoys henceforth the reputation which the pilgrimage ensures.

The scene in the Russian cathedral at Easter time, is striking and instructive. The building is of modern Byzantine architecture, with a fine peal of bells. The walls are painted salmon-colour, with an intricate arabesque in blue and red; the screen in front of the apses is of light oak, with pictures let in and brightly coloured on gold backgrounds; the central gate in this screen is of brass, with silver lamps and candlesticks placed in front.

The congregation generally consists principally of women, but to the right stand the men, unkempt and uncombed, their furrowed features peering out from shaggy locks and long beards, their clothes of dull colours and thickly padded, their feet and legs cased in huge knee-boots. The women wear the same neutral tints, and knee-boots; they have heavy shawls over their heads. The priests are also bearded, with hair down to their shoulders—truly a barbarous priesthood, with a barbarous congregation. The Saviour is represented in Russian pictures with a similar beard and hair.

The religious ecstasy of the congregation was always intense. They took no part in the service, but continued to cross themselves, and knelt at intervals to kiss the floor, many knocking their heads so hard against it as to be heard at the other end of the church. Small tapers were burnt on the great silver candlesticks, and those who stood near the door passed the taper to those in front, each person bowing to the one who handed it, until those near the screen received it; it was then lighted, and when half burnt was put out, and left for its owner to claim.

The ritual was impressive; six choristers in ordinary dress stood round a great lectern just outside the screen, at the top of the steps leading up to it. The bass voice was fine, and the tenor very sweet; the service is frequently attended by Europeans in Jerusalem for the sake of the music.

A tall priest in a rich robe of cloth-of-gold and dark red velvet, stood before the brass gates, a crown on his head, a censer in his hand. His intoned sentences were answered by the responses of the choir. Presently the gates opened, and three priests came out of the mysterious sanctuary, where the golden candlestick and reliquaries could be seen on the altar. The Archimandrite, in flowing robes of black satin, with a broad stole of cloth-of-gold, his head veiled, and his long grey beard covering his breast, swept down the steps; he was preceded by black-robed acolytes, and followed by two other priests scarcely less magnificently dressed. The Gospel was read at a lectern in the middle of the congregation, the censer was swung, and the great bells boomed out during the lesson.

I have attended many religious services, Christian, Jewish, and Moslem, but none more remarkable for barbaric grandeur and pomp. The songs of Latin monks, the shrill nasal clamour of the Armenians, the Jewish gesticulation, are all far less dignified than the solemn chants of the Russian cathedral. The fanaticism of the pilgrims, drawn from the lowest and most ignorant peasant class, surpasses anything in Christendom, and is only equalled by that of the Moslems.

Another large section of the Easter pilgrims in Jerusalem is formed by the wealthy and powerful Armenian sect, to whom the church of St. James on Zion belongs — a very interesting building, carpeted with rich rugs, and lined with tiles and tortoise-shell. The visitor is here sprinkled with rose-water, and valuable jewelled missals are presented for the congregation to kiss.

The remaining nationalities found in Palestine may be briefly dismissed. On Carmel, and in Upper Galilee, the Druses form a large percentage of the population; but their life and habits have been discussed by well-informed writers, and there is no space to enlarge here on their curious admixture of Aryan and Semitic ideas, or on their belief in the duality of the Divine nature, and in incarnations of the Deity. There are also gipsies in Palestine, who engage in the usual occupations of gipsies, and who are called Naury. They have almost forgotten their own language, and speak Arabic as a rule. At sea-side towns there is a curious mixture of mongrel nationalities—Maltese, Greeks, Slavs, and Levantines, with stray specimens of most European nations—a class as uninteresting as they are degraded.

We may now consider the history of the rise and progress of the two German colonies which have obtained a footing in Palestine; for without some account of these enterprises the sketch of the inhabitants of the Holy Land would be incomplete.

The German colonists belong to a religious society known as the "Temple," which originated among the Pietists of Wurtemburg, who, without leaving the Lutheran Church, separated themselves from the world, and engaged in Sunday meetings for prayer and edification. The Pietists accept as their standard the explanation given by Dr. J. A. Bengel (in his Gnomon of the New Testament), of the prophecies in the Revelation. Among the friends and disciples of Bengel was a certain Dr. Hoffmann, who obtained from Frederick, the eccentric King of Wurtemburg, a tract of barren land at Kornthal, where his disciples established a Pietist colony, which he intended to transplant later to Palestine. Hoffmann, however, died, and his followers remained contentedly on their lands; but Hoffmann's son was not forgetful of his father's designs, and instituted a new colony at Kirschenhardthof, with a special view to its final removal to the Holy Land. Among his earliest disciples was Herr G. D. Hardegg, who became in time a leader among the Temple Pietists.

The younger Hoffmann (Christopher) visited Palestine about 1858, and, in 1867, a small trial expedition of twelve men was sent out. They settled in reed huts near Semûnieh, on the edge of the Plain of Esdraelon, west of Nazareth; and in spite of the warning of friends who knew the unhealthy climate of that place, they remained in the malarious atmosphere of the low ground near the springs, until they all died of fever.

On the 6th of August, 1868, Christopher Hoffmann and G. D. Hardegg left Kirschenhardthof, and in October they reached Palestine; after visiting various places, they resolved on settling at Haifa and Jaffa, and bought land in both places. The Haifa colony was the first founded, that at Jaffa being some six months younger. Hardegg became president of the former, and Hoffmann of the latter.

The religious views of the colonists are not easily understood, and I believe that most of them have rather vague ideas of their own intentions. Their main motive for establishing colonies in Palestine, is the promotion of conditions favourable to the fulfilment (which they expect to occur shortly) of the prophecies of the Revelation and of Zechariah. They suppose it to be a duty to separate themselves from the world, and to set an example of a community living, as closely as possible, on the model of the Apostolic age. The spread of infidelity in Germany, appears to be the main cause of this separative tendency among the Pietists.

The tenets of the Temple Society are probably best summarised in the "Profession of Faith of the Temple," published by Herr Hoffmann, and including five articles as below :

"First. To prepare for the great and terrible day of the second coming of Jesus Christ, which, from the signs of the times, is near. This preparation is made by the building of a spiritual temple in all lands, specially in Jerusalem.

"Secondly. This temple is composed of the gifts of the Spirit (1 Cor. xii. 4), which make the true

Church, and every one should strive to possess them.

"Thirdly. The means to obtain these is to seek the Kingdom of God, as described by the prophets (Isaiah ii. 2, xix. 25 ; Ezek. xl. 48).

"Fourthly. The Temple of Jerusalem is not a building of dead, but of lively stones ; of men of every nation (1 Pet. ii. 4—10) united in the worship of God in spirit and truth.

"Fifthly. The Temple service consists of sacrifices such as are described in the New Testament" (Rom. xii. 1 ; Heb. xiii. 15, 16 ; James i. 27).

The writings of Hardegg are far more diffuse and mystic. The main peculiarity which I have been able to extract from them, is the belief that it is not to the Jews, but to the true Israel (by which he apparently understands the Temple Society to be intended), that prophecies of a return to Palestine are to be supposed to refer.

I have stated as far as possible the apparent religious beliefs of the community, but there seem to be many shades of doctrine among them ; all, however, agree in an expectancy of some immediate change in the world's affairs, in the arrival of Armageddon and the Millenium, and in the fulfilment of all prophecy.

In 1875 I had the opportunity of attending one of the Sunday services, in the colony at Haifa. The congregation was devout and earnest ; the service was simple and free from extravagance of any kind. The president offered up a long prayer in German, a hymn was sung with the usual musical good taste of Germans, and a chapter of the prophecy of Zechariah read. The president then delivered an exhortation, announcing the immediate advent of the Saviour, who would "suddenly come to His temple." Other elders followed, speaking with much earnestness, and another hymn was sung, after which the congregation quietly dispersed from the bare schoolroom in which they had assembled. A discussion of the affairs of the colony often immediately succeeds the religious services.

Of the history of the Jaffa colony we gathered comparatively little. They have two settlements —one called Sarôna, about two and a half miles north of the town, consisting, in 1872, of ten houses; the second, nearer the walls of Jaffa, was bought from the surviving members of an American colony which came to grief, and this sentlement included thirteen houses, with a school and an hotel, the latter kept by Hardegg's son who also represents the German Government in Jaffa.

In 1872 the Jaffa colony numbered one hundred men, seventy women, and thirty-five children: two of the colonists were doctors, and some twenty were mechanics, the rest being farmers. They employed a few natives, and cultivated 400 acres of corn-land, paying the ordinary taxes to the Turks. The children are taught Arabic, and

European languages, also Latin and Greek. The houses are clean, airy, and well built, and the colonies wear an aspect of industry and enterprise, which contrasts with the squalor and decay of the native villages.

With the Haifa colony we became more intimately acquainted, by living in one of the houses for three months, during the winter of 1872—3, and again in the hotel of the colony, for about two months, during 1875, when we saw a good deal of the working of the community.

In 1872 the colonists numbered 254—forty single and forty-seven married men, thirty-two single, and fifty-one married women (four widows), and eighty-four children. There were about fifty mechanics, and the settlement consisted of thirty-one dwelling-houses. The land was 450 acres of arable ground, with 140 olives, and 17 acres of vineyard.

In the first three years of its existence only seven deaths occurred in the colony, but the mortality increased later; in 1872 there were eighteen deaths among the 205 colonists at Jaffa, which were due principally to fever, but such a death-rate has never yet occurred at Haifa.

The little village of well-built stone houses is situate west of the walled town of Haifa, under the shadow of the Carmel range. A broad street runs up from the shore towards the mountain, and the greater number of the buildings stand, in their gardens, on either side. Close to the beach is the Carmel Hotel, kept by a most obliging and moderate landlord, and a little farther up are the school and meeting-house, in one building. Mr. Hardegg's dwelling, farther east, is the largest house in the colony. The total number is stated at eighty-five, including buildings for agricultural purposes.

In 1875 the colonists numbered 311, having been reinforced principally by new arrivals from Germany; the increase of accommodation since 1872 was thus far greater than that of settlers. The land had also increased, in the same period, to 600 acres, with 100 acres of vineyards and gardens; but the soil of the newly-acquired property near Tireh, in the plain west of Carmel, is of very poor quality, and the Germans have not yet succeeded, in their favourite scheme of obtaining grounds on the top of the mountain, where the climate and soil are both good.

The live stock consists of 75 head of cattle, 250 sheep, goats, and pigs, and 8 teams of horses. A superior American threshing-machine has been imported. The trades followed are stone-cutting and masons' work, carpentry and wagon-making. Blacksmiths, coppersmiths, tinsmiths, joiners, shoemakers, tailors, butchers, harness-makers, turners, soap-makers, vintners, and quarrymen, are also found among the colonists. There has been an attempt to trade in soap, olive-oil, and olive-wood articles, but, for these undertakings, more capital is required than the Germans at present possess. A good wind-mill, and an olive-press, have been brought from England. A tannery was also being put up in 1875, and a general shop exists, which the natives, as well as the Germans, frequent.

The colonists were many of them employed on the English orphanage at Nazareth, which Mr. Shumacher designed and executed; and all the masons' and carpenters' work was executed by the Germans. The colonists also have done much to clear the road from Haifa to Nazareth, though they have not *made* it, considering that, from a professional point of view, it is not yet a made road at all. Their wagons are now driven between the two places, and the natives employ them for moving grain.

The schools in the colony, for the children and younger men, are two in number. In the upper school, Arabic, English, French and German, arithmetic, drawing, geography, history, mathematics, and music are taught; in the lower, Arabic and German, writing, arithmetic, and singing; in both religious instruction is given; and the girls are taught knitting, sewing, and embroidery.

The colony has thus been sketched in its religious and practical aspects. Though much talk has been expended on the question of colonising the Holy Land, there is no other practical attempt which can compare in importance with that of the Temple Society. It remains to be seen what the success of the undertaking will be.

The colonists belong entirely to the peasant and mechanical classes, and even their leaders are men comparatively uneducated. As a rule they are hard-working, sober, honest, and sturdy; and, however mystic their religious notions may be, they are essentially shrewd and practical in their dealings with the world. They are a pious and God-fearing people, and their natural domesticity renders it highly improbable that they will ever split on the rock which wrecked the former American colony, whose President, it appears, endeavoured to follow the example of Brigham Young by introducing polygamy. The German colonists have also a fine field for enterprise, in the introduction into Palestine of European improvements, which are more or less appreciated by the natives; and, as they have no other community to compete with, they might be able to make capital of their civilised education. The wine which they sell is comparatively excellent, and finds a ready market, as do also many of their manufactured articles.

Such is one side of the picture, but when we turn to the other, we find elements of weakness, which seem to threaten the existence of the colony.

In the first place, there is apparently no man in

the community of sufficiently superior talent or education, or with the energy and force of character, which would be required to control and develop the enterprise. The genius of Brigham Young triumphed over the almost insuperable difficulties of his audacious undertaking, despite even the prejudice which the establishment of polygamy naturally raised against his disciples. However superior in piety and purity of motive the leaders of the Haifa colony may be, they cannot compare with the Mormon chief in the qualities to which his success was due.

In the second place, the colonists are divided among themselves. In 1875 we found that Herr Hardegg had been deposed (temporarily, I understood, till he changed his views) from the leadership of the colony, and he had been succeeded by Herr Shumacher, a master-stonemason and architect, who is, moreover, the representative of the American Government at Haifa. This deposition of the original leader had caused dissensions among the Germans, and several of the influential members did not attend the Sunday meetings.

To internal troubles external ones were added. The colonists are not favourites either with natives or with Europeans, with Moslems or with Christians. The Turkish Government is quite incapable of appreciating their real motives in colonisation, and cannot see any reason, beyond a political one, for the settlement of Europeans in the country.

The colonists therefore have never obtained title-deeds to the lands they have bought, and there can be little doubt that should the Turks deem it expedient, they would entirely deny the right of the Germans to hold their property. Not only do they extend no favour to the colony, though its presence has been most beneficial to the neighbourhood, but the inferior officials, indignant at the attempts of the Germans to obtain justice, in the courts, without any regard to the "custom of the country" (that is, to bribery), have thrown every obstacle they can devise in the way of the community, both individually and collectively.

The difficulties of the colonists are also increased by the jealousy of the Carmelite monks. The Fathers possess good lands, gradually extending along Carmel round their fortress monastery; they look with disfavour on the encroachments of the Germans, and all the subtlety of Italians is directed against the German interests.

The peculiar views of the colonists, moreover, cause them to be looked on with disfavour by influential Europeans in the country, who might do much to help them. They are regarded as religious visionaries, whose want of worldly wisdom might, at any time, embroil their protectors in difficulties not easily smoothed over.

The community has thus to struggle with a positively hostile government, while it receives no very vigorous support from any one. The difficulties are perfectly well known to the native peasantry, who, with the characteristic meanness of the Syrians, take the opportunity to treat with insolence people whom they believe they can insult with impunity. The property of the colonists is disregarded, the native goatherds drive their beasts into the corn, and several riots have occurred, which resulted in trials from which the colonists got no satisfaction.

The indiscretion of the younger men has brought greater difficulties on the community; they have repaid insolence with summary punishment, and finding no help from the Government, have in many instances taken the law into their own hands. Thus the colony finds itself at feud with the surrounding villages, and the hostile feeling is not unlikely to lead to very serious difficulties on some occasion of popular excitement.

There are other reasons which militate against the idea of the final success of the colony. The Syrian climate is not adapted to Europeans; and year by year it must infallibly tell on the Germans, exposed as they are to sun and miasma. It is true that Haifa is, perhaps, the healthiest place in Palestine, yet even here they suffer from fever and dysentery, and if they should attempt to spread inland, they will find their difficulties from climate increase tenfold.

The children of the present generation will, probably, like those of the Crusading settlers in

Palestine, be inferior in physique and power of endurance to their fathers. Cases of intermarriage with natives have, I believe, already occurred; the children of such marriages are not unlikely to combine the bad qualities of both nations, and may be compared to the Pullani of Crusading times. It seems to me, that it is only by constant reinforcements from Germany that the original character of the colony can be maintained; and the whole community, in Palestine and in Germany, is said not to number more than 5000 persons.

The expectation of the immediate fulfilment of prophecy, has also resulted in the ruin of many of the poorer members of the colony, who, living on their capital, have exhausted it before that fulfilment has occurred. The colony is thus in danger of dissolution, by the gradual absorption of the property into the hands of those who originally possessed the most capital; and in any case it is very likely to lose its original character of Apostolic simplicity, some of the members becoming the servants and hired labourers of others.

The natural desire of those members who find themselves without money, is to make a livelihood by any means in their power. Where every man is thus working separately for himself, the progress of the colony, as a whole, is not unlikely to be forgotten, and the members may very probably be dispersed over Palestine, following their various trades where best they can make money.

Such are the elements of weakness in the society. In ten years it has made comparatively little progress, and ten more may perhaps see the colony decaying. Meantime the settlers might be examples to the natives (if Syrians would condescend to learn) of the advantages of European habits of industry and enterprise under very adverse circumstances. The little village of red-cheeked, flaxen-haired peasants, with cheery salutations, and honest smiling faces, is a pleasant place to visit; the women in their short skirts and brown straw hats, and the men in felt wideawakes and grey cloth, contrast most favourably with the dirty, squalid, lying Fellahin. On the Sunday moonlight nights the sounds of the fine old German hymn tunes may be heard, softened by distance, along the beach, as the rings of men and boys stand chanting in the cool night air. A fresh sea breeze blows all day among the acacia trees which flank the dusty street. The long heavy carts come rumbling by, the horses, harnessed with high-peaked yokes, looking rather light in comparison with German cart-horses in Europe. The flags of the Consulates are hoisted on Sundays, and the whole colony is seen soberly marching down to the meeting-house, where they are weekly comforted, with the assurance that the end will soon come, and the Temple Colony be acknowledged, by God and man, to be the example of the whole world, and the true heir of the Holy Land and of Jerusalem.

The colonists freely allow the difficulties which beset their path. Meanwhile, should European attention be ever generally turned to Syria, it may be a matter of no little importance, that men acquainted with the language and the people, and, at the same time, trustworthy and honest, are to be found, who could render material assistance to new-comers, even though not attracted to the land by the belief that it is the natural inheritance of a true Israel, composed of any other nationality except the Jews.

HAIFA.

CHAPTER XII.

THE FERTILITY OF PALESTINE.

THERE is, apparently, a general impression that the Holy Land is, at the present day, a barren and desolate country, and that a great change, due not only to decay of cultivation and to disappearance of former forests, but also to a material decrease in the rainfall, has come over the land. These last pages are, therefore, devoted to a brief résumé of the facts collected during the prosecution of the Survey, which bear on the question.

Palestine is described in the Pentateuch as "a good land, a land of brooks of water, of fountains, and depths, which spring out of valleys and hills;

a land of wheat, and barley, and vines, and fig-trees, and pomegranates, a land of oil-olive, and honey" (Deut. viii. 7, 8); and these verses epitomise the natural features, and the cultivation of modern, quite as well as of ancient Palestine. Two points, then, should be considered: first, is there any change in the water-supply or climate? secondly, is there any decrease in the amount of woodland and forest?

The question of water-supply lies, indeed, at the bottom of the whole inquiry. We have, unfortunately, no ancient observations which can be compared with those now taken, from which comparison positive information as to the *amount* of the rainfall, and the volume of the rivers, might be deduced; but we have very important indications that the *character* of the water-supply is unchanged.

In the first place, we have geological indications. Throughout the country two formations alternate; namely, a hard crystalline limestone of the Neocomian period, and a soft, porous chalk, or marl, of the Cretaceous epoch. Where the hard limestone prevails springs occur, especially at the juncture with the over-lying, porous, and unconformable chalk; but where there is a great thickness of this latter, the water-supply is either from deep wells, or from artificial tanks and cisterns. We have no reason for supposing the geological formation to have undergone any change since the days of Moses; and indeed we have every reason for judging that the distribution of the springs was then the same as now; for those parts which are now dry and desert—the Negeb, or "dry land," the Jeshimon, or "solitude," the wildernesses of Ziph, Maon, and Bethaven—receive titles in the Bible which are derived from the dry and barren appearance that these districts also presented in earlier times.

Secondly, we find that the Hebrew terms, used to express various kinds of natural or artificial sources of water, are still in use, and of these terms no less than eight refer to tanks, pools, or cisterns: the Hebrew words 'Ain (a spring), Nahr (a perennial stream), Bir (a well), Jubb (a ditch), Hufr (a pit), Birkeh (a tank), Bassah (a marsh), are still ordinary words in the language. The springs mentioned individually in Scripture—the fountains of Samaria, and of Jezreel, of Engedi, and Jericho, for instance, are found to be still plentiful and perennial; and it must not be forgotten that there are twelve considerable streams in the country, which contain water even at the end of the dry season, without counting the Jordan.

Thirdly, the great numbers of ancient tanks and cisterns, occurring in the districts where there are no springs, and in connection with Jewish ruins and Jewish tombs, show the necessity which existed, even at an early period, of storing rainwater for the supply of the towns.

Yet further, we can prove that the character of

the seasons is unchanged. In the Mishna, there are minute directions regarding the prayers to be put up for rain. The supplications commenced in October, and continued until the Passover was finished. Three days of fast occurred in the end of October, if no rain had fallen, and three more about the middle of November. "But if these days of fasting be not heard, then shall they leave off selling and buying, the building of houses and the planting of trees, marrying and giving in marriage, and they shall leave off greeting one another . . . . until the end of the month Nizan (the middle of April). For if no rain be given until then, it is a manifest sign of the curse, since it is said, 'Is it not wheat harvest to-day?'" (Mishna, Taanith I.).

From this extract it is clear that rain was expected in October, at which time the first showers now begin, and was not expected later than the middle of April, when the "latter rain" or spring showers now fall; between these limits the rainy season is continuous, the heaviest storms being in January, and the average annual fall between twenty and thirty inches. It is also recorded that years of drought have, from the earliest times, occurred at intervals (as mentioned in the history of Abraham, or of Jacob, or in the time of Ahab), just as dry years still afflict the country from time to time.

As regards the seasons, and the character and

distribution of the water-supply, natural or artificial, there is thus, apparently, no reason to suppose that any change has occurred; and with respect to the annual rainfall, it is only necessary to note that, were the old cisterns cleaned and mended, and the beautiful tanks and aqueducts repaired, the ordinary fall would be quite sufficient, for the wants of the inhabitants, and for irrigation.

The climate has, however, to all appearance materially changed for the worse. The plains of Jericho are no longer a "region fit for gods," and the climate of the maritime plains, in autumn, is little less than deadly; but this would indicate, not a decrease, but, if anything, an increase, in the amount of rain, as the miasma is due to stagnant water collecting in marshes and pools. The main cause of the malarious nature of the climate, seems to be the neglect of proper drainage. The splendid works of the Romans are in ruins; the great rock-cuttings, which let out to the sea the water now soaking in the marshes of Sharon, are filled up with earth; Herod's aqueducts, which irrigated the plains of Jericho, are destroyed, and no attempt is ever made to enforce sanitary regulations, or to promote public drainage or irrigation works.

Turning next to the question of the decrease of timber, it is important first to obtain a clear idea of the character of the old vegetation described in the Bible. It will then appear that the change is not one of kind, but only of degree.

The ordinary words, used in the Hebrew of the Old Testament, for the wild growth of the country are three—Choresh, Jaar, and Etz, none of which are now employed in the modern nomenclature. Choresh means "tangled," and would thus apply to copse, rather than to timber-forest; Jaar signifies "luxuriant," and would also refer to thickets of dwarf trees and of shrubs, quite as well as to forest trees; Etz is a "strong tree," but this does not imply that the tree forms one of a large number, for the word is often used of single trees.

The wild growth of the country now consists generally of single trees, and of scrub or copse. In Galilee there are good-sized trees, but none in Judea, excepting solitary sacred oaks and terebinths, sycamores, and carob trees. The western slopes of the watershed are thickly clothed, with dark lentisk bushes, dwarf oak, spurge laurels, hawthorn, and a variety of other shrubs, which spread over the ridges, and form in parts an impenetrable tangle. There is every reason to suppose that this is the kind of vegetation which, in the earlier times, existed in uncultivated districts, for it seems unlikely that there was ever any greater thickness of soil on the ridges, such as would be required for forest trees.

It must not, however, be supposed that Palestine is entirely devoid of woods. A thick forest of oak extends between Carmel and Nazareth, with underwood below the trees in parts. An open woodland occurs on the low hills south of Carmel, and in the northern part of the plain of Sharon—remains of the "mighty wood" of Strabo, and the "Forest of Assur" of the twelfth century; from these oaks, according to some scholars, Sharon takes its name, and they form some of the prettiest scenery in the Holy Land.

There are indications, throughout the country, of a certain amount of local change in the wild growth, and also of a decrease in the number of trees. The old wine-presses and towers, on Carmel, and in other parts, are now found in the middle of copses, which have evidently spread over ancient cultivated districts; but, on the other hand, there are at present no forest laws, and the peasants hew and even burn down the trees for firewood (Hatab), or cut off the roots (Kormah), which are dug up and also sold for burning; this wanton, and wasteful, annual destruction of the trees, cannot fail to have materially affected the appearance of the land.

The watershed of the country forms the limit of the thickets; the western slopes, exposed to the fresh sea-breeze, are covered with shrubs, the eastern are bare and desert; this natural phenomenon is no doubt unchangeable, and a minute examination of the country tends to show that the eastern districts, which are now without wood, were also treeless in Bible times.

The change in productiveness which has really

occurred in Palestine is due to decay of cultivation, to decrease of population, and to bad government. It is man, and not Nature, who has ruined the good land in which was "no lack," and it is therefore within the power of human industry, to restore the country, to its old condition of agricultural prosperity.

Throughout Palestine the traces of former cultivation are well marked. The ancient vineyards are recognisable by the rock-cut wine-presses, and the old watchtowers are found hidden in the encroaching copse. The great terraces carved out of the soft marl hillsides, or laboriously built up, with stone retaining-walls, as in Italy, are still there, though they are often quite uncultivated, and grow only thistles and thorns, which, by their luxuriance, attest the natural richness of the soil.

The population of the land is insufficient; and it has been calculated that Palestine might support ten times its present total of inhabitants, if fully tilled, even though in the rude and primitive manner of the peasantry only; and that the plains of Sharon and Philistia might, under a proper system of irrigation, become an important corn-growing country. The soil is as good as ever, the crops are, even now, very fine in the cultivated parts: all, therefore, that is wanted is the men and the money to work the land.

The following statements with regard to the present commerce of the country, are taken from an able report by Consul Jago, which was published in 1873, and they include the most reliable details which I have been able to collect.

The Wâly of Syria governs 26,000 square miles, having under him eight Mutaserefliks: namely, Damascus, Jerusalem, Acre, Hamah, Tripoli, Beyrout, the Belka and the Hauran.

The population can only be approximately estimated, as no census is taken, and because every village and town endeavours to conceal its numbers so as to escape taxation. The population of Syria is thought to be about 2,250,000, the principal towns being as follow: Damascus, 175,000; Beyrout, 70,000 (of whom two-thirds are Christians); Jerusalem, 21,000; Jaffa, 8000; Nâblus, 13,000; Acre, 8000; Hebron, 9000; Haifa, 4000; Gaza, 18,000; and Sidon, 10,000. The average of a country village is about 500 souls or rather less.

The majority of the population is Moslem, probably in the proportion of two-thirds, even though counting the large Christian district of Lebanon. The Druses number some 110,000, inclusive of those east of Jordan; the Jews are stated at 40,000 in the whole of Syria; the large majority of the Christians belong to the Greek Church.

The exports of the country are silk, cotton, wool, oil, sesame, millet, maize, wheat, barley, tobacco, madder, sponges, and fruit. The silk is made in Lebanon, and mulberries planted near Beyrout yield two crops, one used for the silkworms, the second for fodder; the wool is purchased from the Bedawîn, especially at Nâblus; the oil is one of the most valuable productions of the country, being of very fine quality, especially that from Nâblus, Nazareth, Sidon, and Safed: 1800 tons were exported in 1871. Half the produce of the oliveyards is made into soap, about a quarter is eaten, and the rest exported. Sesame is another important production, and oil (which is sold for olive oil) is manufactured from it in France. Tobacco comes from the Lebanon district; cotton has never been as yet very successfully grown; a large amount of hemp is annually used up in making rope, and the value of the sponges fished along the coast is said to amount to nearly £1600 every year. The country is fitted for the growth of indigo and of sugar-cane, whilst its fruits, including grapes, figs, melons, bananas, pomegranates, apricots, plums, pears, and apples, oranges, lemons, and dates, are even now plentiful and of good quality.

The imports which find their way into Palestine vary greatly at different times, being chiefly cheap and inferior articles, such as calicoes, cotton, and ironwork, spirits, glass, and hardware, the total amount being about £1,000,000 annually. The want of harbours, and of any encouragement to trade, leaves the country almost without a market. The taxation of raw products, is also said to have killed the native industry of Palestine, and only one attempt has of late been made at mining, namely, near Sidon, where coal (though of inferior quality), was discovered, with copper and tin. Coal was also found in Lebanon, but the works were abandoned after 12,000 tons had been obtained.

Such is the present condition of Palestine—a good country running to waste for want of proper cultivation : truly may it be said, "a fruitful land maketh He barren for the wickedness of them that dwell therein."

There is but one fundamental cause for the ruined condition of the country, namely, the corrupt and inefficient system of government : so long as there is no stability in the upper ranks, and so long as the Governor of Syria is changed each time a Grand Vizier falls, so long will the subordinates be venal and tyrannical, and every attempt at bettering the condition of Palestine will be doomed to final failure.

Attention has been especially directed of late years to the question of colonising the Holy Land. In the last chapter the history of the German colonies has been traced, but these are not the only experiments which have been made. One of the most practical suggestions put forward, was the idea that the Mughrabee Jews might succeed in establishing themselves as agriculturists; but the writer was apparently not aware that this has actually been tried, and has failed. In 1850 there were thirty families of these Jews at Shefa 'Amr in Lower Galilee, north-west of Nazareth, cultivating corn and olives on their own ground: but they gradually relinquished the task, and removed to Haifa where they engaged in trade; for, as the Jews themselves say, agriculture is not their vocation, and it must not be forgotten that their forefathers no sooner became possessed of the land, than they made "hewers of wood and drawers of water" of its primary inhabitants.

At Jaffa also many colonies have been started, the place being convenient from its position on the coast. There is an institution still in existence called the Mikveh Israel, or Agricultural Institution of the Universal Jewish Alliance, cultivating 780 acres, with the object of training children as market-gardeners, and of educating them at a school on the property. The native peasantry are employed, but there is a strong opposition to the institution among the surrounding villagers. It is said that 100,000 plants have been reared in the nurseries, and half a million of vines; but the land is close to the ever-encroaching sand-dunes, which are computed to be advancing inland at the rate of a yard, or even two yards, every year.

By far the most successful experiments yet made have included the employment of the native peasantry. It must not be forgotten that the present climate is quite unsuited to European constitutions, and for this reason all attempts to till the soil, by the employment of European labourers, are destined to certain failure. The plains in autumn are deadly, and the hill climate is not much better. Unseasoned to the fierce heat of the sun, and to the dryness of the climate, a European peasant will certainly fall a prey, sooner or later, to the fever of the country.

The native peasantry are a hardy and naturally energetic race, capable of enduring the climate, to which they are accustomed from their birth; and if directed by capable men, who understand them, and have authority to deal with them, they may be made to work well. The good mining work performed by the men of Siloam, under Captain Warren, is proof of the capacity of the native peasantry for hard work, under competent direction.

The northern half of the plain of Esdraelon belongs to the Greek banking firm of Sursuk, who have factors (generally native Christians) in their various villages. The productiveness of this part of the country has increased, in a most marked manner, ever since the change of ownership has occurred.

Probably the most successful undertaking of an agricultural kind in Palestine is the farm at Abu Shûsheh, belonging to the Bergheims, the principal banking firm in Jerusalem.

The lands of Abu Shûsheh belong to this family, and include 5000 acres; a fine spring exists on the east, but in other respects the property is not exceptional. The native inhabitants are employed to till the land according to the native method, under the supervision of Mr. Bergheim's sons; a farmhouse has been built, a pump erected, and various modern improvements have been gradually introduced.

It is by these means, and not by any invasion of foreign agriculturists, that Palestine might most easily be reclaimed, and might become a rival in fertility even to the most fruitful parts of southern Italy, to which, in the character of its productions and cultivation, it is very similar.

The same hindrance is, however, experienced by the Bergheims which has paralysed all other efforts at improvement in the land. The difficulties raised by the venal and corrupt under-officials of the Government, have been vexatious and incessant, being due to their determination to extort money by some means or other, or else to ruin the enterprise from which they could gain nothing. The Turkish Government recognises the right of foreigners to hold land, subject to the ordinary laws and taxes, but there is a long step between this abstract principle and the practical encouragement of such undertakings, and nothing is easier than to raise groundless difficulties, on the subject of title or of assessment, in a land where the judges are as corrupt as the rest of the governing body.

There must be a radical reform in government, before anything can be done to restore Palestine to its former condition. The undertaking is beyond the power of either private individuals or of semi-religious societies, for it involves the entire opening up of the country, and the creation of public works, which have as yet no existence.

The first requisite would be the construction of roads, for there is not a mile of made road in the land from Dan to Beersheba. This would be a work of comparatively little difficulty; the engineering may be said to have been already done by the Romans, and all that is required is the remaking of the old highways. The streams are narrow, and easily bridged, and the metalling could be accomplished with material ready to hand, namely, the hard limestone and beautiful flint-rock which abounds throughout the hills. It is extraordinary, however, to observe, that even the Romans do not seem to have drained their roads, and to this defect the final destruction of the ancient causeways is no doubt due. Until roads have been made, transport by wheeled vehicles will remain impossible, and the very rudiments of proper communication are thus wanting.

The next great public works would be for irrigation. The lands now covered with pestilent swamp would be reclaimed, and the water would be carried away through the old rocky tunnels made by the great engineers of former times; the climate would probably be sensibly affected, and drought would be almost unknown as soon as the ancient tanks and cisterns had been cleared and repaired. The old aqueducts might be mended, and the complicated network in the Jordan Valley restored; the cultivation of tropical fruits and vegetables would then become possible, in the Ghôr, at least by the use of negro labour, which would be easily obtained.

The third great undertaking would be the planting of the country. Forest laws must be enacted and rigorously enforced, in order to save the natural growth of the hills; the plantation, first of quickly growing grass and then of Indian fig and pines, is required to check the advance of the sand, and finally to reclaim the good soil buried beneath it. The climate of the plains would also, no doubt, be improved by the growth of trees suited to the situation, and the long tract north of Jaffa, now covered with the stumps of a former forest, is, no doubt, capable of supporting timber, such as exists farther north.

Sanitary laws must also not be forgotten, for the unhealthy character of the towns and villages is due almost entirely to the filthiness of the inhabitants.

Such is a slight sketch of the future which might be possible for Palestine; but the formation of a strong, wise, and benevolent government is the first requisite, and without this all partial attempts will effect nothing towards the restoration of the country.

The native population are quite as well aware of these facts, as any one from more civilised lands can be; they lay the blame of their misery on the shoulders of their rulers, and are only too anxious to pass into other hands. There is a very general belief that the land is destined to become once more the property of the Christians, and the Fellahîn often inquire of visitors when this time is to come. It may be that they flatter the vanity of an Englishman, when they declare a preference for an English occupation of the country; but the expression, Kelim Inglecz, "an Englishman's word" (to which I have formerly referred), shows clearly the high esteem in which our English countrymen stand, and reflects the highest credit on our Consuls, and on others, who, by their probity and energy, have created this high public opinion of a nation which is represented by so few individuals.

The happiest future which could befall Palestine seems to me to be its occupation by some strong European power, which might recognise the value of the natural resources pointed out above; but until some such change occurs, the good land must remain a desolation.

"And thorns shall come up in her palaces, nettles and brambles in the fortresses thereof, and it shall be an habitation of dragons, and a court for owls" (Isa. xxxiv. 13).

SKETCH MAP OF PALESTINE.

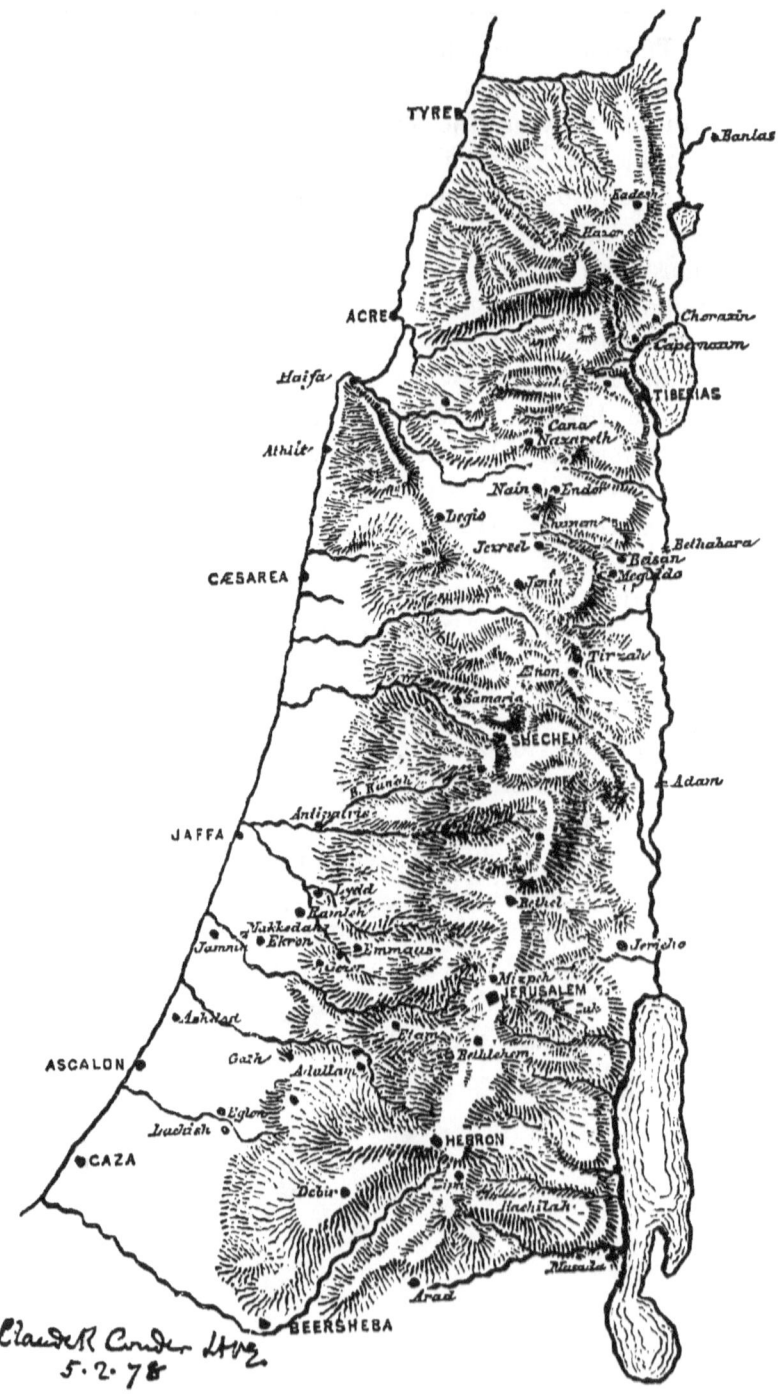

APPENDIX A.

INDEX OF PLACES WEST OF JORDAN MENTIONED IN THE BIBLE AND THE APOCRYPHA.

THE following index of 622 places west of Jordan will, it is hoped, be found pretty exhaustive. Some of the names occurring in the lists of Chronicles and Ezra are omitted, when it is doubtful whether they are names of places or of persons.

The Hebrew names, in italics, are those of places beyond the limits of the Survey. The Arabic names in italics are places for which identifications are proposed, resulting from the Survey work, which, as far as I have been able to discover in the course of study, were previously unknown. It may of course be that, in some work to which I have not had access, similar identifications have been made by others, but the present index is the result of four years of study, and of the information gathered from some fifty standard works on Palestine.

The discoveries elucidating non-Biblical topography in Palestine, made during the Survey work, are quite as numerous as those here given, but will possess less interest to the general reader, with the exception of the list given in Appendix B. They include sites mentioned in the Onomasticon, in the Early Christian and Jewish Pilgrimages, in the Crusading Chronicles, in the Samaritan Chronicles, in Egyptian and Assyrian records, in the Talmud, or in Josephus. Some of the most interesting of these are mentioned in the text of the present work.

It is of course impossible in this appendix, to explain in all cases the reasons for the identifications. The similarity of name is sometimes much closer than appears in the English spelling: *e.g.*, the word *Hudhîreh* is identical in radical letters and meaning, with the Hebrew Hazor, as would appear if both were spelt as they might be, *Hatzer*. It is unnecessary to say that the sites are in all cases, as far as I have been able to make out, suitable, in relative position as regards other places mentioned in connection with them. The name is naturally the deciding indication, and in cases where the name is not radically the same, the reasons which lead to the proposed identification will generally be found in the text of the present work.

It will be seen that out of a total of 622 names 434 are now identified with reasonable certainty, a proportion of more than two-thirds of the whole. And that out of 434 known places 172 are discoveries due to the Survey, a proportion of two-fifths of the whole number identified. This cannot but be considered a very satisfactory result of the Survey work.

Hebrew.	Arabic.	Hebrew.	Arabic.
Abdon	'Abdeh	Anathoth	'Anâta
Abel B. Maacha	Abîl Kumh	Anem	'Anin
Abel Meholah	'Ain Helweh	Aner	'Ellâr
Abez	el Beida	Anim	el Ghuwein
Accho	'Akka	Antipatris	Râs el 'Ain
Aceldama	Hak ed Dumm	Aphek (1)	Tell el Fikieh
Achor (Valley)	W. Kelt	Aphek (2)	Fukûa
Achshaph	el Yâsif	Aphek (3)	
Achzib (1)	er Zib	Aphekah	
Achzib (2)	'Ain Kezbeh	Arab	er Rabîyeh
Adadah	'Ad'adah	Arad	Tell 'Arâd
Adam	ed Dâmieh	Arbela	Irbid
Adamah	Admah	Archi	'Ain 'Arîk
Adami	ed Dâmieh	Arimathæa	
Adar		Aroer	'Ara'rah
Adasa	'Adaseh	Arumah	
Adida	Hadîtheh	Ashan (1)	'Aseileh
Adithaim		Ashan (2)	Hesheth
Admah	ed Dâmieh	Ashdod	Esdûd
Adoraim	Dûra	Asher	'Asireh
Adullam	'Aîd el Ma	Ashkelon	'Askelân
Adummim	Talât ed Dumm	Ashnah (1)	Ghasheina
Ænon	'Ainûn	Ashnah (2)	
Ahlab	el Jish	Asphar (Pool)	
Ai	Haiyân	Ataroth	Tell et Trûny
Aiath	Haiyân	Ataroth Adar	ed Dârieh
Aijalon (1)	Yâlo	Athach	
Aijalon (2)		Aven	Beitîn
Ain	Umm er Ru-	Avim	
Akrabbim	[mâmîn	Aza (Mt.)	Bîr ez Zeit
Alammelech		Azekah	
Alemeth	'Almît	Azmaveth	Hizmeh
Allon Bachrth	'Attâra	Azmon	
Almon	'Almît	Aznoth Tabor	
Aloth	'Alia	Azzah	Ghŭzzeh
Amad		Baal	Umm Baghleh
Amam		Baalah	Sôba
Ammah (Hill)		Baalah (Mt.)	
Anab	'Anâb	Baalath	Bel'ain
Anaharath	en Nâûrah	Baalath Beer	

APPENDIX A.

HEBREW.	ARABIC.	HEBREW.	ARABIC.
Baal Hamon	Belâmeh	Bath Pazzez	
Baal Hazor	Tell 'Asûr	Beth Phage	
Baal Hermon	Jebel esh Sheikh	Beth Rapha	
Baal Shalisha	Kefr Thilth	Beth Rehob	
Baah Tamar	'Attâra	Beth Saida	
Bahurim		Beth Samos	Hizmeh
Balah	Umm Baghleh	Beth Shean	Beisân
Bath Zacharias	Beit Iskâria	Beth Shemesh(1)	'Ain Shems
Bealoth		Beth Shemesh(2)	'Ain esh Shem-
Beer Lahai Roi			*siyeh*
Beeroth	Bîreh	Beth Shemesh(3)	
Beersheba	Bîr es Seb'a	Beth Shitta	
Belmen	Belâmeh	Bethsura	Beit Sûr
Beneberak	Ibn Ibrak	Beth Tappuah	Tuffûh
Berachah	Breikût	Bethuel	Beit Aula
Berea	Bireh	Bethulia	Mithilia
Bered	Bereid	Betonestham	
Besor (Brook)		Bezek (1)	Ibzik
Betane	Beit 'Ainûn	Bezek (2)	Bezkah
Beten	el Bâneh	Bezeth	Beit Zâta
Beth Eked	Beit Kâd	Bileam	Belâmeh
Beth Haggan	Jenîn	Bir Zavith	
Beth Anath	'Ainatha	Bizjothjah	
Beth Anoth	Beit 'Ainûn	Bohan (Stone)	
Bethabara	'Abâra	Bozez (Rock)	el Hosn
Bethany	el 'Aziriyeh	Bozkath	
Beth Arabah		Cabbon	Kubeibeh
Beth Arbel		Cabul	Kâbûl
Bethaven	Beitîn	Cæsarea	Kaisârieh
Beth Azmaveth	Hizmeh	Cæsarea Philippi	Bâniâs
Beth Barah		Cain	Yekin
Beth Basi		Cana	Kefr Kenna
Beth Birei	Bireh	Capernaum	Minieh
Beth Car	'Ain Kârim	Caphar Salama	Sâlim
Beth Dagon (1)	Beit Dejan	Caphenatha	
Beth Dagon (2)	Tell Dâûk	Carem	'Ain Kârim
Bethel	Beitîn	Carmel	Kŭrmŭl
Bethemek		Carmel (Mt.)	Jebel Kŭrmŭl
Bether	Bittîr	Cedron	Katrah
Bethesda	'Ain Umm Deraj	Cedron (Brook)	Wâdy en Nâr
Bethezel		Charashim	Hirsha
Beth Gader	Jedûr	(Valley)	
Beth Haccerem		Caphar Haa-	
Beth Hogla	'Ain Hajlah	monai	
Beth Horon	Beit 'Ur	Chephirah	Kefîreh
Beth Lebaoth		Cherith (Brook)	
Bethlehem (1)	Beit Lahm	Chesalon	Kesla
Bethlehem (2)	Beit Lahm	Chesil	
Beth Mareaboth		Chesulloth	Iksâl
Beth Palet		Chezib	'Ain Kezbeh

Hebrew.	Arabic.	Hebrew.	Arabic.
Chidon		En Haddah	Kefr Adán
Chinnereth	el Ghuweir	En Hakkore	'Ayûn Kára
Chisloth Tabor	Iksâl	En Hazor	Hazîreh
Choba	el Mekhobby	En Mishphat	
Chor Ashan	'Aseileh	En Rimmon	Umm er Rumâmin
Chorazin	Kerâzeh		
Chozeba	Kueiziba	En Rogel	'Ain Umm Deraj
Chusi	Kûzah		
Cola	Kaáûn	En Shemesh	'Ain Haud
Culon	Kolônia	En Tappuah	
Cyamon	Tell Keimûn	Ephes Dammim	Beit Fased
Dabbasheth		Ephraim	Taiyibeh
Daberath	Debûrieh	Ephratah	Beit Lahm
Dalmanutha		Ephron (Mt.)	
Dan	Tell el Kâdy	Esdraelon	Zer'in
Danjaan	Dâniân	Esek (Well)	
Dannah	Idhnah	Eshcol	
Debir (1)	Dhâkeriyeh	Eshean	es Simia
Debir (2)		Eshtaol	Eshû'a
Diblath	Dibil	Eshtemoa	Es Semû'a
Dilean		Esora	'Asîreh
Dimnah	Rummâneh	Etam (1)	'Aitân
Dimonah		Etam (2)	'Ain 'Atân
Docus	'Ain Dûk	Etam (Rock)	Beit 'Atáb
Dor	Tantûra	Ether	'Atr
Dothan	Tell Dôthân	Ezel (Stone)	
Dumah	Dômeh	Ezem	
Ebal (Mt.)	Jebel Eslamîyeh	Gaash (Hill)	
Ebenezer	Deir Abân	Galem	Beit Jâla
Ed (Altar)		Gallim	Beit Jâla
Edar (Tower)		Gareb	
Eder	'Adâr	Gath	Tell es Sâfy
Edrei	Yater	Gath Hepher	el Mesh-hed
Eglon	'Ajlân	Gath Rimmon	
Ekrebel	'Akrabeh	Gaza	Ghŭzzeh
Ekron	'Akir	Gazara	Tell Jezer
Elah (Valley)	Wâdy es Sunt	Geba	Jeb'a
Eleasa	Ilása	Gebim	
Eleph		Gederah (1)	Jedireh (1)
Elon	Beit Ello	Gederah (2)	Katrah
Elon B. Hanan	Beit 'Anân	Gederoth	Jedireh (2)
Eltekeh	Beit Likia	Gedor	Jedûr
Eltekon		Gelilloth	Jiljûlieh
Eltolad		Gennesaret	el Ghuweir
Emmaus	'Amwâs	Gilead (Mt.)	Jálûd
Enam	'Alin	Gerar	Umm el Jerâr
Endor	Andûr	Gerizim	Jebel et Tôr
En gannim (1)	Jenîn	Gethsemane	
En gannim (2)	Umm Jina	Gezer	Tell Jezer
Engedi	'Ain Jidy	Giah	

APPENDIX A. 337

Hebrew.	Arabic.	Hebrew.	Arabic.
Gibbethon	Kibbieh	Hebron (2)	'Abdeh
Gibeah (Saul)	Jebá	Helbah	
Gibeah (1)	Jebîa	Helbon	Helbôn
Gibeah (2)	Jeb'a	Heleph	Beit Lîf
Gibeah (Phinehas)	'Awertah	Helkath	
		Helkath Hazzurim	W. el 'Askar
Gibeon	el Jîb		
Gidom		Hepher	el Mesh-hed
Gihon	Silwân	Heres (Mt.)	Kefr Hâris
Gilboa (Mt.)	Jelbôn	Hermon	Jebel esh Sheikh
Gilgal (1)	Jiljûlieh (1)	Heshmon	
Gilgal (2)	Jiljilia	Hezron	Umm Kheshram
Gilgal (of Goim)	Jiljûlieh (2)	Hinnom (Valley)	Wâdy en Nâr
Giloh	Jála	Holon	Beit 'Alâm
Gimzo	Jimzû	Horem	Hûrah
Gittaim		Hormah	Hôrân
Goath		Hosah	'Ozzîyeh
Gob		Hukkok	Yâkûk
Golgotha	el Heidhemîyeh	Hukok	
Gomorrah	'Amrîyeh	Humtah	
Goshen		Ibleam	Belámeh
Goshen (Land)		Idalah	ed Dâlieh
Gur		Iim	
Hachilah (Hill)	el Kôlah	Ijon	Khiyâm
Hadad Rimmon	Rummâneh	Ir Nahash	Deir Nakhkhâs
Hadashah		Iron	Yârûn
Hadattah (Hazor)	Hazzârah	Irpeel	Râ-fât
		Ir Shemesh	'Ain esh Shems
Hadid	Hadîtheh	Ittah Kazin	
Halak (Mt.)		Ithnan	
Halhul	Halhûl	Jabneel (1)	Yebnah
Hali	'Alia	Jabneel (2)	Yemma
Hammath	el Hûmmâm	Jagur	
Hammon	'Ain Hammûl	Janoah	Yanûh
Hammoth Dor	el Hummâm	Janohah	Yânûn
Hananiah	Beit Hanina	Janum	Beni Naim
Hannathon	Kefr 'Anân	Japhia	Yâfa
Haphraim	el Farrîyeh	Japhleti	
Hareth	Kharâs	Jarmuth (1)	Yermûk
Harod (Spring)	'Ain el Jemm'in	Jarmuth (2)	Râmeh
Harosheth	Harithîyeh	Jattir	'Attir
Hazar Addar		Jearim (Mt.)	'Armah
Hazar Gaddah	Judeideh	Jebusi	el Kuds
Hazar Shual		Jehosaphat (Valley)	Wâdy en Nâr
Hazar Susim	Beit Sâsîn		
Hazezon Tamar	'Ain Jidy	Jehud	el Yehûdiyeh
Hazor (1)	Hudhîreh	Jericho	'Ain es Sultân
Hazor (2)	Hazzûr	Jeruel (Wilderness)	
Hazor Hadattah	Hazzârah		
Hebron (1)	el Khŭlil	Jerusalem	el Kuds

HEBREW.	ARABIC.	HEBREW.	ARABIC.
Jeshanah	'Ain Sinia	Lod (Lydda)	Ludd
Jeshimon	el Bukei'a	Luz (1)	Beitîn
Jeshua	S'awi	Luz (2)	Luweizeh
Jethlah	Beit Tûl	Maarath	Beit Ummar
Jezreel (1)	Zer'in	Machpelah	el Haram
Jezreel (2)		Madmannah	Umm Deimneh
Jiphtah		Madmenah	
Jiphtah El (Valley)		Madon	Madîn
Jokdeam		Magdala	Mejdel
Jokmeam		Mahaneh Dan	
Jokneam	Tell Keimûn	Makaz	
Joktheel		Makkedah	el Mŭghâr
Joppa	Yâfa	Mamre	
Juttah	Yutta	Manahath	Málhah
Kabzeel		Manocho	Mâlhah
Kanah	Kâna	Maon	Tell M'aîn
Kanah (Valley)	Wâdy Kûnah	Maralah	
Karkaa		Mareshah	el Mer'ash
Kartah		Maroth	
Kartan		Masaloth	
Kattath		Mearah	
Kadesh Barnea		Megiddo	Mujedda
Kedesh (1)	Kades	Megiddon (Valley)	Wâdy Jâlûd
Kedesh (2)	Tell Abu Kadeis	Mejarkon	W. el 'Aujeh
Kedesh (3)	Kadish	Mekonah	
Keilah	Kila	Meonenim (Plain)	Mŭkhnah
Kerioth (Hezron)	Umm Kheshram	Merom (Lake)	el Hûleh
Kezez (Valley)		Meroz	
Kibzaim		Michmash	Mukhmâs
Kinah		Michmethath	
Kirjath	Kuriet el 'Anab	Middin	
Kirjathaim		Migdal-el	Mujeidel
Kirjath Arba	el Khŭlîl	Migdal Gad	Mejdel
Kirjath Baal	Sôba	Migron	W. Suweinît
Kirjath Jearim	Sôba	Misrephoth Maim	Surafend
Kirjath Sannah	Dhâherîyeh	Mizpeh (1)	Sh'afât
Kirjath Sepher	Dhâherîyeh	Mizpeh (2)	
Kishion		Mizpeh (Valley)	
Kishon (River)	el Mŭkŭtt'a	Mochmur (Brook)	W. el Ahmar
Kithlish		Modin	el Medyeh
Lachish	Tell el Hesy	Moladah	
Lahmam	el Lahm	Moreh (Plain)	Mŭkhnah
Laish	Bâniâs	Moreh (Hill)	
Lakum		Moreshah Gath	
Lasharon	Sârôna	Moriah	el Haram
Lebaoth		Mozah	Beit Mizzeh
Lebonah	Lubben		
Libnah			

APPENDIX A.

HEBREW.	ARABIC.	HEBREW.	ARABIC.
Naamah	Na'aneh	Rimmon (1)	Rummâneh
Naaran	el 'Aûjeh	Rimmon (2)	Umm er Ruma- mîn
Naarath	el 'Aûjeh		
Nachon		Rimmon (Rock)	Rummôn
Nahalal	M'alûl	Salcah	
Nain	Nein	Salim	Sâlim
Nasor (Plain)		Salmon (Mt.)	Jeb. Sh. Selmân
Nazareth	en Nâsirah	Salt (City)	Tell el Milh
Neah		Sansannah	Beit Sûsîn
Neballat	Beit Nebâla	Saphir	Sûâfîr
Nebo	Nûba	Sarepta	Surafend
Neiel	Yânin	Sarid	Tell Shadûd
Nekeb	Sciyâdeh	Scythopolis	Beisân
Nephtoah	Lifta	Secacah	Sikkeh
Netophah	Umm Tôba	Sechu	Suweikeh
Nezib	Beit Nusib	Seir (Mt.)	Bâtn es Saghîr
Nibshan		Seirath	
Nob	Sh'afât	Sela Ham Mah- lekoth	W. Mâlaky
Olivet	Jebel et Tôr		
Ophni		Senaah	
Ophrah (1)	Taiyibeh	Seneh (Rock)	W. Suweinit
Ophrah (2)	Ferâta	Shaalbim	Selbit
Oreb (Rock)		Shaaraim	S'aireh
Parah	Fârah	Shahazimah	Tell Sh. Kâsim
Perez Uzzah		Shalem	Sâlim
Phagor	Beit Faghûr	Shalem (Land)	
Pirathon	Fer'on	Shalisha (Land)	Kefr Thilth
Ptolemais	'Akka	Shamir (1)	Sômerah
Rabbah	Rabba	Shamir (2)	
Rabbith	Râba	Sharon (Plain)	Sahel Yâfa
Rachal		Sharuhen	Tell esh Sherî'ah
Rakkath	Tabarîya	Shaveh (Vale)	
Rakkon	Tell er Rakkeit	Shechem	Nâblus
Ramah (1)	er Râm	Sheba	
Ramah (2)	Râmia	Shebarim	
Ramah (of South)		Shema	
		Shen	
Ramath Lehi	'Ayûn Kâra	Shicron	
Ramathaim Zophim		Shihon	'Ayûn Sh'ain
		Shihor Libnath	Wâdy Shaghûr
Ramathem		Shilhim	
Ramoth	Râmeh	Shiloh	Seilûn
Rehob (1)		Shimron	Semûnieh
Rehob (2)		Shimron Meron	Semûnieh
Rehoboth	Ruheibeh	Shochoh (1)	Shuweikeh (1)
Rekem		Shochoh (2)	Shuweikeh (2)
Remeth	Râmeh	Shunem	Sûlem
Rephaim (Valley)		Siddim (Vale)	el Ghôr
		Sidon	Saida
Riblah		Siloam	Silwân

Hebrew	Arabic	Hebrew	Arabic
Siphmoth		Zaanaim	*Bessûm*
Sirah (Well)	'Ain Sârah	Zanoah (1)	Zanûh
Sitnah (Well)		Zanoah (2)	*Z'anûta*
Sodom		Zarephath	Surafend
Sores (Thebes)	Sarîs	Zaretan	
Sorek (Valley)	Sûrik	Zartanah	*Tell es Sârem*
Succoth		Zeboim	
Sychar	'Askar	Zeboim Valley	Shukh ed Dub'a
Taanach	T'annuk	Zebulon	
Taanath Shiloh	*Th'ala*	Zeeb ("hollow	
Tabor (Mt.)	Jebel et Tôr	place of")	
Tabor (Plain)		Zelah	*Rummôn*
Tamar		Zelzah	
Tappuah	Tuffûh	Zemaraim	es Sumra
Tappuah Enam		Zemaraim (Mt.)	
Tappuah (Land)		Zenan	
Taralah		Zephath	*Sueifât*
Tatam		Zephathah	
Tekoa	Tekû'a	(Valley)	
Telem		Zer	
Thamnatha	Tibneh	Zereda	*Surdah*
Thebez	Tûbâs	Zeredathah	*Tell es Sârem*
Thether	*Bittîr*	Zererath	
Tiberias	Tabarîya	Ziddim	Hattîn
Timnah (1)	Tibnah	Ziklag	
Timnah (2)	*Tibneh*	Zior	S'aîr
Timnah (3)	*Tibna*	Ziph (1)	Tell er Zîf
Timnath Heres	*Kefr Hâris*	Ziph (2)	
Tirzah	*Teiâsîr*	Ziz (Cliff)	el Husâsah
Tyre	Sûr	Zoheleth(Stone)	Zahweileh
Yemini (Land)		Zoreah	Sûr'ah
Ummah	*Ummich*	Zuph	*Shûfa*
Uzzen Sherah	Beit Sira		

APPENDIX B.

THE BATTLE OF MEGIDDO.

By far the most important illustration of the Biblical geography, in modern times, is that supplied by the decipherment of the Hieroglyphic inscriptions on the walls of the Temple of Karnak in Egypt.

These inscriptions give the history of the conquests of the great monarch Thothmes III., who lived before the time of Joshua, and made an expedition into Palestine. The whole account of his marches and victories is recorded on the walls of the Temple, and a list of the cities he conquered is thrice repeated in different parts. Thus, not only do we see before our eyes the names as written by the sculptor thirty-four centuries ago, but the comparison of the different copies seems to eliminate the chance of any ancient clerical error which might have been made by the Egyptian scribe.

In these geographical lists, published by Mariette Bey in 1875, we are at once interested to find that many well-known Bible names occur, and a further study shows that a large proportion of the captured towns are to be found noticed in the Old Testament, and that the order of the lists shows the position indicated to be that which may be separately deduced from the Bible narrative. The list is older than the date of the Book of Joshua, for the conquests of Thothmes III. appear to have been made before the Exodus. Thus it is the ancient Canaanite nomenclature, adopted afterwards by the conquerors under Joshua, which we find preserved in the very handwriting of some Egyptian sculptor, who must have lived before that conquest had been effected.

The plain of Sharon appears, at this period, to have been under Egyptian control, and it was in it that Thothmes assembled his army. The object of the expedition, undertaken in the twenty-second year of the King's reign, was the conquest of Magedi and Kadeshu, which are supposed to be Megiddo and Kadesh, and the tablet known as the "battle of Megiddo," also from the walls of Karnak, describes this invasion and the spoils which were taken. The King's army advanced to a fortress called Aaruna, and reached Kaina, south of Megiddo, which they took on the following day. The list of names indicates that the expedition afterwards crossed over Jordan and went as far as Damascus. Aaruna and Kaina are not identified with certainty, but they seem most probably to be the present 'Arâneh and K'aûn, the first immediately east of the plain of Esdraelon, the second in the Jordan Valley a few miles south of Mujedd'a, where I have proposed to place Megiddo.

The route thus followed by Thothmes III. is the same afterwards taken by Necho; and his great battle at Megiddo preceded that in which Josiah was slain.

We may go yet further and say that if any important battle be fought in Palestine in future times it is at Megiddo, or in its neighbourhood, that it is likely to occur, in fact, "Ar-Mageddon" is a military probability in case of a contest in the Holy Land. The same physical causes which led to the two former battles in this district would again come into operation. An army would find its way across the watershed of the country most easily in the neighbourhood of the plain of Dothan, where the greatest elevation is only 800 feet above the sea, or a little farther north by the chalk downs of the "Breezy Land," where the slopes are gentle, and the greatest elevation only 1200 feet.

An army advancing from Damascus on Egypt would cross the Jordan Valley near the Sea of Galilee, and would advance with the greatest ease up the broad highway of the Valley of Jezreel, where Megiddo (if at *Mujedd'a*) now stands in ruins. Thus it is in the neighbourhood of this place that the two contending forces might still meet, and the old highway of kings from Egypt to Assyria would be the line of advance for armies of the nineteenth century.

Mariette Bey has published the list of 119 towns in Palestine, which were conquered by Thothmes III. He supposes them to be divided into six groups, including the districts of Sharon, the Hauran, Galilee, Moab, Judea, and the Negeb, or "South." Among the names there are ten which may be identified with so much certainty as to form indications which enable us to fill in many others. Thus the Egyptian *Damesku* is unmistakably Damascus, and there is no other known place of similar name in the country attacked by Thothmes III., with which it may be confused. This naturally leads to the identification of *Adara* and *Abila*, which follow it, with Edrei and Abila, places south of Damascus. Not less clear are the names *Cinnaratu* (Chinneroth) and *Aeshaph* (Achshaph); *Taanac* again is unmistakably the Hebrew Taanach, and *Anukheru* cannot well be anything but Anaharath. These five names show that the country from the neighbourhood of Acre to Damascus was conquered, and we have therefore no hesitation in accepting *Khemtu* as the Biblical Hammath on the Sea of Galilee.

A little farther down the list we find *Iphu* (Joppa), *Luden* (Lod), *Hana* (Ono), and are thus evidently transported to the maritime plain. Finally the names *Rakhebu* (Rehoboth), and *Taphunu* (Beth Tappuah) show, with great certainty, that the list extends over the south of the Judean hills, and over the district called Negeb ("Dry land") in the Bible.

Out of the identifications proposed by Mariette Bey, forty-two in all seem to me so well founded as to be almost indisputable, but in the additions which I have ventured to make there appears to me to be an improvement on his development of the identifications; for whereas, according to him, the list goes from south to north and from east back to south-west, it will be found that the arrangement here proposed shows half the list to allude to places in Galilee and in the Hauran, or near Damascus, the other half to refer to places south of Jaffa, including the Negeb and the Shephelah. Thus the only unconquered districts were, apparently, the rugged hills of Judea and Samaria, the Carmel range, and the mountains of Phœnicia, which lay remote from the general line of march. No name is found which could be twisted to represent Tyre or Sidon, Jerusalem or Bethlehem; moreover, these are places which would not lie in the way of an advance on Damascus.

Many of the unidentified places may easily be filled in by conjecture, but I have preferred to give only those which seem best founded—42 of Mariette Bey's and 29 of my own. The proportion of 71 out of 119 is sufficient to vindicate the important character of this invaluable series of inscriptions, and to put the general accuracy of the explanation almost beyond doubt, though individual names may perhaps be questioned. The most satisfactory indication, afforded by internal evidence, of the correctness of the identifications seems to me to be in the case of Nos. 53 and 54. Here we find two names following one another, which are identically the same, *'Aphla* and *'Aphla*, equivalent to the Hebrew Ophel, a "swell of ground;" they follow the name Anaharath, which is apparently the modern *en N'aûrah*. Now immediately west of *en N'aûrah* there are two villages close together, one called *'Afûleh*, evidently an ancient Ophel, the second corrupted into *el Fûleh*, "the bean;" both stand on low mamelons or swelling eminences in the plain, and thus what might at first sight appear to be a clerical error, by which a name is twice repeated inadvertently, is, in fact, a strong indication which, once seized, leads to the identification of *Gelümna* and *Nekelu* with places in lower Galilee.

A work treating, however slightly, of the ancient geography of Palestine, would, I think, be incomplete without the present list, the oldest known record of the Canaanite cities before the time of Joshua. The italics distinguish my own suggestions.

LIST OF THE TEMPLE OF KARNAK

EGYPTIAN.	HEBREW.	ARABIC.
1. Kedeshu	Kadesh	Kades
2. Magedi	Megiddo	*Mujedd'a*
3. Khai		
4. Gethu (na)	*Gitta*	*Jett*
5. 'Anshu		
6. Thebukh		
7. Bam'ai		
8. Gam'ata		
9. Thutina		
10. Raba (na)	*Rabbith*	*Reba*
11. Kerettenau	*Kirjathaim*	
12. Marama	Merom	
13. Damesku	Damascus	esh Shâm
14. Adara	Edrei	edh Dhr'a
15. Abila	Abila	Abil
16. Khemtu	Hammath	Hummâm Tabariya
17. Akidua		
18. Shem'anau		
19. Barthu		
20. Madna	Madon	*Madin*
21. Sarana	Lasharon	*Saróna*
22. Thebi		
23. Batzna	*Bitzaanaim*	*Bessûm*
24. Amashna	*Amathus*	*Amata*
25. Masakh		
26. Kaana	*Kenath*	*Kunawât*
27. 'Arana		
28. Ashtaratu	Ashtaroth Carnaim	es Sunamein
29. Anaurpha		
30. Makata	Maachath	
31. Lausa	Laish	Baniâs
32. Khatzor	Hazor	*Hudhîreh*
33. Pha. Khura	*Horem*	*Hûrah*
34. Cinnarathu	Chinneroth	
35. Shem'ana		
36. Adam	Adami	ed Dâmieh
37. Katuna		

APPENDIX B.

EGYPTIAN.	HEBREW.	ARABIC.
38. Shenam	Shunem	Sùlem
39. Mashala	Misheal	
40. Acshaph	Achshaph	el Yasîf
41. Geb'atu'an	Gabatha	Jebat'a
42. Taanac	Taanach	T'ânnuk
43. Ibla'amu	Ibleam	Bel'ameh
44. Genthuashna		
45. Ratau 'Araka		
46. 'Aina	Anem	'Anîn
47. 'Aac	Accho	'Akka
48. Rash Kadesh	Kedesh	Tell Abu Kŭdeis
49. Geliimna		Jelameh
50. Bar		
51. Shemesh Adum		
52. Anukheru	Anaharath	en N'aûrah
53. 'Aphla		'Afûleh
54. 'Aphla		el Fâleh
55. Kheshbu		
56. Datzulat		
57. Nekebu	Nekeb	Sciyâdeh
58. Ashushkhen	Shihon	'Ayûn Shâîn
59. Ranama	Rimmon	Rummâneh
60. Irata		
61. Makhata		
62. Iphu	Joppa	Yâfa
63. Gentbu		
64. Luden	Lod	Ludd
65. Aana	Ono	Kefr 'Ana
66. Aphuken	Aphek	
67. Suca	Sochoh	Shuweikeh
68. Ikhma	Emmaus	'Amwâs
69. Khabata		
70. Genetu		
71. Magdal	Migdal Gad	Mejdel
72. Aphden		
73. Shebtuna		
74. Diai		
75. Naun	Naamah	N'aneh
76. Khudida	Hadid	Hadîtheh
77. Har		
78. Ishphar	Saphir	Snâfir
79. Rakata	Rakkon	Tell er Rakkeit
80. Gerara	Gerar	Umm el Jerâr
81. Harar		
82. Lebau	Lebaoth	
83. Num'ana		
84. N'am'ana		
85. Marama	En Rimmon	Umm er Rumamîn
86. 'Ani	Ain	

EGYPTIAN.	HEBREW.	ARABIC.
87. Rakhebu	Rehoboth	er Ruheibeh
88. Akara		
89. Higlaim	Eglon	'Ajlân
90. Abala	Balah	Umm Baghleh
91. Adar'a	Adoraim	Dûra
92. Abara	Beth Birei	Bîreh
93. Gentu		
94. Makerphut		
95. 'Aina	Anim	el Ghuwein
96. Caraman	Carmel	Kurmul
97. Badia		
98. Taphu(na)	Beth Tappuah	Tuffâh
99. Abila		
100. Ilathu		
101. Hargala	Giloh	Jâla
102. Pakbamra		
103. Kaphuta		
104. Katira	Gederah	Katrah
105. Rabatu	Rabbah	Rubba
106. Makratu		
107. 'Amekt.		
108. Sarda		
109. Balatu	Baalath	
110. Bet Shara	Shaarain	S'aîreh
111. Bet Anta		
112. Khar Kata	Gath	Tell es Sâfi
113. 'An Kan'amu	Engannim	Umm Jina
114. Keb'au	Gibeah	Jeb'a
115. Tsalla		Beit Sallâh
116. Tzaphtza		Sâfa
117. Berakena	Berachath	Breikût
118. Hum...		
119. Agmesh		

APPENDIX C.

LIST OF WORKS CONSULTED.

The following books have been consulted in writing the Memoirs to the Survey and in the present work:

LEXICONS.

Gesenius' Hebrew and Chaldee Lexicon to the Old Testament Scriptures.
Buxtorf's Lexicon Chaldaicum Talmudicum et Rabbinicum. 1639.
Lane's Arabic and English Lexicon.
Freytag's Lexicon, Arabico-Latinum. 1830.
Smith's Bible Dictionary. 1830.

HEBREW LITERATURE.

Biblia Hebraica, Editio a Judah D'Allemand. 1825.
Septuagint, Vatican Text Edition. 1839.
New Testament, Tauchnitz Edition. 1869.
Josephus Opera Omnia, Oberthür. 1782.
Surenhusius' Mishna, with commentaries of Maimonides and Bartenora. 1698.
Barclay's Talmud. 1878.
Constantine l'Empereur's Middoth. 1630.
Neubauer's Géographie du Talmud. 1868.
Carmoly's Itinéraires de la Terre Sainte. 1817.

SAMARITAN LITERATURE.

Juynboll's Chronicon Samaritanum. 1848.
Neubauer's Chronique Samaritaine (in the "Journal Asiatique," December, 1869).
Nutt's Sketch of Samaritan History, etc. 1874.
Mill's Modern Samaritans.

EGYPTIAN AND ASSYRIAN LITERATURE.

Marieth Bey's Listes Géographiques des Pylônes de Karnak. 1875.
Chaba's Voyage d'un Egyptien. 1866.
Records of the Past.

EARLY CHRISTIAN AND CRUSADING LITERATURE.

Eusebius' and Jerome's Onomasticon, French Edition. 1862.
Tobler's Palestinæ Descriptiones. 1869.
Bongar's Gesta Dei per Francos. 1611.

Early Travels in Palestine (Bohn's Series). 1848.
Chronicles of the Crusades „ „ 1871.
William of Tyre (Guizot's Translation). 1824.

JERUSALEM LITERATURE.

Ordnance Survey Notes (Major Wilson). 1865.
Recovery of Jerusalem. 1871.
De Vogüé's Temple de Jerusalem.
Willis' Holy Sepulchre. 1849.
Williams' Holy City.
Thrupp's Ancient Jerusalem.
Lewin's Siege of Jerusalem.
Fergusson's Ancient Topography of Jerusalem. 1847.
„ Holy Sepulchre. 1865.
„ Temples of the Jews. 1878.
Warren's Underground Jerusalem. 1876.

MISCELLANEOUS.

Reland's Palestina ex Monumentis Veteribus Illustrata. 1714.
Robinson's Biblical Researches. 1841–56.
Quarterly Statements, P. E. Fund. 1866–78.
Our Work in Palestine, 1873.
De Vogüé's Eglises de la Terre Sainte. 1860.
Rey's Monuments des Croix en Syrie. 1871.
Tristram's Land of Israel, 1876.
Stanley's Sinai and Palestine. 1856.
„ Sermons in the East. 1856.
Finn's Byeways in Palestine. 1868.
Thomson's Land and the Book. 1873.
Munk's Palestine. 1863.
Murray's Handbook to Syria and Palestine. 1875.
Bædiger's „ „ „ 1876.
Père Lievin's Guide des Sanctuaires. 1869.
De Sauley's Dictionaire Topographique de la Terre Sainte. 1877.
Besant and Palmer's Jerusalem. 1871.
Lartet's Géologie de la Palestine. 1869.
Fergusson's Handbook of Architecture. 1855.
Coste's Architecture Arabe.
Cassell's Bible Educator.

INDEX TO VOL. II.

	PAGE		PAGE
'Arârah	64	Beit Jibrîn	149
Abel Meholah	62	Belvoir (Castle)	79
Abu Dahûk	143	Bethabara	17, 64
Admah	16	Bethany	27
Adullam	156	„ beyond Jordan	67
Adventure at Gath	154	Bethel	104
Ænon	57	Bethsur	76
Ai	108	Birds of Jericho	3
'Ain Hajlah	19	Brickmaking	238
„ el Jem'aîn	69	Brook Cherith	21
„ es Sultân	3		
„ Tâbghah	185	Calf Temples (at Bethel)	107
Altar of Ed	53	Camels	263
'Aly Agha 'Allân	195	Camps of Arabs	274
„ Merwân	170	Capernaum	182
Ancient Cultivation	323	Caphar Nahum	182
Apples of Sodom	135	Castle of Good Samaritan	27
Arab Camp	49	„ Philistines	163
„ Sheikhs	280	„ St. Lazarus	27
„ Women	283	Cave of Adullam	158
Archi ('Ain 'Arîk)	104	„ Machpelah	80
Armenians	300	Cavern of the Fenish	150
Ascalon	163	„ Umm et Thoimin	268
Ashdod	166	Character of the Arabs	277
Ashkenazim (Jews)	294	„ „ Fellahin	209
Ataroth Adar	105	Cherithites	163
Attack on Corporal Brophy	92	Children of Fellahin	252
„ at Safed	191	Choresh Ziph	89
		Chozeba (Kueizîba)	76
Ballûtet Sebta	85	Christian Traditions among	
Balsam Tree	2	Fellahin	223
Baniâs	35	Cities of the Plain	13
Bedawîn (The)	270	City of Brass	11
Beersheba	94	Climate of Jericho	26
Beisân	69	Climate of Palestine	320
„ Plain	61	Colonisation of Palestine	326

350　　　　　　　　　　*INDEX.*

	PAGE		PAGE
Cost of the Survey	122	Gath	153
Costumes of Arab Women	283	Gaza	169
,, (Christian)	245	Geba of Benjamin	110
,, (Female)	242	Gebal	23
,, (Jewish)	296	Geology of Palestine	40, 317
,, (Male)	240	German Colony	301-314
Crops	256	Ghazû (Raids)	285
Crown of Thorns	2	Gibeah of Saul	114, 115
Crusading Monasteries	23	Gibeon	120
Cupros (Tower)	6	Gilgal	7
		Goats	262
Dancers	253	Gomorrah	15
David and Goliath	160	Government of Palestine	234, 324
Dead Sea	20, 45	Granaries	260
Debir (Dhâherîyeh)	93		
Derwishes	231	Hachilah (Hill)	91
Dhirweh	76	Haifa (Colony)	306
Dialect of Arabs	277	Haram at Hebron	80
,, Fellahîn	213	Hareth	88
Docus (Fortress)	53	Harvest	258
Druses	301	Hebron	79
		Henna	245
Ekron ('Akir)	174	Horses	285
Emir of Mes'aid Arabs	50	Hûleh (Lake)	35
Engedi	134	Hûlbûl	76
Ephes Dammim	160	Huts (Reed)	275
Eriha	7		
		Ignorance of Fellahîn	230
False Names	162	Imâm 'Aly	11
Fantazia (Dance)	286		
Fâr'ah (Valley)	55	Jaffa (Colony)	305
Farm at Abu Shûsheh	328	Jebel Tûr'an (view)	179
Fasts	234	Jericho (Byzantine)	7
Feddân (Land measure)	256	,, (of Joshua)	6
Fenish (Tradition)	225	Jerid (Game of the)	254
Feshkhah (Spring)	21	Jerû'ah (Corner of Field)	259
Fever in Camp	27	Jewish Colony in Galilee	326
Field of Damascus	84	,, Sacrifices	297
Flowers of Jordan Valley	54, 58	,, Sects	293
Folk-lore	208	,, Women	296
Food of Fellahîn	239	Jordan (Course of)	36
Foreign Words	217	,, (Fords of)	65
Forests	321	,, Valley (Formation of)	40
Fountain of Capharnaum	185		
,, Eunuch	76		
Future of Palestine	332	Kâdy (or Judge)	265
		Karaite Jews	294
Garden of Abraham	7	Keilah	88
Garden of the Fenish	150	Kelim Ingleez	210

INDEX. 351

	PAGE		PAGE
Kelt Valley	21	Ramathaim Zophim	116
Kôd Sacrifices	221	Râmeh	85
Kufeiyeh (Head-dress)	280	Râs Jâdir	60
Kurn Sŭrtŭbeh	51	Raven's Nest	10
		Religion of Arabs	288
Lachish	168	,, Fellahîn	218
Land Tenure in Palestine	255	Retem (Broom)	54, 58
Legends of Arabs	11, 291	Rijm el Bahr	20
,, Fellahîn	228	Roads in Palestine	330
Lepers	247	Roman Camps (Masada)	141
Level of Sea of Galilee	177	Rueikbeh (Er)	126
		Russian Cathedral	298
Makkedah	174	,, Pilgrims	297
Mamre	83		
Mankalah (Game)	252	Sacred Trees	233
Masada	140	,, Tombs of Arabs	289
Megiddo (Mujedd'a)	68	,, ,, of Jews	297
Meidân el 'Abd	44	Saint John of Choseboth	22
Mejdel	163	,, John-on-Jordan	17
Mensa (Mountain)	187	,, Michael (Chapel)	12
Meshâhed (Monuments)	233	Sand Grouse	99
Meshâsh (El)	99	Sandals	281
Michmash Valley	110	Scythopolis	69
Mikveh Israel	327	Sea of Galilee	55, 180
Minai (Sect of)	183	Seasons in Palestine	319
Mizpeh	116	Sela Ham-mahlekoth	91
Moreg (Sledge)	259	Semitic Peculiarities	207
Mother of Steps (District)	56	Seneh and Bozez	113
Mukâms (The)	219	Sephardim (Jews)	294
Muntâr, El	170	Shafât	117
		Sheep-cotes	262
Neby Samwîl	118	Shefa 'Amr	178
Negeb (District)	87	Sheikh Jemíl	49-50
Nimr (Leopard)	19	Shejeret el Ithleh	9
Nob	116	Shkârah (Glebe-land)	256
		Shunem	72
Olives	260	Shûsheh (Top-knot)	233
Osheh (Hûsheh)	178	Sirah (Spring of)	86
		Sowing	258
Phasaelis (Fusâil)	49	Spring of Harod	69
Pilate's Aqueduct	76	Stink-stone	2
Pilgrims' Bathing-place	19	Storks	61
Ploughing	257	Succoth (Sâkût)	62
Population of Palestine	324	Sugar Cultivation	292
,, a Village	239	Sulphur Springs	137
Public Works required	330	Superstitions of Fellahîn	233
		Sursuk (Family)	328
Quarantania (Mount)	12		
Raised Beaches	43	Tahum (or limit)	256

INDEX

	PAGE		PAGE
Taxes	. 265	Valley of Elah .	. 157
Tell el Milh (Malathah)	. 100	,, Sorek .	. 174
,, es Sâfi (Gath)	. 153	,, Thorns .	. 112
Tells (Jordan Valley) .	. 46	Village (Described)	. 237
Temple Society .	. 301	Vows .	. 221
Tents of Arabs .	. 275		
Tires (Moon-shaped) .	. 244	Wâdy Hasâsch .	. 125
Threshing Floors	. 259	,, Mâlch .	. 57
Trade of Palestine	. 324	Water Supply of Palestine	. 317
Treasure (Buried)	. 291	Weapons of Arabs	. 282
Tribes of Arabs .	. 273	Wedding Ceremonies .	. 249
Tomb of Nahum .	. 184	Wild Goats .	. 140
Tombs of Patriarchs .	82, 226	Wusm (Tribe-mark) .	. 290
Usury .	. 268	Yagur (El Jûrah)	. 166
		Yebnah (Jamnia)	. 172
Vale of Siddim .	15-16		
,, Tears	. 84	Zeboim .	. 16
Valley of Achor .	. 21	Zeffeh (Procession)	. 250

THE END.

BILLING AND SONS, PRINTERS, GUILDFORD, SURREY.

www.ingramcontent.com/pod-product-compliance
Lightning Source LLC
Chambersburg PA
CBHW020224240426
43672CB00006B/412